AUSTRALIA'S
SECOND
CHANCE

ALSO BY GEORGE MEGALOGENIS

The Australian Moment
Faultlines
The Longest Decade
Quarterly Essay 40: Trivial Pursuit

GEORGE MEGALOGENIS

AUSTRALIA'S SECOND CHANCE

What our history tells us about our future

To John —
With very best wishes.

Also best wishes
from John Richards
Glebe NSW Aust.

HAMISH HAMILTON
an imprint of
PENGUIN BOOKS

HAMISH HAMILTON

UK | USA | Canada | Ireland | Australia
India | New Zealand | South Africa | China

Penguin Books is part of the Penguin Random House group of companies
whose addresses can be found at global.penguinrandomhouse.com.

 Penguin
Random House
Australia

First published by Penguin Group (Australia), 2015

10 9 8 7 6 5 4 3 2 1

Text copyright © George Megalogenis 2015

The moral right of the author has been asserted.

Cover and text design by John Canty © Penguin Group (Australia)
Cover photographs: Quentin Bryce: nla.int-nl40093-gp8/ courtesy of National Library of
Australia; Arthur Calwell: nla.pic-vn4978639/ courtesy of National Library of Australia;
Anh Do: Tamara Dean/ Fairfax Media; national serviceman: courtesy of AWM/ P01392.017;
Evonne Goolagong Cawley: Jones/Daily Express/Hulton Archive/Getty Images; Billy Hughes:
nla.pic-vn3065078/ courtesy of National Library of Australia; Effie: Chris Ivin/Getty Images;
Caroline Chisholm: State Library of New South Wales, DG 459; detail of portrait of Nanultera:
Rex Nan Kivell Collection, the National Gallery of Australia and the National Library of
Australia; Daniel Mannix: MDHC Catholic Archdiocese of Melbourne; Chinese hawker: nla.
pic-an24615958, courtesy of National Library of Australia; Bachar Houli: Michael Wilson/AFL
Media; Queen Elizabeth II: Fox Photos/Hulton Royals Collection/Getty Images; Dame Edna:
Paul Hawthorne/Getty Images Entertainment; George Megalogenis: ABC TV
Typeset in Adobe Caslon Pro by Samantha Jayaweera © Penguin Group (Australia)
Colour separation by Splitting Image Colour Studio, Clayton, Victoria
Printed and bound in Australia by Griffin Press, an accredited ISO AS/NZS
14001 Environmental Management Systems printer.

National Library of Australia
Cataloguing-in-Publication data:

Megalogenis, George
Australia's second chance / George Megalogenis
9781926428574 (paperback)
Australia – Economic conditions
Australia – Emigration and immigration – Economic aspects

325.94

penguin.com.au

In loving memory of Amalia and Erasmia

CONTENTS

Introduction

In the twenty-first century Australia staged one of the great recoveries in human history: from a nation to be pitied to one that is considered the envy of the world. No other economy has had a comparable winning streak to ours, and at a time of global instability. Twenty-four years have passed since our last deep recession, and since we were subjected to the taunt from Singapore's president, Lee Kuan Yew, that Australia risked becoming the 'poor white trash of Asia'.

Yet we no longer feel comfortable in our prosperous skins. There is a palpable fear in the community that our luck will soon run out, and that we will revert to our former state of mediocrity: a people to be ridiculed for wasting their fortune. Liberal Party pollster Mark Textor describes the surly public mood as a form of performance anxiety. 'Australians realise they have been in a privileged position but feel stressed about it,' he says. 'When you are sitting on an economic pedestal, you ask yourself, "How do I maintain this?" The only way is down.'

We have been here before. These first surprising, unsettling decades of the new millennium have brought Australians back to the position they enjoyed as the world's richest people in the nineteenth century. For the second time, an entire generation of Australians has been raised with no experience of the economic or social hardship currently felt in the United States or Europe. Once again, our society reflects the best of the world back to it. In the 1870s, when

Australia enjoyed its greatest advantage in living standards over the United States and Britain, the population split almost fifty-fifty between migrants and local-born. Today, almost half the population can be counted as first- or second-generation migrants – 28 per cent were born overseas and another 20 per cent have at least one parent who was a migrant.

The question of who we are has never been more fascinating, or confronting. And seldom have we been less able to discuss it. Most of us react to the subject of 'national identity' as we do to fingernails on the blackboard. Debate has polarised to the point where one Australia is made deliberately unrecognisable to the other. We are either irredeemably racist, or the greatest people on earth. To those in the former camp it is impossible to compute Australia's success. To those in the latter, it is unAustralian to even acknowledge the violent dispossession of the people who were here before us, or the revolving door of xenophobia that greets each new arrival.

This book will seek to avoid the false choice between a good and a bad Australia, and explore, instead, the answer to the more interesting question of why this settlement exceeds at both ends of the economic cycle. In our most recent period of poor performance, in the 1970s, Australia was one of the few nations to suffer rates of unemployment and inflation above 10 per cent. Australia experienced the hardest landing of any country in the global depression of the 1890s, and in the Great Depression of the 1930s endured the humiliation of an austerity program imposed by the Bank of England. The cuts to wages and pensions back then were as severe as the Greeks are being forced to accept in the twenty-first century.

Our national contradictions mirror the extended booms and busts of the economy. We are a confident people who can't articulate what it is to be Australian beyond the clichés of mateship and the fair go; an affluent people pretending to be battlers. Our politics has a proud history of world-leading reform, but our leaders have disappointed more often than we care to count.

Australia's Second Chance considers our place in the world in three parts, from rise to fall and back to the present day. In Part One we will see how Australia made the relatively quick journey from open-air prison to the very top of the global income ladder in the nineteenth century, with a people willing to inspire the world with democratic reforms. Part Two will delve into our longest bust, from the end of the 1880s to the start of the Second World War, offering a new theory for why we shrank as a people. And Part Three brings us up to now – at the crossroads between relapse and national maturity.

The thread that connects the past to the present and future is the ongoing conversation between those who came to these shores, and those who received them. This dialogue has always been central to the national story, but it is too often reduced to its social dimensions only. The economic side of the equation is rarely considered, even though Australians would acknowledge they obsess about economics more than most people. Our blindness in this respect is a curious national trait. Americans view migration as essential to their nationhood, recognising that migrants literally made the United States. Australians are more likely to define the benefits of migration in cultural terms – the food.

We worry that the new arrival will not become 'Australian', while the Americans never doubt that the migrant will embrace their identity. Meanwhile, every new arrival has a version of the first contact story of James Cook. When the Yorkshire-born sailor claimed the east coast of Australia for Great Britain in 1770, the locals rejected the gifts he offered and took aim with their spears. 'All they seem'd to want was for us to be gone,' he wrote. Once the migrants join the mortgage belt and send their children to the top of the class, these first impressions begin to dissolve because the country has both remained familiar and grown more wealthy.

Our periods of strong migration have been our most successful; our busts are distinguished by the closing of our doors, through policies of racial selection and import protection. This is not to say that the new arrival is somehow superior to the local, but rather that Australia's least productive and most divisive eras have been those when migration was at its lowest ebb – in the early decades of convict settlement and in the half-century-long stagnation of White Australia, from the 1890s until the end of the Second World War.

Our economic winning streak will end, as streaks always do, and there is much to be genuinely concerned about. Property prices in Sydney and Melbourne have reached levels that past experience says will lead to a crash. National politics has surrendered to its own cynicism, and China, the country that helped give Australia its extra decade of good times, can no longer be relied on to prop up the global economy. Here is the critical challenge for Australia: whenever the next shock comes, will we revert to our old sheltered, internationally maligned self and endure another lost decade like the 1970s, or worse, the isolation of White Australia? Or can we learn something from how we reacted to previous setbacks, and build on the success of our longest boom? Migration is the greatest compliment that can be paid to a nation, and for only the second time in history a significant share of skilled arrivals are choosing Australia over the United States. The changes these people will bring to the nation will be more profound than those brought by the postwar waves from southern Europe and South-East Asia. The test is to keep them coming, and to avoid repeating the mistakes of the past. Whether we will be anxious or excited about the future can't be answered by minerals, or the global economic cycle. The question of whether Australia can make something of its second chance turns on whether we can remain the place the world wants to be.

August 2015

PART ONE

THE RISE

I

ARTHUR PHILLIP, THE ACCIDENTAL EGALITARIAN

No two peoples could have been further apart when the British and the Indigenous population first met at Sydney Cove in 1788. The First Australians represented the world's oldest continuing culture; the new arrivals came from its most technologically advanced society. Their very understanding of life was at odds.

The First Australians had a lineage stretching back fifty thousand years. They had spent the previous seventeen thousand years in splendid isolation, after the Australian continent had been separated by rising seas from New Guinea in the north and Tasmania in the south. In that time, they missed the revolutions that transformed the European, Middle Eastern, Asian and American societies – large-scale farming, the settlement of towns and cities, and, later, nation states and empires with standing armies. They had no conception of the newcomers' values: the faith in a single god, and attachment to property. Even if these things could have been grasped, the gulf between the two cultures was perhaps unbridgeable. How could a people who had occupied a continent for millennia understand that the new arrivals would turn their country into an open-air prison?

The first British Australians thought of humanity in biblical terms, with a time span of six thousand years. They saw the locals as savages, one developmental stage below their own. They intended to treat them kindly as fellow humans, but not as equals. They lacked the knowledge to appreciate the ingenuity of the locals, from their art to the land management system that sustained a population of up to one million people.

In these initial encounters the template was established for the interaction between old and new Australia that survives to this day. It begins with a misunderstanding on both sides. A well-meaning engagement follows, which, ultimately, leads to a settlement on the migrant's terms.

Arthur Phillip, the first governor of New South Wales, had expected to come across no more than a handful of 'natives'. He thought his party of 750 convicts, 200 marines and a small number of officials and their family members, including future governors John Hunter and Philip Gidley King, was large enough to establish a village in virgin territory. However, he found that the locals were 'more numerous than they were supposed to be'. 'I think they cannot be less than fifteen hundred in Botany Bay, Port Jackson, and Broken Bay, including the intermediate coast,' he wrote in an early dispatch home to London. The smoke he saw on 'Landsdown Hills, which are fifty miles inland, I think leaves no doubt but there are inhabitants in the interior parts of the country'.

Nevertheless, he assured London 'we have never yet seen any other weapon than the spear, which is certainly very inferior to our guns'.

The governor's written instructions from King George III envisaged a peaceful occupation. The land should be taken without resort to arms, and settled without a treaty. The locals were to be respected, and Phillip was to punish any convict or guard who interfered with them.

Phillip took his orders literally. He would not, if he could help it, ever kill a local. 'It has been my determination from the time I landed, never to fire on the Natives, but in a case of absolute necessity,' he wrote to Sir Joseph Banks, the colony's original patron, in July 1788. 'I think better of them from having been more with them. They do not in my opinion want personal Courage, they very readily place a confidence & are, I believe, strictly honest amongst themselves.'

Phillip developed a technique he thought would assure the First Australians of his benign intentions. He would walk up to an armed local with an open hand, offering it in friendship. In one revealing early meeting, Phillip thought he had won the confidence of a local elder. He rewarded the old man's friendly behaviour with a hatchet and other gifts; the local reciprocated with 'a dance and a song of joy'. But when the local stole a spade a few days later, the governor was determined to register his disapproval, again with his open hand. He pushed the old man away when next they met and slapped him two or three times on the shoulder.

'This destroyed our friendship in a moment, and seizing a spear he came close up to me, poised it, and appeared determined to strike; but whether from seeing that his threats were not regarded – for I chose rather to risk the spear than fire on him – or from anything the other natives said who surrounded him, after a few moments he dropped his spear and left us. This circumstance is mentioned to show that they do not want personal courage, for several officers and men were then near me.'

Phillip was so impressed with the locals that he named Manly Cove after them, for 'their confidence and manly behaviour'. In line with the inclinations of the day, he also wanted to civilise the 'natives', and in November 1789 he had two men captured for the purpose of observation and tutoring. One, named Colby, escaped; the other, Bennelong, remained for six months, learning to speak like the British, wear their clothes, eat their food and down their drink, before he also fled.

When Phillip and Bennelong reunited at Manly Cove in September 1790, the governor almost certainly misread what his friend had in mind. Bennelong appears to have arranged the meeting to deliver a ritual punishment to the governor for breaching laws the newcomers were not aware of. Phillip presumably thought this gathering was to be like all the others. He would offer his hand in friendship, and the two peoples would resume their dialogue. Bennelong placed a spear on the ground for one of his group to pick up. Phillip was expected to pick up a smaller implement to deflect the spear to be thrown at him. But he walked unarmed towards the group, offering his customary handshake. The man Bennelong had designated for the task replied by spearing the governor in the shoulder. The frontier war might have started right there, but Phillip kept his head. He had instructed colleagues Captain David Collins, the judge advocate of the penal settlement, and Marine Lieutenant Henry Waterhouse to leave their muskets on the boat. Phillip did have a gun concealed in his pocket, and he discharged what was perhaps intended as a warning shot as he and his two men scampered back to the boat.

Bennelong might have feared that the governor would issue the order for payback. Phillip knew that many of his men 'would be desirous of punishing what was generally deemed an act of treachery' but he assured them he 'did not see the transaction in that light' and issued instructions that there be no retaliation for a simple misunderstanding. While this argument 'seemed at first to threaten the colony with a loss that must have been for some time severely felt,' Collins wrote, '[it created] an opening of that amicable intercourse with these people which the governor had always laboured to establish.'

Assured that he would not be recaptured, Bennelong resumed contact with Phillip and, along with other locals, became a regular visitor to the yard of Government House. The governor built his friend a hut in 1791, and when Phillip returned to England at the end of the following year, he took Bennelong with him to meet King George III.

It might have seemed a genuine possibility to the governor that the rest of the locals would follow Bennelong's example and assimilate in the face of the self-evident superiority of European civilisation. Viewed from the perspective of the First Australians, however, the newcomers were little more than a curiosity. The locals might have grasped the power of the musket, but they also saw a slow-moving intruder who did not understand their environment. The British were poor hunters, and could not turn the soil to their advantage to grow sufficient crops to feed themselves. On the brink of starvation, these miserable representatives of empire were not the role models they might have imagined themselves to be.

New South Wales had been conceived in response to the American Revolution of 1776 and virtually abandoned following the French Revolution of 1789 as Britain was consumed by the threat of rebellion at home, and its war with France. The second date is as important as the first, because the early character of the settlement was shaped by imperial neglect. Almost nothing went according to plan in those formative years, either at London's end, or on the unfamiliar ground of Sydney Cove.

Transportation was Britain's attempt to scrub its own ethnicity clean. The habit had formed earlier in the eighteenth century when convicts were sent to what are now Virginia and Maryland. Many were sold as slaves to free settlers. By 1775, some fifty thousand felons had been exported, at a rate of two thousand per year. When the American Revolution stopped that trade, prisoners were held on decommissioned navy ships, called hulks, anchored on the banks of the Thames and at ports across the country, until a new colony could be found to receive them. New South Wales, the territory Captain Cook had claimed for Britain sixteen years earlier, was finally selected in 1786.

Arthur Phillip did not intend for 'convicts to lay the foundation of an Empire'. His plan for the colony envisaged that free settlers would develop the vacant country. He also believed that Britain's class structure could be transplanted to New South Wales, with a rigid hierarchy that placed free settlers above the felons, even after the prisoners had served their sentences. The convicts, he wrote before the First Fleet sailed, should remain forever 'separated from the garrison and other settlers that may come from Europe'.

In reality, Britain's conflict with its own people, and with France, meant that no free settlers would land in New South Wales until 1793, five years after Phillip had arrived and a month after he left for home with Bennelong. By this time the colony's egalitarian character was taking root, with some convicts enjoying a standard of living superior to that which a free man could obtain in Britain. Even once the free settlers arrived, they were so small in number that subsequent attempts to graft Britain's class structure onto these roots proved futile. In each year until 1837 (by which time the entire continent had been claimed by Britain), more convicts arrived than free settlers, setting Australia on a path that would make the colonies unrecognisable to the mother country within a generation.

The convicts were a mix of hardened urban criminals and rural misfits. The latter had been drawn to the cities by the lure of the Industrial Revolution and the loss of previously communal farmland under the system of enclosure. Historians have long abandoned the heroic assumption that most convicts were innocent victims. A large proportion had been career crooks before the legal system marked them for export to New South Wales. One-third of the First Fleet intake had received sentences of death, commuted to transportation.

They carried none of the righteous energy of the pilgrims of the *Mayflower*, who fled religious persecution in England to establish a new settlement on Plymouth Rock in 1620. The pilgrims celebrated their landing with a prayer of thanksgiving. Australia's founding felons marked theirs with an orgy.

After a relatively peaceful eight-month journey from Portsmouth in England, the First Fleet arrived in Botany Bay on 18 January 1788. But the site was deemed unsuitable for settlement. Phillip then explored nearby Port Jackson, where he found 'the finest harbour in the world, in which a thousand sail of the line may ride in the most perfect security'. He selected Sydney Cove as the site for the settlement, which he named after the home secretary Lord Sydney. The national holiday is 26 January, when Phillip planted the British flag at Sydney Cove, but the first full day of settlement was 6 February, when the women joined the camp that had been established by the male convicts. 'They were dressed in general very clean, and some few amongst them might be said to be well dressed,' surgeon Arthur Bowes Smyth wrote in his journal. 'The men convicts got to them very soon after they landed and it is beyond my abilities to give a just description of the scene of debauchery and riot that ensued during the night.' Having arrived at the literal end of the earth – a moral terra nullius – it is hard to imagine them behaving any better.

Australia began as America's migrant opposite, in leadership as well as morality. The pilgrims had signed a compact before disembarking, agreeing that the laws they would observe 'for the general good of the colony' would be put to a vote. The colony in New South Wales was reliant on the judgement of one man, a 49-year-old naval officer. The London-born Phillip was a somewhat unlikely first ruler. He had not been raised in privilege: his father was a language teacher and his mother was the former wife of a captain of the Royal Navy, which may have influenced Phillip's career path. His own record had been solid, but not outstanding. Interestingly, he was opposed to the death penalty in most cases. The exceptions were murder and sodomy, which he thought should be punished by the offenders being handed over to be eaten by the 'natives of New Zealand'.

On the day after the foundation orgy, Phillip laid down the law. Having ordered the convicts to sit on the ground, like primary school children at morning assembly, he told them he 'was now thoroughly convinced there were many amongst them incorrigible, and that he was persuaded nothing but severity would have any effect upon them, to induce them to behave properly in future,' Smyth reported. 'He also assured them that if they attempted to get into the women's tents of a night there were positive orders for firing upon them.'

Five couples were wedded on the first Sunday after the romp; the arranged marriages were a powerful metaphor for the society the convicts would have to construct without London's help.

Phillip's frustration soon turned to the marines. 'Most of them have declined any interference with the convicts, except when they are employed for their own particular service,' Phillip wrote in a letter to Lord Sydney dated 16 May 1788. He thought he had made a reasonable request for his men to 'occasionally encourage' the diligent convicts and 'point out for punishment [those] they saw idle or straggling in the woods'. The officers had replied that they were soldiers, not policemen or prison guards. They 'did not understand that any interference with the convicts was expected'. With London eight months away by ship, Phillip had no choice but to work around the lazy marines.

Phillip did not become a benefactor of convicts because of an innate humanitarianism. His liberalism was forged by the circumstance of having no one else available. He turned prisoner into guard to maintain discipline. Convicts acted as hangmen and night watchmen until the mother country answered his appeal 'for proper persons' to take over. This first page of Phillip's pragmatic compact, giving convicts a small say in the running of the settlement, was written by necessity. The second page was written as an act of survival.

In two follow-up letters to Lord Sydney, on 5 and 9 July that year, Phillip admitted the infant colony could not feed itself in the short term without regular provisions from the mother country. Self-sufficiency would only come when he had skilled migrants who could farm and make things. He placed a modest request for a better class of migrant: 'If fifty farmers were sent out with their families they would do more in one year in rendering this colony independent of the mother country, as to provisions, than a thousand convicts.'

These two requests – to replace the marines with a new military force, and for a small number of free settlers – predicted one of the essential differences between Australia and the United States in the nineteenth century. America offered to improve the lot of the migrant. It claimed every other nation's tired, poor, huddled masses yearning to breathe free, the wretched refuse of their teeming shore. Although the Americans did sometimes restrict entry on the basis of race, the American identity as a migrant nation was never doubted; all new arrivals had the pilgrims, and later the Statue of Liberty, to act as their guide. Australia, by contrast, wanted the migrant to improve the national stock as the first few boatloads of convicts and marines had been deemed unworthy. Transportation gave Australians an inferiority complex and made them innately suspicious of the next arrival. The oft-stated fear of colonial governors, and later the democratic politicians who courted public opinion, was that migration could reduce the Australian standard of living. Given the choice between more or fewer boats, authorities would consistently err on the side of fewer, even from the mother country. Phillip established the pattern in those early dispatches when he told Lord Sydney he would prefer 'few convicts will be sent out for one year at least' unless they had skills such as carpentry, bricklaying or farming.

The convicts and their reluctant guards were united by starvation. They survived mainly on what they had brought with them. They were not suited to hunting, and while they could catch fish, those were in short supply. The initial weekly allowance of food was seven pounds of salt beef or four pounds of pork, three pints of dried peas, seven pounds of bread, six ounces of butter and half a pound of rice, with women on two-thirds the male ration. It was a hopeless diet: heavy in salt, it did not provide sufficient energy for the healthy to work a full day and made the sick sicker.

As soon as he realised their plight, Phillip insisted on equality of rations. It effectively obliterated the governor's own plan for a class-based settlement. He would eat no more than the most miserable felon. Anyone who broke this social contract by stealing food would be sentenced to death. And in March 1789, six marines were hanged between the two storehouses they had plotted to rob. There was hardly an officer or man that did not shed a tear that day, Private John Easty wrote. The condemned were outraged that one of their fellow conspirators had been spared death in return for giving evidence 'as he was the first that bagan the Said Roberry'. But they accepted their fate, and their grieving colleagues did not take up arms against Phillip.

National character is made in moments such as these. The hunger of a small, stranded community created an extremist egalitarianism, rigorously enforced. Phillip could not compel the marines to supervise the convicts, but he could execute those who endangered the settlement. If Americans can draw a straight line from the pilgrims to their modern self as a religious people distrustful of government, the Australian line goes the other way: from a querulous group of convicts and marines to an intemperate people with a paradoxical dependence on government.

As the colony completed its second year, both the Indigenous and the First Fleet populations were falling. A large number of the 1500 locals Arthur Phillip had counted on landing were struck down by a smallpox epidemic, while almost one in four of the recent arrivals succumbed to starvation. At the final muster for 1789, there were just 645 migrants present – 211 fewer than had been counted the previous year. Another year of privation, and the settlement might have been abandoned.

The menace of starvation was alleviated by the ships of the Second Fleet, which arrived one at a time in the middle of 1790. They brought beef, pork, flour, sugar, oil and liquor; and the officers and soldiers of the New South Wales Corps, the newly formed military regiment to replace the work-averse marines. This part of the intake would reinforce the boisterous side of the Australian personality once Phillip left the colony, when they became better known as the Rum Corps.

The ships of the Second Fleet represented both salvation and death for the troubled settlement. The mother country had not forgotten its colonial child, but still managed to mistreat it. Three of the ships, the *Surprise*, *Scarborough* and *Neptune*, had effectively become floating coffins, with 261 men, eleven women and two children perishing on their journey to Sydney Cove. In total, more than one in four of the thousand convicts sent had been sacrificed due to the most extraordinary administrative blunder. The contractors who loaded the convicts onto the Second Fleet had been paid on the number who boarded, not, as had been the case with the First Fleet, on those who disembarked at the other end.

'No interest for their preservation was created in the owners and the dead were more profitable – if profit alone was consulted by them, and the credit of their house was not at stake – than the living,' David Collins wrote. The total migrant population was now above two thousand, with almost one in four sick.

'The melancholy scenes which closed the last month appeared unchanged at the beginning of this,' Collins wrote in his diary for July 1790. 'The morning generally opened with the attendants of the sick passing frequently backwards and forwards from the hospital to the burying-ground with the miserable victims of the night. Every exertion was made to get up the portable hospital; but, although we were informed that it had been put up in London in a very few hours, we did not complete it until the 7th, when it was instantly filled with patients. On the 13th, there were four hundred and eighty-eight persons under medical treatment at and about the hospital – a dreadful sick list!'

Despite Phillip's requests, there were no free settlers in the Second Fleet. There was a handful of skilled convicts, but some had died along the way. And in early 1791, the arrival of the Third Fleet amplified the problems, arriving with a similar death toll that placed an even greater strain on the settlers.

Yet despite these handicaps, Phillip managed to fashion a form of leadership in hard times that would become uniquely Australian. A more stubborn, less stable governor might have taken out his frustrations on the felons themselves. Phillip chose to motivate the convicts to become productive members of the settlement by giving them land. After some dismal early attempts, the colonists were generally of the view that the soil was not fit for agriculture, and Phillip wanted to prove that diligence would overcome natural disadvantage. With no free settlers to make the case, he turned to James Ruse, a Cornwall-born farmer.

Ruse had been sentenced to death for burglary in 1782, commuted to seven years' transportation, and in 1789 he insisted that his term had expired. While Phillip was waiting for confirmation from London, he agreed to provide some land to Ruse on a trial basis. In November 1789, two acres of ground was cleared for him near Parramatta, a small hut built, and he was loaned tools, grain and some livestock. By February 1791, and with his freedom confirmed, he was able to support both himself and his convict wife, Elizabeth Perry. Ruse was granted the colony's first land title in April 1791. Slowly, other former convicts began to apply to join this primitive pastoral economy. By the end of 1792, there were seventy-three landholders in the colony.

Although he seemed to vindicate Phillip's judgement, Ruse was, in fact, disappointed with the soil he had and sold his parcel of land in 1793, after the governor had returned to England. In 1794, Ruse asked for another land grant, this time in the new settlement on the Hawkesbury River. There he grew the first wheat in the colony, foreshadowing one of Australia's major exports, and although he never became a major figure in his day, he is remembered in the name of a leading agricultural high school.

Significantly, London tolerated, even encouraged, the practice of granting land to convicts, as a way of discouraging them from returning to Britain, while prohibiting government staff and marines from owning land so as not to be distracted from their jobs. In the absence of free settlers, the convicts rose by default. Without an effective private economy as a foundation, the base for the settlement was laid by government, with convict hands. David Collins, who as judge advocate was responsible for the colony's legal system, observed the transformation with a suspicious eye. 'Some settlers had themselves declared, on its being hinted to them that they had not always been so diligent when labouring for the whole, "We are now working for ourselves".'

London's neglect was moderated by Phillip's pragmatism. He created, more by chance than inspiration, the egalitarianism that still binds Australia today in defiance of his own upbringing in England's governing class. Yet this distinctive ethos came with a catch. Phillip's relative kindness to the convicts would unwittingly kill his policy of amity to the First Australians. The frontier wars between the locals and the migrants commenced soon after his departure at the end of 1792, on the superior agricultural lands of the Hawkesbury where the model convict James Ruse was one of the founding farmers.

2

DISPOSSESSION
AND WINDFALL:
THE COLONY EXPANDS

The Hawkesbury flood plain north of Sydney was discovered early in the life of the colony, in 1789. Although it soon became apparent that the land was extraordinarily fertile, Arthur Phillip chose not to establish a settlement in the area because it was too isolated and he did not trust the former convicts with its riches. He would wait until the arrival of 'proper people' who were skilled at farming and did not carry the stain of transportation. But those who ran the colony after Phillip left had no such reservations. Eager to unleash the private economy after the slow crawl of Phillip's government economy, authorities gave ex-convicts and free settlers a licence to develop the Hawkesbury. In doing so, they signalled the end of the starvation years and predicted Australia's affluent future, in which wealth could be created without apparent effort.

Here the land seemed to be so accommodating that the pioneers who farmed it devoted more effort to 'drinking and rioting' than to tilling the soil. Those who had taken land closest to the river were the laziest, David Collins wrote in early 1795. They trusted 'the extreme fertility of the soil would produce an ample crop at any time without much labour'. Collins felt these people were 'so silly and thoughtless' that they did not deserve their good fortune.

In the two and a half years it took London to replace Phillip with his successor John Hunter, the New South Wales Corps ran the colony. This greedy period provided the next building block in the national psyche, and its dual characteristics were aggression and prosperity. The commander of the corps, Francis Grose, indulged his men, replacing civilian magistrates with his own officers, and granting land and convict labour to his troops without London's consent. Grose even abandoned Phillip's policy of equality of food rations so the military got fatter than the convicts they supervised and exploited.

The Rum Corps earned its nickname through its use of alcohol to control the economy. Once the allotted food, clothes and rum had been distributed to the colonists, officers bought up the surplus and sold it at whatever price they could get away with. A profit margin of 100 per cent was considered the starting point, and mark-ups as high as 700 per cent were commonplace. Phillip had restricted the availability of alcohol but the military created a new economy around its consumption. Rum became the de facto currency, and convicts demanded it as payment for the extra work they were allowed to do in their private time. David Collins observed that they valued alcohol over 'every other article of provisions or clothing that could be offered them.'

Many serving and former convicts drank themselves to death. Whether they couldn't control their intake, or had chosen suicide as an early release from exile, their binges almost certainly contributed to another reduction in the total settler population, the second time in seven years that the colony had lost more people than it gained. At the December 1795 muster there were 3446 present, 113 fewer than twelve months earlier. Phillip's friend Bennelong returned from England that year, and he too would eventually succumb to the grog. And yet the migrants had never felt wealthier: the colony was experiencing its first bittersweet taste of trade with the outside world. The very presence of rum was due to the overseas merchants who began coming to Sydney Cove with alcohol and other goods to sell to the colony. Even though the Rum Corps exploited this exchange at the expense of fellow colonists, it was not the only group to extract a profit. Grose indulged others with grants of land. Critical to his policy of private expansion was his approval for a settlement on the Hawkesbury in January 1794. The initial party of twenty-two farmers included former convicts such as James Ruse, and some of the first free settlers to arrive in the colony. They dubbed the Hawkesbury the Nile of New South Wales, and their early success encouraged others to join them. Almost five hundred migrants had moved into the area by the winter of 1795, or about one in seven of all the colonists at the time.

Grose and his officers did not share Phillip's concern for the Indigenous population – at best, they were indifferent – but nor did they give much thought to the Hawkesbury settlers. Their approach was to let the migrants and the locals fend for themselves, and when disputes inevitably escalated, send in the troops to restore order in favour of the settlers. And so the toxic mix of the Hawkesbury was established: a money-hungry military, newly rich settlers full of rum, locals would who not surrender their land without a fight and a disengaged London.

David Collins catalogued a tragic cycle of settler provocation, local raid and settler reprisal that led to 'open war' within months. In September 1794, a settler and his servant were ambushed in their hut, and almost clubbed to death. Collins wrote: 'A few days after this circumstance, a body of natives having attacked the settlers, and carried off their clothes, provisions, and whatever else they could lay their hands on, the sufferers collected what arms they could, and following them, seven or eight of the plunderers were killed on the spot.'

A retaliation on this scale was unlikely to have occurred under

Arthur Phillip's rule. If it had, the settlers would probably have been punished to assure the locals that justice had been served. Under Phillip, a convict typically received 150 lashes if found guilty of attacking an Aboriginal. Then again, the Hawkesbury settlers might have behaved differently if the area had been developed more systematically, with troops living alongside them, and a humanitarian governor to negotiate with the locals.

Collins blamed the former convicts for the troubles. He detailed horrible examples of settler violence, including the torture and murder of a local child in October 1794. 'The presence of some person with authority was becoming absolutely necessary among those settlers, who, finding themselves freed from bondage, instantly conceived that they were above all restrictions.'

But there was no respite from the violence. Francis Grose departed the colony in December 1794 due to ill health, but John Hunter did not board the ship that would bring him back to Sydney until late February 1795. This left the second-in-command of the Rum Corps, William Paterson, as acting governor until Hunter finally arrived in September. Paterson was the wrong man to mind the colony. In May 1795, with Hunter still at sea, Paterson received a report of another raid by locals in which one free settler and one former convict had been killed. He responded with an order to massacre the locals.

Paterson dispatched sixty members of the New South Wales Corps from Parramatta 'with instructions to destroy as many as they could meet with of the wood tribe (Be-dia-gal); and, in the hope of striking terror, to erect gibbets in different places, whereon the bodies of all they might kill were to be hung.'

The Rum Corps achieved the first part of the mission, killing several people, including women and children, but they failed to secure the bodies of tribal warriors for display. Whether Hunter would have acted differently cannot be known. The military were now permanently stationed on the Hawkesbury. Collins wrote,

'And the soldiers were distributed among the settlers for their protection; a protection, however, that many of them did not merit.'

The questions of who actually ran the colony, and for whose benefit it had been established, were not easy to answer. The governor
had the power of a dictator, but struggled to exercise that authority
while the military controlled the economy between 1793 and 1809.
John Hunter, Philip Gidley King and William Bligh, respectively
the second, third and fourth rulers of this tiny convict settlement,
each failed to reign in the Rum Corps. Hunter and King were out-
manoeuvred by the military, while Bligh proved more stubborn
and was overthrown in a coup on the twentieth anniversary of the
colony's founding, 26 January 1808. London swung between inat-
tention and futile micromanagement during this insolent era, with
orders from the Home Office taking up to a year to be delivered by
sea mail.

What London did not appreciate was that once the military
was brought down to earth, only the convict could rise in its place.
There were simply not enough free settlers to take advantage of the
next phase of colonial expansion. The problem for the locals was
that this expansion to the west of Sydney would follow the same
deadly pattern as on the Hawkesbury.

The governor sent to restore order was the Scottish-born Lachlan
Macquarie. Unlike his predecessors, who had all been naval officers, Macquarie was a soldier. London believed this would make
a difference as it was assumed military men better understood the
value of compromise.

Macquarie arrived in January 1810 and found the colony upbeat,
but in disrepair. It was 'barely emerging from infantile imbecility',
he wrote. 'The Country impenetrable beyond 40 miles from Sydney; Agriculture in a yet languishing state; commerce in its early
dawn; Revenue unknown; threatened by famine; distracted by

faction; the public buildings in a state of dilapidation and moulding to decay; the few Roads and Bridges, formerly constructed, rendered almost impassable; the population in general depressed by poverty; no public credit nor private confidence; the morals of the great mass of the population in the lowest state of debasement, and religious worship almost totally neglected.'

Sydney and its surrounding settlements were confined to a strip of land that could be covered in a day's riding, with the Pacific Ocean to the east and nature's imposing wall of the Blue Mountains to the west, which would not be crossed until 1813. Along the narrow paths of the capital, animals jostled with people for right of way. 'Horse and foot passengers in the streets of Sydney sustain great inconvenience and danger by pigs, goats and dogs being permitted to wander at large through the town,' Macquarie observed.

He widened the streets, introduced footpaths on either side and made a symbolic change to the main drag. Sergeant-Major's Row, which ran through the centre of the town, was renamed George Street 'in honour of our revered and gracious sovereign.' Putting convicts to work to tidy up the settlement seems like an innocuous, logical thing to do. But Macquarie took his instructions liberally. He saw himself as a nation-builder, and with no one to tell him otherwise, he wrote the second chapter of Australian egalitarianism: state-led growth, with grand projects across Sydney and the surrounding settlements. He built Sydney's first hospital, relying, ironically, on the rum trade to pay for it after London refused to fund the venture. He then introduced a coin-based currency to replace rum, and despite London's objections, opened a people's bank – the Bank of New South Wales. When he had finished his career as governor in 1821, after eleven years and eleven months in charge, Macquarie tallied up the public works he had delivered. He counted 265 in total, including a new military barracks, a new church, a refurbished Government House, public buildings for officials, a lighthouse, schools and lunatic asylums for Sydney, as well as roads, bridges and the opening of half a dozen new townships.

The most far-reaching change came in his first year in office, and it was to the colony's social structure. Macquarie was struck by the injustice of Arthur Phillip's policy of keeping the former convicts apart from the free settlers. The former convicts did have land, but, with a handful of exceptions, were excluded from important official positions. Macquarie thought those who had been sentenced for trivial offences, and who had behaved well, deserved full restoration to their former rank in society. His plan was initially approved by Lord Bathurst and a select committee of the House of Commons. But London had second thoughts once it realised that the colony was being run for the benefit of the convict. New South Wales was supposed to punish the felon through transportation and deter crime at home, not act as a social laboratory. Each advance made by a former convict drove another wedge between the colony and the mother country, separating the egalitarian son from the class-conscious parent.

As with Phillip's pro-convict policies, Macquarie's were enabled by imperial neglect. Britain was still distracted by its rivalry with France and the colonial population stagnated in Macquarie's first six years, growing by just 600 per year – 150 people per year fewer than the convict intake of the First Fleet. Of those 600, about 400 were prisoners, a handful were free settlers and the remainder were born locally.

It was only after Napoleon met his Waterloo in 1815 that London gave the settlement any serious thought. The soaring crime rate in the mother country meant that between 1815 and 1819 the colonial population more than doubled from 15 063 to 31 472, as the boats carried ever larger intakes of felons, but still only a small portion of free settlers. The arrival of so many people after what seemed like an eternity of hardship created the colony's first housing shortage.

The private economy couldn't cope with the influx. There were not enough free settlers to provide jobs for the newly arrived convicts, so Macquarie conveniently took seven out of every eight for himself, and stepped up his public works program. He employed the convicts in 'numerous Gangs in all parts of the Colony; repairing the old public Roads and Bridges, and constructing new ones'. The remainder was sent to the government farm at Emu Plains.

Lachlan Macquarie would soon incur London's wrath for elevating the former convict, and historians have often drawn attention to this as a pivotal moment in the development of Australia's egalitarian culture. What is less well reported is that he also made the fatal official decision to place the convict above the Indigenous person, and signed that contract with an order for a massacre. The confrontation was an inevitable result of Macquarie's program of settlement expansion, which placed former convicts on land that the locals did not want to give up.

Macquarie had intended to treat the locals kindly, and his early diaries contain repeated references to warm meetings with tribal leaders. At 'Aboriginal Feast Day' held in Parramatta on 28 December 1814, the governor entertained up to sixty people of all ages. He advised the tribes of the advantages they would derive if they changed their 'manners' and applied themselves to 'moderate industry'. They lunched on roast beef, washed down with 'a cheering jug of ale'. The governor had expected more people to turn up, but some stayed away because they feared they would be 'forcibly deprived of their children and themselves sent to labour'. There was a precedent for this: at the Hawkesbury, settlers had said they were taking Indigenous children for their safety, and had not returned them when their parents asked for them. Macquarie assured the locals he had no such plans. The governor wanted to protect the children, especially in winter 'when the weather is cold, the woods afford them little or no food, and they become a prey to many loathsome diseases which poverty entails upon the human frame'. He was aware that the 'clearing of immense forests' for settler farming had deprived the locals of customary food sources – kangaroo, and more recently possum meat.

From Macquarie's perspective, his was a policy of compassion, providing shelter and education. But from the Indigenous perspective it was the second act of dispossession. First the land had been taken, and now the white man wanted their children.

The governor must have understood that the land had a prior occupant. The First Fleeters even had some inkling of the Indigenous attachment to the country. Macquarie may have been familiar with the exhaustive summary of the locals and their customs written by David Collins in 1796. Under the heading 'Property', he explained, 'They have also their real estates. Bennillong [sic], both before he went to England and since his return, often assured me, that the island Me-mel – called by us Goat Island – close by Sydney Cove was his own property; that it was his father's, and that he should give it to By-gone, his particular friend and companion. To this little spot he appeared much attached; and we have often seen him and his wife Ba-rang-a-roo feasting and enjoying themselves on it. He told us of other people who possessed this kind of hereditary property, which they retained undisturbed.' Governor Philip Gidley King had told William Bligh that he always considered the Indigenous people 'the real Proprietors of the Soil'.

The troubles on the Hawkesbury should have given Macquarie pause. Yet Macquarie proved to be no more benevolent than the acting governors of the Rum Corps, even though he hoped to be seen as the humanitarian heir to Arthur Phillip.

The relationship broke down at Appin, south-west of Sydney, after the locals had launched a number of raids on settlers in the autumn of 1816. Macquarie accused them of committing 'murders, outrages, and Depredations of all descriptions'. He had pleaded with them 'to discontinue their hostile Incursions'. He did not specify which incident forced him to act. But, he wrote in his diary, he had 'to protect the European Inhabitants in their Persons & Properties against these frequent and sudden hostile and sanguinary attacks from the Natives'. The governor issued the order for a massacre on

16 April, telling his troops to clear the area of the 'Native Blacks of this County' and drive them 'across the mountains'.

He declared mission accomplished on 4 May with fourteen locals killed, and five taken prisoner. The local warrior Kanabygal was hanged from a tree and later beheaded. His skull was sent to Edinburgh as a trophy of war.

Macquarie gave his account to the Home Office in a letter to Lord Bathurst, dated 8 June 1816. He said that only two of those deemed guilty had been killed. The other twelve to lose their lives were 'innocent Men, Women and Children'. He regretted their deaths but hoped their example would 'eventually strike Terror amongst the surviving Tribes, and deter them from the further Commission of such sanguinary Outrages and Barbarities.'

The line Lachlan Macquarie had drawn across the settlement was based on colour, not class. He treated former convicts as the equals of free settlers. But the locals could only be accepted on the same terms as the migrants if they became like the migrants, agreeing to work for the greater good of the colony as farmers or servants.

After Macquarie, the policy of open war became the imperial preference.

A second penal colony had been founded in 1803 at Van Diemen's Land, and for two decades the authorities maintained some order without taking sides. In 1826, the colony's lieutenant governor George Arthur vowed to punish all wrongdoers equally whenever the two cultures clashed. As the violence escalated through that year, he took the side of the settlers, even though they were often the aggressor. He abandoned his program of 'amity and kindness' at the end of 1826. Those locals who were hostile to settlement were declared 'open enemies' and were to be rounded up for deportation to Flinders Island in Bass Strait. Late in 1830, Arthur drew a 'black line' across Van Diemen's Land, thus making every local an enemy of the settlement, whether they had taken up arms or not. The last 123 members of the Indigenous community were exiled to the island in 1835. Charles Darwin visited the colony shortly afterwards, and found the venture cruel but unavoidable. 'All the aborigines have been removed to an island in Bass Strait, so that Van Diemen's Land enjoys the great advantage of being free from a native population,' he wrote.

As the Hawkesbury had shown, free settlers held no higher moral standards than soldiers or ex-convicts. Western Australia proved another case in point. It had been established as a free colony in 1829, and by 1834 its first lieutenant governor James Stirling was leading a 25-strong force of police, soldiers and settlers to deal with the Pindjarup tribe, which had threatened to destroy all the whites within the district. Although outnumbered three-to-one, Stirling's posse had guns; the locals carried only spears. The official record states that fifteen of the seventy-strong tribe were killed, but witnesses said thirty locals trapped in a waterhole were executed.

Queensland was established as a prison colony in 1824, but the main bloodletting did not come until the second half of the decade, when free settlers and former convicts expanded into more populated areas. In the free colonies of Victoria (founded in 1835) and South Australia (1836), authorities attempted to avoid the errors with limited success.

The decline of the Indigenous people was shockingly rapid. A local population of up to one million across Australia in 1788 was reduced to fewer than ninety-five thousand by 1901. This was the year of federation, when the six existing colonies formed a nation of almost 3.8 million people. The locals were not counted in that first Commonwealth census, but if their number is added to the 'official' population, they accounted for 2.5 per cent of the total. Disease is assumed to have been the biggest killer, but many were slain by the settlers; perhaps twenty thousand, according to a summary by historian John Hirst. Others have suggested a significantly larger number. There is less debate about the two thousand settlers and convicts who were killed in return.

A migrant nation was built on top of the old one, in which even the most wretched arrival could aspire to a good life. But the key to colonial upward mobility – the grant of land – was based on the convenient but erroneous assumption that the country had no prior owner.

It became clear to London by 1817, with New South Wales not yet thirty years old, that Lachlan Macquarie was trying to create a convict paradise. This was abhorrent to the ruling classes, yet the view from the bottom of British society reflected another reality. Criminals appearing before Britain's courts were asking to be sent to the colony on the not unreasonable expectation that they would prosper once they had completed their sentence.

Slowly London came to believe that Macquarie had exceeded his mandate, but the corrective action took so long that it was impossible to restore the colony to its original brutal purpose as a prison.

Lord Bathurst, secretary of state for the colonies in the Tory government of Lord Liverpool, appointed John Thomas Bigge royal commissioner and sent him to Sydney in 1819 with instructions to put the convicts back in their place.

'You are aware of the causes which first led to the Formation of the Settlements in New Holland [New South Wales]. As they were peculiar in themselves, these Settlements cannot be administered with the usual Reference to those general Principles of Colonial Policy, which are applicable to other Foreign Possessions of His Majesty. Not having been established with any view to Territorial or Commercial Advantages, they must chiefly be considered as Receptacles for Offenders.'

Lord Bathurst asked Bigge to look at how convicts might be kept separate from 'the Mass of the Population'. He also canvassed the fallback option of starting afresh with new penal settlements 'on other parts of the Coasts, or in the Interior of the Country'.

This was the two-tier society Phillip had in mind before the First Fleet left Portsmouth in England in 1787. But it was too late to recreate that snobbish ideal because the colony had already crossed an important threshold. By 1820, as Bigge was writing the first volume of his report, the majority of the New South Wales population – 53 per cent – was already free. But free settlers represented just 7 per cent of the total population. Former convicts were double their number (17 per cent) and the local-born were four times larger (29 per cent).

And so London found itself caught between its preference for transportation and its need to give the free population political rights. Bigge would recommend an end to the autocratic power of the governor. A small legislative council was established after Macquarie left which could modify the governor's laws, but not initiate any of its own. The members of this parliament were appointed, not elected, and they would include former convicts. The upward mobility that had so offended London could not be reversed; in fact, it would accelerate for those lucky enough to have served their sentences under Macquarie or his predecessors.

The first volume of the Bigge report, delivered in 1822, found that land was the key to respectability in the colony. The prospect of acquiring and enjoying property gave the convict a 'great incentive to reformation and moral improvement'. Bigge might have stopped there, with an implicit endorsement of Macquarie's egalitarian policies. But he saw the advances made by former convicts as an affront to the free settlers.

'Yet it has been remarked in the colony, and so often, till at last it has become proverbial, that the surest claim to the favour and confidence of Governor Macquarie was that of having once worn the badge of conviction for felony,' Bigge advised the House of Commons.

'In bestowing upon the emancipated convicts so great a mark as that of introduction to society,' Macquarie had insulted the free settler. The levelling of hierarchy, Bigge wrote, was 'an act of violence to those of the free population'.

But Bigge undermined the free settlers he wished to encourage with recommendations that increased the flow of convicts to New South Wales and Van Diemen's Land, and led to the establishment of new prisons in Queensland. Free settlers were reluctant to move to Australia while transportation remained London's main priority.

Fifty thousand convicts were sent to Australia in the fifteen years after the report's release, between 1823 and 1837, while only thirty thousand free settlers migrated in that time. The convicts had fewer rights than their predecessors because governors no longer had the discretion to award early pardons, or make generous grants of land and they were subjected to a regime of arbitrary cruelty. In 1835, for instance, twenty-three thousand serving convicts had more than one hundred thousand lashes applied to their backs.

The real act of violence was from the mother country to the colonial child. The extension of transportation retarded Australia's cultural development, even as a new bounty was about to reveal itself in the wool trade that drove the settlement deeper into traditional lands.

Many of the elements for a civilisation were still missing. Australia could not shed the baggage of its convict foundation until it corrected the population shortages in free settlers and women, and harnessed the critical ingredient for a prosperous migrant nation – diversity.

3

THE BEGINNING
OF DIVERSITY

The first thing the new arrival notices about Australia is the space. The country beckons to be exploited. Deep in the subconscious there must be some recognition that the migrant nation rose at the expense of the Indigenous nation, because the white man has always worried that the next arrival would overrun him. The source of this anxiety is complex. It is influenced by the continent's distance from the mother country, and the vulnerability felt by a small settler population. Another factor is the foundation shortfall left by transportation. The convicts were excessively English and male, creating a homogeneity that was bound to be challenged by the arrival of people of different backgrounds. The first intake to test that identity in Australia's formative years was the Irish.

There had been Irish convicts on the First Fleet, but it wasn't until the turn of the nineteenth century that the transport ships deposited them in large numbers. They came as political prisoners after the failed Irish Rebellion of 1798, forcing a social experiment on the penal colony that mixed England's exiles with its tribal enemy.

These Irish almost certainly carried a grudge against London. Their uprising at home had been brutally suppressed by soldiers from the same military culture that would be guarding them in New South Wales. Up to twenty-five thousand Irish insurgents and civilians had been killed in the one-sided battle, while the British and loyalist troops lost six hundred of their comrades. Local rebel leaders were executed without trial, their severed heads stuck on spikes or on buildings in the most public places, to remind the locals who was in charge. The Rum Corps had deployed the same extreme force on the Hawkesbury three years earlier, on the orders of William Paterson.

The architect of the Irish massacre was Earl Camden, the lord lieutenant of Ireland. At his own request, he was replaced by General Lord Cornwallis, who called a halt to the summary killings. In a letter to a friend in London that year, 1798, Cornwallis complained that 'our people' in the military had been committing 'numberless murders' by the hour 'without any proper process or examination whatever'. 'Their folly in making it a religious war added to the ferocity of our troops who delight in murder,' he wrote.

But Cornwallis still wanted to be rid of the insurgents and their sympathisers. Rebels were offered a deal: surrender, and they would be transported to New South Wales for the term of their natural lives. The first group was received by John Hunter. On his retirement in 1800, he was replaced by another First Fleeter, Philip Gidley King. In one of xenophobia's first dispatches against the Irish, King wrote a vicious letter to the Duke of Portland in March 1801 demanding that London send no more rebels to him. In the governor's estimation, the transport *Anne* had just delivered '137 of the most desperate and diabolical characters that could have been selected throughout the Kingdom'. This brought the total number of Irish in the colony to six hundred, out of a population of almost six thousand.

'I am well aware, my Lord, that this colony was formed for the reception of such characters as could not with safety be kept in Ireland or England,' King explained. '[But] if many more of the Irish Republicans are sent out here I do not know what will be the consequences.'

He argued that the Irish were 'certainly not a proper description to people an infant colony with', echoing the concern Arthur Phillip had expressed about the English convict. Once again, the needs of empire and the grinding demands of holding the settlement together appeared to be at odds.

King's opinion changed quickly once he made contact with the objects of his apprehension. In November 1801, he praised the good conduct of the Irish under his guard, and pleaded for clemency for those sent to him on false charges. 'I have great pleasure in informing your Grace of the general regular and quiet behaviour of those deluded people, the Irish,' he wrote.

What King did not say, but which can be deduced by the colonial record, is that many of the Irish rebels came with much-needed skills. Among the political prisoners to prosper under King was James Meehan. He had arrived in 1800 and was put to work as a servant for the colony's acting surveyor Charles Grimes. Meehan thrived in the job, and by 1803 was trusted to run the office when Grimes went on extended leave.

King also appreciated a point that London could not from its perspective as an imperial power. The Irish were less likely to repeat the troubles of the old country if their faith was respected. In 1803, the governor lifted the ban that applied to Catholics practising their religion in New South Wales. King came to trust James Dixon, a Catholic priest from Ireland's County Wexford, and in April that year granted him a conditional emancipation. The first public mass was held less than a month later, on 15 May 1803. The arrangement worked so well that King put Father Dixon on the official payroll, giving him more rights as a former convict in New South Wales than a free Irishman in the United Kingdom. Catholics did not enjoy full rights in Britain or Ireland at the time. Although they could practise their religion, they were barred from parliament and public office.

However, New South Wales was not entirely immune from

the conflict between England and Ireland. The reconciliation that King had pursued was interrupted less than twelve months later, in March 1804, when hundreds of convicts staged an uprising at the government farm of Castle Hill, north-west of Sydney. It was a jailbreak with a political purpose, and appeared to reflect King's original assessment that the Irish posed an unacceptable threat. The insurgents were roused by the news they had just received of a second failed rebellion in Dublin the previous year. The two hundred convicts at Castle Hill intended to link up with men on the Hawkesbury, forming a combined force of eleven hundred. They would march to Parramatta and then Sydney, where they would board ships back to Ireland.

But even here, as the rebels came face-to-face with the trigger-happy Rum Corps, Australia refused to repeat the history of the old country. The plot had been an open secret and Father Dixon, among others, had urged his compatriots to call off the uprising. His pleas were ignored. The military dealt with the rebels swiftly and brutally, killing nine, stopping short of the massacres their comrades had unleashed in Ireland, and that they themselves had indulged in on the Hawkesbury. The critical difference was the role of Governor King. He wanted to avoid a slaughter, and the troops, perhaps feeling a kinship with the Irish that they did not share with the Indigenous population, demonstrated a level of restraint that was unusual for men in their uniform. It is also likely that the religious fervour within the affluent Rum Corps was less pronounced than in the equivalent, less well-remunerated detachments serving in Ireland.

The first group of Castle Hill leaders to be tried included a number who claimed to have been coerced into taking part in the uprising. The court wasn't swayed, and all ten were executed. Four of the condemned happened to be Irish Protestants, and another two were English. Yet the Irish Catholics suffered a disproportionate share of the recriminations. King withdrew public support for

Father Dixon, and ordered all convicts to attend Anglican services. But this illiberal ban wasn't adhered to. Here was the ultimate contrast with the old country. Even as the governor reverted to sectarianism, the people of the colony found a way to get along. Father Dixon continued to practise privately, without harassment. The 1806 muster recorded him as 'Roman Catholic priest, self-employed'. He returned to his old parish in Ireland two years later.

Castle Hill was the exception that proved a deeper point: migrants in Australia had the ability to come together in cultural pairings that would have been unthinkable at home. It was the solitary Irish uprising in the colony, and it was quashed with an un-British benevolence. Catholic and Protestant had defied their parents by preventing Australia from becoming another front in the civil war. This and the rejection of the mother country's class structure under governors Arthur Phillip and Lachlan Macquarie are the two defining traits that distinguished Australia from Britain and the United States – it was egalitarian for the white man and wary of religious extremism. The difficulty came in extending the principle of equality to women.

There were three men for every woman on the First Fleet, and Arthur Phillip had worried that this gender imbalance would imperil the settlement if left uncorrected. 'The very small proportion of females makes the sending out of an additional number absolutely necessary,' Phillip wrote to Lord Sydney on 15 May 1788, in the same dispatch in which he requested troops to guard the convicts and skilled migrants to raise the colony's productivity.

However, when his call was answered with the women of the Second Fleet, Phillip's officers seethed into their diaries. David Collins recorded the arrival of the *Lady Juliana* in June 1790 as an affront to the starving men. 'In the distressed situation of the colony, it was not a little mortifying to find on board the first ship that arrived, a cargo so unnecessary and unprofitable as two hundred and twenty-two females, instead of a cargo of provisions.'

Women were seen by the governors as a distraction from the task of nation-building. Phillip's successor, John Hunter, saw the issue through the economic lens. In a dispatch to the Duke of Portland written in November 1796, he hoped that a boat then on its way to Sydney Cove would contain no female convicts at all.

'I must express my hope that the three hundred are all men, and not part men and part women, for of the latter we have already enough,' Hunter wrote. 'We have scarsely [sic] any way of employing them, and they are generally found to be worse characters than the men; if we had more work for them it would often be difficult to employ them, for we generally find those of a certain age taken up in the indispensible dutys [sic] of nursing an infant.'

The male convict could redeem himself through work. The penal colony employed him as a builder or a farmer and when his term ended, he was given land. The female convict, by contrast, had a narrower path to respectability: marriage. The settlement had almost no use for her as a worker unless she was taken into a settler's home as a servant, or placed in a government factory. If she was dismissed from a settler's home, she slept out in the town, placing her at immediate risk of mistreatment.

Most convict women had been transported to the colonies for petty crimes. None had been sentenced for prostitution, because this was never a transportable offence. But some did fall into prostitution once in the colonies.

When royal commissioner John Thomas Bigge landed in Sydney in 1819, he was shocked by the crudity of the settlement. 'As long as the great disproportion continues to exist between the male and female population in New South Wales, the temptations to illicit intercourse in both, and all the crimes that are committed for the purpose of supporting it, must be expected to prevail,' he wrote. But he had no viable plan to close the gender gap. Nine out of ten convicts sent to New South Wales and Van Diemen's Land following the Bigge inquiry were male, erasing whatever small gains were being made towards gender balance through natural birth and the slow trickle of free settlers. By 1831 the gap across the colonies was still no different to what it had been on the First Fleet – three males for every female. The difference now was the majority of men were free, yet the mistreatment of women persisted, suggesting the problem was deeper than just transportation. By the 1830s, women were ten times more likely to be raped in New South Wales than in England. To put that figure in the perspective of the time, rape was as common in the colony as petty larceny was in the mother country.

All settler societies are founded with an excess of men, but Australia's gender gap persisted because of the staggered nature of colonial development. Each new settlement after New South Wales – Van Diemen's Land (1803), Queensland (1824), Western Australia (1829) and Victoria (1835) – was founded with more males than the Australian average at the time. The exception was the free settlement of South Australia (1836), which received not one of the 137 000 male convicts and 25 000 female convicts sent to Australia between 1788 and 1868.

Australia would remain the most masculine of the migrant countries throughout the 1800s. As late as 1881, long after transportation had ceased, Australia was still 54 per cent male when the United States and Canada were approaching fifty-fifty splits.

A little-known aspect of the population story of this era is the role that Britain's own demography played in Australia's blokey demeanour. Britain's population was majority female across the nineteenth century because it lost more men than women to emigration. Given that Australia was one of the main destinations for those men, the difference between mother country and colonial son – between the refined, class-conscious Briton and the plain-spoken, egalitarian Australian – was reinforced with each boat.

The gender gap reflected the distance still to be covered between settlement and civilisation; between an open-air prison that served Britain's narrow interest in cleansing its own ethnicity, and a migrant nation that could attract Europe's newly mobile working and middle classes. While London remained attached to transportation, the free settler would be discouraged. For the foundation shortfall of Australia to be redressed, the colonies had to demonstrate their worth as something other than a dumping ground for felons. They needed an economic purpose.

The mother country's view of Australia began changing in the 1830s, as Britain's own economy and politics were being radically transformed. The combination of peace after the Napoleonic Wars and the rapid advances of the Industrial Revolution had overturned the old agricultural order. New technology was reducing the cost of manufacturing cloth, while the Corn Laws had put a floor under the price of grain to protect farmers, which artificially inflated food prices. This made the sheep on the British Isles more valuable for their meat than their fleece. To keep the textile mills spinning, the raw materials had to be sourced from overseas. New South Wales had been trying to enter the wool trade since the earliest years of settlement and by 1831 had claimed 8 per cent of the British wool market.

The long Tory rule in Westminster ended in November 1830, when Earl Charles Grey's Whig Party came to power with the most radical agenda Britain had known. Voting rights were to be extended to one-sixth of the British population and slavery abolished across the empire. Transportation did not fit into this moral universe and, inevitably, it would be reviewed.

The Whigs took office at the very moment when Britain's problems of overcrowding, unemployment and income inequality reached a tipping point. The working and middle classes began a mass emigration that would eventually see about ten million people leave England, Scotland and Wales, and a further seven million depart Ireland between 1830 and 1930.

Almost sixty thousand people left the United Kingdom in 1830. More than eighty thousand followed in 1831, and a further one hundred thousand in 1832. Nine in ten went to the United States. This exodus to the former American colonies finally forced London to reconsider the role of its unloved Australian colonies.

The Tories might have said good riddance to the British masses yearning to be Americans, but London no longer had the luxury of indifference. If no effort was made to divert some emigrants to Australia, Britain would have populated its US rival at its own expense, while leaving Australia permanently retarded.

The Whigs asked the obvious question: why would an emigrant choose America over Australia? The answers were clear enough: price, distance and familiarity. America was nearby – just six weeks' sailing time. Australia was three or four months away, and the boat fare was the equivalent of two-thirds of the annual wage that a labourer could expect to make at the other end. Migrants to America reported favourably back to their friends and relatives in Britain while Australia's reputation as a convict paradise continued to discourage free settlers. Of the nearly 250 000 emigrants who had left the United Kingdom in the 1820s, less than 4 per cent, or 8935, went to Australia.

To change this equation, the government would have to intervene in the market to reduce the cost of moving to Australia. The Whigs would not do this out of their own pockets, but they could give New South Wales the authority to raise special taxes to help cover the cost of the boat fare to Sydney. The decision was taken in 1831 to create a land fund. Revenue would be set aside from the sale of Crown land in the colonies to assist the passage of Britons to Australia. This policy also removed the power of governors to grant land, so the new arrivals would come as free migrants but not free settlers. They would be motivated workers and professionals, not pampered landholders.

It is interesting to note that gender was cited as one of the main reasons for the scheme, although it would inevitably address the wider problem of attracting free migrants. The Home Office advised the Treasury Office that the land fund would help remedy the 'serious evil' of too many men. 'Their Lordships are doubtless aware how necessary it is for the moral improvement of the Colony to correct the existing disproportion of the sexes, which has produced such unhappy effects.'

Among the first to receive assisted passage were young women hand-picked to work as servants. Three boats arrived during 1833 and were greeted by governor Richard Bourke, the colony's first Irish-born ruler, who had been appointed by the Whigs in 1831.

Bourke told the Home Office that the first two boats were well received, but the third to dock that year, the *Layton*, had brought shame to the colony. His dispatch recycled the complaint of John Hunter about the value of female migrants. Of the 232 women and girls on board the *Layton*, only fifty were of good character. 'It appears from the statements of Mr. Beilby, the Superintendent, and the Surgeon Mr. Bule that an almost unlimited intercourse existed between the seamen and a great number of the female passengers during the voyage.'

Bourke blamed the London broker who wanted to fill the ships as quickly as possible. This unhappy experience led to a new scheme, which moved the governor from passive recipient of new arrivals to an active recruiter. For the first time in almost half a century of settlement, the colony would determine the composition of its population. Migrants were to be selected by an agent of the colony not connected to the shipping company. The ship's captain was paid for each person who landed safely in Sydney.

The system was unique at the time, with the colonial economy dictating the migrant that would be sought. Later, Canada would copy it when it was fed up with losing its own people to the United States. What it gave the colonies in the 1830s and 1840s was an injection of creativity that laid a new foundation for Australia as a high-income, urban settlement. But this came through a lucky break that no one could have predicted when the scheme was first mooted in 1831. Australia went shopping for free migrants just as a global wool boom was underway. Wool unleashed a cycle of rising export income and rising land values that created the need for more migrants.

The first list of free migrants drawn up in New South Wales sought mechanics, butlers, maids and unmarried women, reflecting both the needs of landholders with an interest in wool and the governor's desire to close the gender gap. The only families accepted had to have a skilled breadwinner, and no more than three children. The scheme made history in 1837 when the colony received five thousand free migrants and four thousand convicts: the first occasion on which the felons had been outnumbered in a single year.

As the wool boom accelerated, the government and private interests expanded their list of wanted migrants to include shepherds, stockmen and agricultural labourers. Employers were offering wages double or treble the going rate in England. The numbers attracted by this suddenly viable settlement were staggering. Almost eighty thousand free migrants landed from January 1838 to December 1841. To put that number in perspective, it had taken the settlement forty-six years from 1788 to establish a colonial population of one hundred thousand, the majority of whom had been convicts.

Under the old system, Australia could have expected to receive less than 10 per cent of the people leaving the United Kingdom at the time. The super intake of almost eighty thousand would have been less than thirty thousand in the absence of assisted passage, and the difference would have gone to the United States.

Theoretically, they had been lured by the pastoral economy,

specifically the wool boom. Yet they had no intention of living an agrarian life. Among them were lawyers, public servants, politicians and media proprietors. They were the disgruntled and ambitious working and middle classes of Britain and Ireland, fleeing high unemployment for a fantastic new Promised Land that would pay their boat fare and guarantee them a well-paid job on arrival. But they were more than just migrants in search of a better life for themselves. They wanted to make a better society than the one they had left. The economic and the social motivation of this group can been seen in four powerful case studies.

Henry Parkes, a failed businessman from Birmingham, spoke for his generation when he wrote a farewell poem to England, cursing the society whose injustices compelled men like him 'to seek the means of existence in a foreign wilderness'. He and his wife Clarinda had moved from Birmingham to London in search of a fresh start in 1838, but were frustrated by the lack of opportunities and, in March 1839, they boarded a ship for assisted passage to Sydney. They struggled at first before Parkes found work as a labourer on a farm. They returned to Sydney, where slowly Parkes moved from working for others to running his own business, and then into media and politics. His newspaper *The Empire* was the leading journal of its day in New South Wales. He became premier of New South Wales, and ultimately the most influential colonial politician of the nineteenth century.

London-born Mary Colton, nee Cutting, was seventeen when she went to Adelaide in 1839 with her widowed father, her brother and sister. She married John Colton in 1844, and became one of South Australia's best-known community workers. Her defining achievement came later in life as the president of the Woman's Suffrage League, which helped secure the vote for women in 1895.

Another of the class of 1839 was Redmond Barry, a young lawyer from Ireland. He was barely making a living in the overcrowded legal profession of Dublin. In Melbourne, he joined the establishment as a judge of the Victorian Supreme Court in 1852.

Irish-born Robert Torrens disembarked in Adelaide in December 1840, where he soon joined the public service as collector of customs. He was a nominated member of the SA Legislative Council in the 1850s, and later premier. His greatest contribution to colonial life was the reform of the land titles system, which remains the basis of property law today.

These recruits are one of the most fascinating pieces in the Australian puzzle, an urban people who came to idealise the bush. They brought with them the idealism of the age, when Britain's technological, military and cultural power was approaching its zenith.

One of the immediate consequences of these migrants as the new majority was that London now had a much-needed incentive to halt transportation to the Australian mainland. Without assisted passage, the issue might not have been settled for many more years. The Whigs had appointed the young radical William Molesworth to review the system, and his committee began taking evidence in 1837, the year the free migrants outnumbered convicts for the first time. Molesworth found that transportation had become a costly and cruel failure. It would be cheaper to build more jails at home than to send another convict to Australia.

He tabled his report in 1838, but it was his speech to the British parliament two years later that jolted the Whigs into action. Molesworth delivered a moral and practical argument.

Transportation had contributed to the 'depraved character of the [Australian] population', he said. 'Abolish transportation, and there will be no difficulty in procuring emigrants for those colonies . . . The amount of emigration should be such as would, within a very short period, entirely swamp the convict population and completely alter the moral character of those communities.'

Molesworth spoke on 5 May 1840. Seventeen days later the head of the Colonial Office, John Russell, ended transportation to New South Wales, leaving just Van Diemen's Land and Norfolk Island open for the old business of punishment.

Yet even as the free migrants were swamping the convict population, the gender gap persisted because the Australian economy's immediate needs for shepherds and labourers overwhelmed all other considerations.

Assisted passage was not a female-friendly policy in practice. It hadn't occurred to Richard Bourke or his successor as governor, George Gipps, to give the newly arrived migrant any help if they failed to find immediate work or shelter. This made the trip to Sydney more a game of roulette than the lottery win being promoted by the migration agents in London. The most vulnerable free migrants were the young single women.

English philanthropist Caroline Chisholm saw the problem more clearly than the officials, and began to agitate for reform. She and her husband, Captain Archibald Chisholm of the East India Company, had only intended to take leave in New South Wales. They landed in 1838, but when Captain Chisholm was recalled to active duty in 1840, Caroline remained behind with her three sons.

She became a one-woman welfare and employment agency, greeting each ship that arrived in Sydney. Chisholm took care of young migrant girls, arranging suitable employment, and provided shelter for many of them in her own home. In 1841 she established a girls' home, paid for entirely by public subscriptions.

She told London that the colony would never have a 'good and virtuous people' while the gender gap persisted. 'For all the clergy you can dispatch, all the schoolmasters you can appoint, all the churches you can build, and all the books you can export, will never do much good, without what a gentleman in that colony very appropriately called "God's police" – wives and little children – good and virtuous women.'

But her campaign kept hitting the brick wall of demography. As the colony acquired its new reputation as a workers' paradise in the 1840s, the ships continued to carry many more men than women.

The gender gap was ultimately reduced, although not quite closed, by a tragic set of circumstances in Ireland.

The move from a penal settlement to a free one was lightning fast. It took the assisted passage wave of the late 1830s and early 1840s just five years to correct the half-century-long imbalance of transportation. Free migration changed the nation's ethnic face from predominately Anglo to almost equal parts Anglo and Celt. Although the English, Welsh and Scottish free migrants were excessively male, one tribe defied the gender gap: the Irish.

The collective Australian memory associates the Irish of the nineteenth century with men of resistance: the hero of Eureka Peter Lalor, and the bushranger Ned Kelly. But these caricatures are as statistically misleading as the notion that Australia's true identity resides in the bush. The Irish were the only major migrant group of the nineteenth century to land with more women than men. The mother of the Australian nation was not really England, but Ireland, and it made its mark almost half a century after the English convicts and Irish rebels negotiated the first tentative truce between the two tribes.

The exodus of the free Irish began some years after the free British, on terms that were bound to test the Anglo-Celtic union in Australia. Ireland was effectively an agrarian colony of Britain at the time. Four decades as part of the United Kingdom had failed to close the development gap between England, Wales and Scotland on the one hand, and Ireland on the other. The old hatreds remained, and when Ireland suffered the failure of its potato crop from 1845, London's blunders turned it into a catastrophic famine.

The Tories were back in power, and they were slow to appreciate the magnitude of the crisis. In 1846, the prime minister Robert Peel tried to speed up the relief effort by abolishing the Corn Laws to reduce the price of bread. This reform would come to be seen as the moment Britain embraced free trade. However, Peel split his own party and brought down his government. The Tories lost the next major parliamentary vote, bringing the anti-slavery Whigs back to power under Lord Russell.

But these Whigs had lost their moral compass. The official now in charge of the relief effort was Charles Trevelyan and he saw the famine as a message from God, telling the Irish to get off the land and stop relying on government handouts. 'The judgement of God had sent the famine to teach the Irish a lesson,' he explained in 1847. It wasn't his job to interfere 'too much' in God's work. 'The real evil which we have to contend with is not the physical evil of the Famine, but the moral evil of the selfish, perverse and turbulent character of the people.'

Trevelyan thought like a laissez-faire Karl Marx, seeing famine as a necessary step to a utopian Ireland. His book *The Irish Crisis* was even published in the same year as *The Communist Manifesto* – 1848.

One million Irish perished in the famine, and another two million abandoned the country between 1841 and 1855. The Irish population had been 8.2 million in 1841 – three times larger than Scotland's 2.6 million, and almost forty times larger than the colonial population of just over two hundred thousand. By 1911, both Scotland and Australia had surpassed Ireland's population of 4.4 million.

Most of the Irish went to the United States. But enough men, and many more women, came to the colonies to ensure Australia did not miss out on this migrant wave of opportunity. The first famine intake came between 1848 and 1851, as Australia embarked on its next big round of assisted passage. The colonies received ninety-four thousand free migrants from the United Kingdom in that four-year period, breaking the previous record of seventy-eight thousand between 1838 and 1841. It was the smallest, most vulnerable part of that intake which generated the greatest controversy and set the tone for Australian xenophobia in the free migrant age – the bigotry of the affluent.

Earl Grey had asked the Irish workhouses to find mechanics and servants to go to Australia. The United Kingdom would have fewer mouths to feed, and the colonies would have their incessant demands for skilled labour appeased. The workhouses replied with a warning and a recommendation. The young men were no better than the 'ordinary Irish labourer'. But there were a 'large number of well conducted young women' who deserved a new life in Australia.

Earl Grey promptly filled three boats with about two hundred girls each. The first vessel arrived in Sydney in May 1848, the second in Port Adelaide in July, and the third in Port Phillip in December. The girls were congratulated on 'their healthy, respectable appearance' by the Melbourne newspaper, *The Argus*. 'They have our best wishes that their lot in the land which is to be their future home and country will be a happy one.'

But the *Sydney Morning Herald*, the journal of the once-poor migrant John Fairfax, embarked on what may have been the first Australian media campaign against a vulnerable migrant group. No misdeed attributed to these girls went unpublished by the newspaper. Every court appearance, every rumoured outrage was reported in the most sensational terms. The readers obliged with polarised letters to the editor. One side wanted to defend the girls; the other wanted to throw them out.

Typical of the arguments that raged at the time was an exchange of letters to the *Sydney Morning Herald* in early 1850 between 'A Bushman' and a 'Looker On'.

The man from the bush thought the girls should be sent to what is now Queensland. 'If a vessel was dispatched immediately to Wide Bay with 200 of these girls, I have no hesitation in stating the whole of them would be married in two months.' The Sydney-based 'Looker On' replied that these girls were part of an elaborate conspiracy to conquer New South Wales from within.

'The lower orders of the Roman Catholics are now heard to boast in Sydney, that though the Protestants have succeeded in stopping

the importation of overwhelming numbers of grown up Roman-
ists . . . the priests have beaten them by getting out these girls, who
they anticipate will, with their offspring, give us, not many years
hence, a Popish ascendancy in New South Wales.'

On the day the 'Looker On' was having his say in the *Sydney
Morning Herald*, 105 girls were nearing the end of their two-week
journey from Sydney to the town of Yass. The local *Goulburn Herald
and County of Argyle Advertiser* embraced their arrival on 2 March
1850 with the warmth of the bush.

'In the afternoon great numbers of the towns people, especially
bachelors desirous of becoming Benedicts, crowded the opposite
banks of the river, to feast their eyes on the "dear creatures" as they
promenaded, danced or gamboled arm-in-arm on the recreation
green before the depot.'

When word was received in early 1850 of 'another ship load of
female orphans from Ireland' heading for Port Phillip, *The Argus*
urged its readers to protest on the grounds that it was an 'outra-
geous prostitution of the immigration fund'. But it wasn't only
about the money. 'We feel it to be our duty to state that further
experience has but shown that the evils we before referred to are
increasing, and that now, from the general disinclination of the
colonists to have anything to do with them as servants, they hang
on hand at the depot till a very considerable proportion of their
number join the ranks of the prostitutes infesting the more public
streets of the city.'

Undeterred by the genial encounter in Yass earlier that month,
the *Sydney Morning Herald* had also had enough. On 13 March, the
newspaper said it was not opposed 'to a fair proportion of immigrants born on Irish ground and professing the Romish faith. [But]
here we have an excess monstrously unreasonable. It is worse than
excess, it is absolute monopoly. Of British female orphans we do
not complain that we have had a disproportion, but that we have
had none at all.'

The editorial betrayed the chauvinism of the age. 'It is not an immigration of mere labour, but of sex; of females, and of young females. The destiny of these girls is understood by everybody. Their ostensible vocation is domestic service [and] domestic service is but a stepping stone to the higher and more influential position of wives and mothers.'

What colonists objected to, the newspaper claimed, was 'that their unmarried youth are coerced into matrimonial alliances with Irish Roman Catholics'.

Earl Grey read the mood and abandoned this particular scheme in 1850, after only a few thousand girls had been sent to the colonies. Nevertheless, the larger Irish wave carried sufficient numbers to ensure that the English did not dominate Australia's ethnic mix in the second half of the nineteenth century. In fact, the famine ensured that Australia and the other settler countries became more Irish than the United Kingdom. In the United States, for example, three out of four migrants from the United Kingdom in the second half of the nineteenth century were from Ireland.

While the Irish made up just 15 per cent of the UK population by the 1880s, the tribes remained more or less in balance across Australia. The English and Welsh comprised 55 per cent of the UK-born population living in the colonies; the Irish 31 per cent and the Scots 14 per cent. The Irish provided the only intakes with consistently more women than men, reflecting informal colonial restrictions on the latter. The mixed marriages the *Sydney Morning Herald* feared not only occurred, they made Australia more cohesive.

The convict intakes had been excessively Anglo – 70 per cent were English. The shift to free migration created a new, open Australia that built on the foundation of egalitarianism, a country that would prosper because of its diversity.

But the national temperament remained male, and it was the encounters between English and Irish men in the new settlement

of Melbourne, and later, between Irish diggers and English authorities on the Victorian goldfields, that would determine Australia's
future as a rich migrant nation.

4

CRACKING THE CODE: THE SETTLEMENT OF MELBOURNE

A decade before Sydney was conceived for the illiberal purpose of transportation, a prophecy for Australia as the world's richest settlement was written. First published in 1776, Adam Smith's *Wealth of Nations* contains one of those fantastic accidents of economic forecasting when hyperbole is exceeded by reality.

'The colony of a civilized nation which takes possession either of a waste country, or of one so thinly inhabited that the natives easily give place to the new settlers, advances more rapidly to wealth and greatness than any other human society,' he wrote.

According to Smith, the colonists carry knowledge, laws and habits of governance that give the new settlement a jumpstart in development. The land they take is too vast to cultivate by their own hand, so they hire 'labourers from all quarters, and reward them with the most liberal wages'. These labourers quickly acquire their own land, and, in turn, 'reward with equal liberality other labourers, who soon leave them for the same reason that they left their first master'.

It reads like the Australia of the mid-nineteenth century, which rose from far-flung outpost to the top of the global income ladder in less than two decades. This fable became fact not in Sydney, but in Melbourne, as two ambitious waves of migration arrived at the same time and accelerated Australia's prosperity.

Sydney had been established by England's exiles and took almost half a century to find its feet. But it was the sons of those convicts who settled the boomtown of Melbourne. They had three advantages their parents lacked – local knowledge, luck and London's benevolence. And their timing was immaculate because they created a new centre of growth for Australia just as the assisted-passage waves from Britain and Ireland were being enticed to the colonies.

The seed for the venture had been planted in the first failed attempt to colonise the area in 1803. David Collins had brought three hundred convicts to what is now the wealthy Victorian seaside town of Sorrento, but the site was unsuitable, lacking adequate fresh water and a safe harbour for ships to dock. Collins gave up within six months and took his expedition across Bass Strait to try again at the new penal settlement of Van Diemen's Land.

Among the felons in this original attempt was John Fawkner, a London-born metal refiner sentenced to fourteen years' transportation for receiving stolen goods. It was his son, John Pascoe Fawkner, who led one of the expeditions to reclaim the territory three decades later, at the more favourable location near the Yarra River.

The father received a conditional pardon in 1806, and with it a grant of fifty acres of land, and led a respectable life while the son found trouble. In 1814, John Pascoe Fawkner received five hundred lashes and three years' hard labour for conspiring with seven convicts who wanted to escape to South America. Following his release, he tried to make a fresh start in Sydney but struggled to find work. Penniless, he begged his way onto a ship returning to Van Diemen's Land in 1818. Fawkner eventually found his calling in journalism as the founder of the *Launceston Advertiser* in

1828, which he used to champion the cause of former convicts, and expose the shortcomings of officials and free migrants.

The destiny of the self-made newspaper proprietor and future father of Melbourne became entwined in Van Diemen's Land with that of another convict son. John Batman was born in New South Wales in 1801 to a convict father and a free-settler mother. Batman moved to Van Diemen's Land in late 1821, where he made his name as a grazier and found favour with authorities for the almost improbable double feat of hunting bushrangers and attempting to improve relations with the locals. He was rewarded for his services with additional grants of land, but it was of poor quality.

The 1820s were relatively strong in Van Diemen's Land due to the wool trade, and in 1825 the island secured its independence from New South Wales to become Australia's second stand-alone colony. Settlers had plotted an expansion to the mainland as early as 1827, when Batman applied to move his stock to what early reports from explorers said was superior grazing land. That request was turned down, but he and others kept returning to the topic.

By 1835 the population of Van Diemen's Land had grown so quickly that it accounted for one in three of all colonists. All the available grazing land was now occupied, yet the colony required more livestock to help feed its people. Settling the southern part of the continent became a matter of necessity.

Men like Batman and Fawkner were driven by ambition, but they could not have known the true potential of the territory they aspired to. The land had been prepared for a wool boom by an unsuspecting Indigenous population. Thousands of years of cultivation by fire had created a 'park-like' estate that was well suited to running sheep.

Batman and Fawkner would be running ahead of the law because London had not yet authorised that part of the mainland for settlement. But Batman did want the consent of the Indigenous population, to avoid a repeat of the conflict between settlers and locals in Van Diemen's Land. This was a curious inversion of the self-serving practice of empire, which relied on the monarch's approval to take the land without regard to the locals.

The Batman party departed Launceston on 10 May 1835 with a plan to buy the land. The *Hobart Courier* reported that Batman had taken 'seven natives' with him to assist in the negotiations. 'He proposes to purchase from the Chiefs of that part of the country such a territory as he may require, of which he will himself become the Chief, with the best of all possible titles, that of the real proprietor.'

The following month the newspaper cheerfully announced the acquisition of five hundred thousand acres. 'Almost immediately after landing, Mr. B fell in with a tribe of forty, who at first evinced a disposition to oppose him, but after a short parley, the natives he had with him effected an understanding, and he was received by them with open arms, and every manifestation of good feeling.'

Batman offered annual rent of 'one hundred pair of blankets, one hundred knives, one hundred tomahawks, fifty suits of clothing, fifty looking glasses, fifty pair scissors and fifty tons flour' in exchange for the land.

The Fawkner party intended to travel in April, a month before Batman's. But its chief had to face court on a charge of assault. He also had debts to clear. Fawkner's crew left without him in August and they anchored near what is now Spencer Street. A representative of Batman's party told them they were trespassing on land purchased from the natives, but had no power to evict their fellow colonists, and the two camps were no doubt both aware that the government in Sydney viewed them all as trespassers.

When Fawkner joined the camp in October, he was impressed by its serenity. 'On the 30th August 1835, our horses and cattle, and men were landed, and a hut built,' he wrote. 'Our fruit trees and garden plants planted – ground ploughed, seeds sown – and upon our own arrival in October, we found fine acres of promising wheat, grown most surprisingly for the time, and enjoyed cress, lettuce and radishes, the first grown at Melbourne.' It was a world away from the hardships faced by the First Fleet.

Historian James Boyce believes that Melbourne did not suffer the high death rates of previous settlements because the pioneers understood the land. 'It obviously helped that Van Diemen's Land was close by, and that people, animals and supplies could be easily moved across a well-known trade route,' he wrote. 'But even more important was that by 1835 Van Diemonian Britons had been through three decades of environmental adaptation in a land with many similarities to Port Phillip.'

The example of the Swan River settlement in Western Australia demonstrates Boyce's theory. Swan River was established six years earlier than Melbourne, by free settlers sent with London's blessing, but the environment proved much less friendly, and the settlers arrived with no local knowledge and no other colony close by.

Lieutenant Governor James Stirling complained of the 'winds and rain of a boisterous winter' in one of his first dispatches home on 9 September 1829. 'Among the settlers since arrived, some disappointment has arisen in consequence of their being in general but little accustomed to encounter hardships, and in all cases too sanguine in the expectations they have entertained respecting the country,' he wrote.

'The background of most was middle class, respectable in character and property, but unaccustomed to the problems of making virgin country habitable and profitable,' RM Hartwell wrote of the Swan River intake. 'They dreamt of a squirearchy, but their attempts to reproduce English society . . . were often hopelessly unpractical.'

London hoped it would avoid the mistakes of the west when it settled South Australia. The would-be pioneers formulated a detailed plan, based on the work of British politician Edward Wakefield, after a number of years of haggling. Wakefield was so impressed with the final model that he hailed South Australia as 'the first attempt since the time of the Ancient Greeks to colonise systematically'. The colony was given final approval in 1835, and the first 546 settlers arrived the following year. But they also saw their optimism wilt in an unfamiliar terrain. 'The colonists had little idea of the difficulties of pioneering, of the physical problems of a bad harbour, of building roads and bridges, of combating the strange insect life, floods and drought,' according to Hartwell.

The free settlers of Western and South Australia were more suited to urban living. They were ideal second-wave migrants, like those who went to Melbourne under assisted passage later in the 1830s, after the convict sons had extracted the first windfall from the land.

Even in those early days, before the extent of the full bounty was understood, Melbourne seemed to spark with an unusual energy. The arrival of Batman and Fawkner in Port Phillip provoked perhaps the first intercolonial rivalry, between the governor of New South Wales, Richard Bourke, and the lieutenant governor of Van Diemen's Land, George Arthur, over who would get to administer the settlement. Each leader made a pitch to London to secure retrospective approval on behalf of their respective colonies. Their arguments revealed the opportunity Melbourne presented for both an enlightened and economically rational settlement. The cosmopolitan side of the Australian personality, which supports both multiculturalism and markets, was predicted in these very dispatches.

Arthur's pitch contained the telling admission that he should have pursued a 'treaty' with the locals of Van Diemen's Land. Whether he sincerely regretted the brutality of his 'black line' campaign or was merely trying to impress the Whig government at the time cannot be known. What is clear is that Batman's treaty cannot be taken too seriously. The land was not his to buy, nor were the terms just. Yet even the appearance of negotiations marked Melbourne as a relatively tolerant venture compared to the three previous examples of Sydney, Van Diemen's Land and Western Australia.

The New South Wales governor appealed to London's financial rather than moral interests. Bourke advised that it would be impractical to force the Batman and Fawkner parties off the land. He reminded the Home Office that the colony needed even more land made available for Australia to continue prospering. 'The wool of New South Wales forms at present, and is likely long to continue, its chief wealth. It is only by a free range over the wide expanse of native herbage, which the Colony affords, that the production of this staple article can be upheld at its present rate of increase in quantity, or standard of value in quality.'

The ruling in favour of expansion was received in September 1836, a year after the Fawkner camp was enjoying its cress, lettuce and radishes. New South Wales was granted control of what would be known as the Port Phillip district. Bourke visited the settlement the following March. He was accompanied by surveyor Robert Hoddle, who traced the outline for a grid system of roads and lanes. Bourke named the village after the then Whig prime minister William Lamb, who was better known as Lord Melbourne. The governor noticed one immediate similarity with the township of Sydney.

'Attended Church at Melbourne,' he wrote in his diary for 26 March 1837. 'Congregation less numerous than on the first Sunday I attended. The Sabbath is not well observed any where in N S Wales except by a few Persons of sober habits.'

It was in Melbourne that the first unequivocal link between migration and prosperity was established. The export income generated from wool was used to import the working and middle classes of Britain and Ireland through assisted passage, who, in turn, created what quickly became the richest metropolis in the world.

The first Melburnians were better educated than their Sydney brethren. Unsurprisingly, there were more free migrants and fewer convicts in their ranks. By 1846, the new town enjoyed a clear advantage over its older rival across the social indicators. Eight in ten adult males in Melbourne (84 per cent) could read and write against seven in ten in Sydney (76 per cent). Melbourne's free migrants were 72 per cent of the total population against Sydney's 58 per cent. Only 4 per cent of Melbourne's males were convicts, either former or serving, compared to 13 per cent of Sydney's.

Yet as the early settlers on the Hawkesbury had demonstrated, rapidly acquired wealth comes with anxieties. Melbourne was Australia's first non-Anglo settlement, but initially more volatile because of it. The Irish-born were the single largest group, followed by the English-born and then the Australian-born. In Sydney, the order was reversed: the local-born were first, the English-born second and the Irish-born third.

Melbourne's burgeoning Irish community comprised both Protestants and Catholics. On one mad winter's afternoon in 1846 they almost broke the half-century-long truce between Protestant and Catholic in Australia. Significantly, the resolution of their dispute, imposed by the colonial parliament in Sydney, extended the policy of egalitarianism to the religions themselves.

On 13 July, the Protestant community prepared to celebrate a 156-year-old battle with a grand dinner at the Pastoral Hotel in Queen Street, while the Catholic community was enjoying a game of hurling at nearby Batman's Hill. The Protestants gathered under the banner of the Orange Order, which had been formed in Ireland's Ulster province in the late eighteenth century to counter the Irish Defenders. The Orangemen took their name from King William of Orange, and chose his final decisive assault on the Catholic King James II at Boyne, near Dublin, on 12 July 1690 as the date for commemoration.

Melbourne's Orangemen had a licence to stage a dinner only, but they found a way to antagonise the Catholics outside. At 2.30 p.m., the banners of the Orange Order were placed on the windows of the Pastoral Hotel, in full view of passers-by on Queen Street. This 'immediately operated as a signal to the opposite party, who soon after assembled in force on the spot, and demanded that the colours should be withdrawn', Melbourne's mayor James Palmer wrote in his report to Port Phillip superintendent Charles La Trobe. The banners stayed up, prompting heckles from the protestors outside. Word spread to those at the hurling game, who joined the throng outside the hotel.

Palmer had been at the council office, and on hearing of the disturbance, dashed across town to the hotel, arriving at 3.30 p.m. He asked the Orangemen to hand the colours over to him. They refused his order, telling him he must be mad. As the Catholics tried to rush the hotel, the first shots rang out. The mayor made a run for it as a full-scale battle erupted.

Palmer returned at 4 p.m. with the military, read the Riot Act and persuaded both sides to lay down their arms. Fortunately no one was killed, but four people were wounded. The dinner was called off, promoting loud cheers from the street. The next day, the tribes reassembled near the Flagstaff Gardens to resume the fight. The military was called out again, and the Riot Act had to be read twice before the mob dispersed. The police remained on the sidelines on both days. All but one member of the force was of Irish extraction, each with friends in both camps.

While a number of people were subsequently arrested for possessing firearms, nobody was charged with rioting, which proved not only the most pragmatic course available to authorities, but also the most effective way of preventing further sectarian violence. There were no martyrs in prison to fan resentments.

The importance of this encounter was in the response of the New South Wales authorities, who immediately introduced legislation banning any further gatherings that might incite religious hatred. This effectively enshrined equal treatment of Protestant and Catholic across the colonies. Previously, Richard Bourke had guaranteed equality of funding for the churches but this new legislation went further. The Party Processions Bill banned street parades and all other gatherings that celebrated or commemorated 'any festival, anniversary, or political event, relating to or connected with any religion or other distinctions or differences between any class of her Majesty's subjects'. No one could carry firearms or other offensive weapons, or publicly display 'any banner, emblem, flag, or symbol' which might 'provoke animosity between her Majesty's subjects of different religious persuasions'. The playing in public of religious music was also prohibited.

It is impossible to imagine a similar piece of legislation being contemplated in the United States, where religious freedom in every sense is a considered a birth right. In later decades, the Americans would witness their own Orange Riots, with much deadlier consequences. In New York in 1870 and again in 1871 more than seventy people were killed in clashes between Irish Protestants and Catholics.

In Australia, it was the absence of mass killings that vindicated the ban on processions. The Australian governing culture from Arthur Phillip onwards had distinguished itself by its pragmatic approach to social cohesion. Equal treatment had, from the first, proven an effective way of quelling dissent. The same appeal to order could be made in the abject poverty of Sydney Cove, or in the boom conditions of Melbourne. In another setting on the goldfields of Ballarat a few years later, unfair treatment could provoke a revolution.

Australia was only able to crack the code for economic growth through migration after the settlement of Melbourne. The fertile pastures of Port Phillip turned Adam Smith's prophecy into a reality, but not in the way he imagined. He assumed the 'natives' were irrelevant. Yet without them, the land would not have been cleared for grazing. He assumed that British knowledge of farming would be superior. But it was the Australian-born who ensured that Melbourne began with a burst of confidence.

The windfall was in the land, yet the true wealth was in the people who came to the colony. Most of the grazing land developed was, in fact, grabbed by a small number of squatters, and they abused their political power. It would be many decades before colonial parliaments caught up with them and reformed land policy. Yet a more regulated advance might have slowed the wool industry, and through it the migration that delivered the critical mass for a flourishing civilisation.

Port Phillip could count its success in sheep. The number grew from a foundation flock of twenty-six thousand in 1836 to almost eight hundred thousand in 1841, and then to more than 5.3 million by 1850. That short period covered a boom, a global depression and a recovery.

New South Wales had an even larger flock, and all the colonies combined to replace Germany as the main supplier of wool to the mother country over the course of the 1840s. By 1850, they had 53 per cent of the British market.

Many of the nation-building migrants who came under assisted passage had no intention of living an agrarian life. The population of Port Phillip surged from 177 in 1836 to 76 000 by 1850, and about one in three people lived in Melbourne itself, which was a very high rate of urbanisation for its time. Port Phillip had eclipsed the colony it sprang from: by 1850, Van Diemen's Land had been demoted to the third colony, with a population of 68 870. In 1851 Port Phillip separated from New South Wales and took the name of the Queen, Victoria.

South Australia had a slow start, but began attracting people following the discovery of copper in 1842. From a demoralised base of 546 people in 1836, it reached 63 700 by 1850. It also had wheat to sell to the world. Western Australia, on the other hand, had no exports to speak of. It had just 5886 people in 1850, a net addition of 233 per year since its shivering foundation in 1829.

These extremes between rapid advance and stagnation would become more familiar to Australia as the settlement matured. At the mid-point of the nineteenth century, Australia was still discovering the boom side of its personality.

The most astonishing fact of this period is that Australia boasted the world's fastest growing economy when the great and rising powers were in turmoil. To paraphrase Charles Dickens, these were the best of times for Australia and the worst of times for the United Kingdom and the United States.

The statistics are now reliable enough to build a global income ladder that compares living standards across Europe, North America and Australia. Taking the long view from the founding of Melbourne in 1835 to 1850, the picture is of one economy soaring above all others. Australia's GDP per person jumped by 73 per cent over that fifteen-year period. The next best was Denmark, which improved its national income by just 28 per cent. The United States stagnated, with its GDP per person improving by a miserly 6 per cent while the United Kingdom lost 4 per cent. The 1840s were known as the 'hungry forties' across Britain and Ireland. Across Europe, they were a decade of revolution.

Australia had created its own economic cycle, which was resistant to international shocks. It would feel the global depressions like the rest of the world, but it would recover more quickly because exports and migration kept pushing national income higher.

Foolishly, London tried to tamper with the formula by reintroducing transportation to the mainland in 1848. The old free settlers and squatters with big estates were a powerful political force in the colonies, and they petitioned Earl Grey to send them skilled convicts as a means of obtaining much cheaper labour. Port Phillip reluctantly accepted the first group, even though the settlement had been founded free. But when the *Hashemy* convict ship, carrying 212 male exiles, set sail for Sydney in early 1849, something snapped. Former convicts, their children and free migrants found common voice in telling London to take back its refuse, and to send, instead, the paperwork for self-government for the colony.

More than five thousand people gathered on 11 June to demand the right to decide who came to this country. The town had not witnessed a protest rally on this scale before. The chairman of the meeting, Robert Lowe, said convicts 'had been the source of wealth to many' and that these sectional interests wanted to get rich again. But the law-abiding workers of New South Wales just wanted to make an honest living. 'They, the men of Australia, had wives, and children, and they would be content to subdue the land and replenish it, without the introduction of British crime and its attendant British misery.'

A five-point petition was drawn up, calling on London 'to respect the will of the majority'. Sending convicts was 'incompatible with our existence as a free colony, desiring self-government'. The final line of the resolution left hanging the threat of an American-style revolt: 'We greatly fear that the perpetration of so stupendous an act of injustice by Her Majesty's Government will go far towards alienating the affections of the people of the colony from the mother country'.

Journalist Henry Parkes earned the loudest cheer when he rose to speak on behalf of 'the largest class of men in the colony – the working class'. There was more meaning in that cheer than any other declaration made that day. Transportation had boiled down to a labour dispute. The workers wanted to maintain their high-wage society, the first of countless calls that would be made against migrants who threatened to undercut their standard of living. There was also an anti-convict sentiment at play. Parkes expressed 'his deep feeling of indignation at the insult that had been offered to the community at large'. The only just remedy would be for 'the convict ship and cargo to be sent back'.

The *Hashemy* wasn't sent back, but the convicts were packed off to the countryside and north to the Queensland settlement. The next boat to meet with public protests was the *Randolph*, in August of the same year. It carried 295 exiles bound for Port Phillip. Superintendent Charles La Trobe disobeyed his orders and refused to let the ship unload the convicts. He sent it on to Sydney on 9 August 1849.

The Argus greeted the news with a good riddance, under the headline of 'No Pollution'. 'We have the proud gratification of being able to announce to our readers that the moral plague which threatened us is averted.'

Ten days later, a public meeting was held to send the strongest possible message to two audiences. The first motion addressed London: 'The Mother Country has no right to tax free British Colonies for Imperial purposes, which she does when she requires them to maintain any part of [her] criminal system.' The second was aimed at Sydney: 'Australia Felix [Port Phillip], although it has been for a temporary purpose attached to New South Wales, has never been in any sense or way a penal colony.' They were 'now prepared to undergo any extremity, rather than submit to the degradation either of the name or the reality of a penal settlement'.

The language in the Melbourne resolution had an edge that was missing in the Sydney petition. Yet the provocations for an uprising were simply not there. There were no British troops demanding obedience, as in Boston in 1774. There was no restless underclass, or army of intellectuals to rouse them. The colonies were notably free of the mass urban poverty that had been the fuel for revolutions in Europe in the previous year, 1848. The resolutions were framed from the perspective of affluence. In Sydney and even in Melbourne, the cry of freedom was more a plea to preserve the high-wage society than a warning of rebellion.

The time lag between the colony and London created its own pressure release valve. The people sent their messages, and waited for the mother country to consider them, and send her replies. This process could take up to a year, and the decision to finally abolish transportation to New South Wales did not come into effect until October 1850. Convicts continued to be sent to Van Diemen's Land unti 1853, while Western Australia was a late entrant to the business, receiving almost ten thousand felons from London between 1850 and 1868.

In between transporting the convicts and receiving the protests, Earl Grey had given the House of Lords a stirring account of how Australia had become the model colony. He noted that the 'thriving community' of Port Phillip 'had been established without one shilling of expense to the mother country'. The progress of all the Australian colonies was 'really marvellous' when compared to the American colonies in the previous century, he continued. 'The population of Sydney, in 1836, was 19 000; in ten years it was actually doubled, and in 1846 was 38 000. Comparing this with the old colony of Boston, its population in 1790 – 170 years after its foundation – was 18 000. The population of the city of New York, in 1773 – immediately before the breaking out of the war – was only 21 896, being 17 000 less than Sydney at the present day. The population of Philadelphia, in 1790, was 28 528.'

These numbers were tweaked to make the loss of the American colonies seem like no big deal. In fact, the United States had a population of almost twenty-one million in 1846, and it would soon be larger than the United Kingdom's. Australia would need another 160 years to reach that figure. Also, it was mischievous to compare growth across two entirely different centuries, essentially before and after the Industrial Revolution.

But Earl Grey's chest-puffing did contain a more valuable truth. The American people had been a third richer than the Australians when Melbourne was founded in 1835. Thirteen years later, Australia had the higher standard of living.

Australia had already passed Sweden, Norway and Canada on

the global income ladder by 1840. It overtook a further eight European countries by 1850, including France and Germany, as well as the United States. Only the Netherlands and the United Kingdom sat above Australia before the next driver of migrant-led growth revealed itself: gold.

5

THE ECONOMICS
OF EUREKA

A new foundation story was being written for Australia in Melbourne. This Australia was confident and globally connected, and it had no past to weigh it down. No transportation, no Rum Rebellion, and no governor-ordered massacres of the locals. By chance, this open Australia was rising in the nineteenth century at the very moment the world was searching for a new model civilisation to project its dreams on: a society free of Europe's extremes of wealth and poverty, of hereditary privilege and political oppression. The United States seemed the most logical place to answer this call for liberty, but Australia became its unexpected rival.

Victoria carried the apparent handicap of a late start because its gold rush began almost three years after California's, and three months after New South Wales'. It was the smallest of the trio in 1851, with a population a third smaller than California's and half that of New South Wales. Yet Victoria had passed California within a year of its rush, and had caught New South Wales after just two years. By the third year, 1854, Victoria had more than trebled in size to 280 000 people, compared to a New South Wales population of 240 000, and California's 210 000. Melbourne was suddenly the new capital of the Australian colonies, and one of the most talked-about cities in the world.

California had more in common with New South Wales than Victoria, with a foundation stained in blood. The United States had claimed the territory under the treaty that ended the Mexican-American War in February 1848. Although gold had been found only days beforehand, the discovery was kept secret for a short while.

California had no laws in place when its rush commenced in 1849, which left prospectors to settle disputes over claims between themselves. Violence was a constant part of life on the goldfields, and in the towns that sprang up around them. A form of policing was introduced by local vigilante groups and at least four migrants from Sydney were among the scores of criminals who were lynched by the dreaded San Francisco Committee of Vigilance.

The United States actually produced more gold than the Australian colonies over the course of the 1850s. But the settlement that held the world's attention, and enticed and retained the most migrants in that astonishing decade, was Victoria.

No people were better prepared for transformation by gold than the Victorians of the mid-nineteenth century. They had already achieved a high-income society by the 1840s, so the discovery of a new source of wealth did not carry the same risk of social disorder as it did in the previously undeveloped territory of California. Yet no leaders were less able to cope with the challenge of success than the governors who ruled the colonies. They simply did not trust the people with gold, fearing it would entice law-abiding men to abandon their work, and the criminally minded to unleash a reign of terror on the community.

Geologist and Anglican clergyman William Clarke had explored the rocks from the Blue Mountains to as far west as Bathurst, and was convinced the colony was 'abundantly rich in gold'. He took his evidence to a startled Governor George Gipps in 1844. 'Put it away, Mr. Clarke, or we shall all have our throats cut,' the governor replied.

The Californian rush had attracted thousands of Australians from 1849, forcing George Gipps' successor as governor, Charles FitzRoy, to reassess the official policy of denial. Weighing the risk of anarchy against the loss of the colony's men, FitzRoy decided that a homegrown gold rush was the lesser evil. He offered a generous reward to anyone who discovered a commercially viable deposit in New South Wales. The bounty was claimed by Edward Hargreaves, who had returned to the colony in January 1851 after an unsuccessful stint as a prospector in California. News of his find at Summer Hill Creek, near Bathurst, reached the public in May and within days the first Australian rush was on.

'A complete mental madness appears to have seized almost every member of the community,' the *Bathurst Free Press* wrote on 17 May 1851. 'Any attempt to describe the numberless scenes – grave, gay and ludicrous – which have arisen out of this state of things, would require the graphic power of a Dickens, and would exceed any limit which could be assigned to it in a newspaper.'

Blacksmiths could not produce picks fast enough for the men who lived in the area. 'A few left town on Monday equipped for the diggins, but on Tuesday, Wednesday and Thursday the roads to Summer Hill Creek became literally alive with new made miners from every quarter, some armed with picks, others shouldering crow bars, or shovels and not a few strung round with wash-hand basins, tin-pots and cullinders. Garden and agricultural implements of every variety either hung from the saddle bow or dangled about the persons of the pilgrims to Ophir.'

The price of flour almost doubled overnight, from a low of twenty-six shillings per hundred pounds to forty-five shillings. The price of tea and sugar spiked by a similar rate, and most of the wheat in the district was bought by speculators.

These inflationary shocks had already been felt in California. 'Agricultural matters are entirely neglected, the price of provisions enormous, and labour expensive,' according to one account, published in October 1849. 'High wages are counterbalanced by the exorbitant price of every necessary article, and people are very glad to crawl into any place for shelter.'

California's example terrified Australian authorities. Although the American circumstances were peculiar to the time and place, they informed the excessive regulation that was imposed on the diggers in New South Wales, and then Victoria.

Charles FitzRoy met the rush to Bathurst with threats. He asserted Crown ownership of all gold, whether on private property or not. Anyone who distributed the soil in search of gold without permission would face a double prosecution, for civil *and* criminal offences. But prospectors would be free to dig if they took out a mining licence and paid a tax of thirty shillings per month, the equivalent of a week's wages. The fee would apply whether a prospector found gold or not. The idea was that unsuccessful miners would quickly return to their day jobs as they could not afford to keep paying the tax without finding gold.

Once California achieved statehood in 1850 it did move to regulate the goldfields, but on behalf of American prospectors. The state legislature imposed a 'foreign miner's license' at the punitive rate of twenty dollars per month. It was designed to deter Chinese and Mexican miners, but had the unintended consequence of sending penniless migrants off the goldfields and into San Francisco, creating even further social strife in the town. This selective Californian tax was withdrawn in 1851, just as the hated mining tax was being applied to all prospectors in Australia.

The initial stampede to Bathurst had unnerved the district formerly known as Port Phillip. Newly separated from Sydney's rule with its own lieutenant governor and parliament, and with a name to fit its destiny, Victoria risked a pyrrhic independence if its menfolk deserted to the mother colony, or to California. To keep the people at home, Victoria's first lieutenant governor, Charles La Trobe, engineered a reverse rush by offering a reward of two hundred pounds for the discovery of gold within two hundred miles of Melbourne. As in California, Victoria's first gold strike had initially been kept a secret. William Campbell discovered gold in Clunes, north of Ballarat, in 1850, but the find was not revealed until July 1851, one month after La Trobe offered the reward.

Victoria's rush was underway by the late winter of 1851. *The Argus* sent a reporter to Anderson's Creek, near Melbourne, and he returned with an account of the now-familiar divide between the savvy and the first-time prospector.

'Hardly a man on the Creek is without gold, that is if he has gone the right way to work to get it,' according to the article published on 11 August 1851. '[But we also] have the old Bathurst and Californian farces rehearsed at Anderson's Creek, by men who come almost unprovided, and with nothing to wash [the gold] in but a tin dish, the bottom full of holes punctured by a nail. Such absurdities as these can be attended with nothing but disappointment.'

La Trobe visited the Ballarat goldfields when the rush was still in its infancy. Over two frenzied days, he saw men extract gold worth the equivalent of ten years' wages for the typical Englishman. The lieutenant governor reported the mayhem in an anguished letter to Earl Grey, dated 10 October 1851. 'It is quite impossible for me to describe to your Lordship the effect these discoveries have had on the whole community,' he wrote.

'Within the last three weeks the towns of Melbourne and Geelong and their large suburbs have been in appearance almost emptied of many classes of their male inhabitants; the streets which for a week or ten days were crowded by drays loading with the outfit for the workings [on the goldfields] are now seemingly deserted.' Cottages were left empty, businesses shut down, even schools closed.

The market economy ceased to function for those with money and no interest in gold. Servants could not be hired at any wage. Boats lay idle in the harbour, their masters unable to keep their crew for the next leg of their journey. Even the pastoralists who ruled the global wool trade were left without men. They asked La Trobe to suspend the issuing of gold licences at least until that season's wool clip had been sheared, and the wheat had been harvested. But there was no point even trying, La Trobe told Earl Grey.

'It would be quite impossible to withstand such a general popular movement, excited by such a cause, by any practicable measures whatever. There is but one way, and that is, to let the current spend itself, and meanwhile that as far as possible, it is kept within proper bounds.'

To keep his own administration running, La Trobe pulled the only lever available to him in a high-wage society without workers – he doubled the salary of public servants. It was one of the few decisions he made that had any logic.

The very character of the American and Australian rushes would be shaped by how much land was made available to individual prospectors. California's laissez-faire approach had allowed men to claim relatively large plots, which created an immediate class system between landholders and the labourers they employed. In New South Wales and then Victoria, diggers were restricted to an area of ground no larger than a contemporary Australian garage. This stingy division of land was meant to reinforce the message that there was no point remaining on the goldfields but had the radical effect of giving tens of thousands of men equal rights to the gold. It was accidental egalitarianism, and it provided New South Wales and especially Victoria, where the greatest deposits were to be found, an immense advantage over California in the global contest for migration in the 1850s.

However, La Trobe seemed determined to kill the rush, even before the first migrant boats arrived. He decided to double the monthly tax to three pounds to send a clear message to diggers to return to their former lives. This panicked, short-term response betrayed a leader out of his depth. New South Wales, already worried about the loss of men to Victoria, was moving in the other direction by proposing to cut its fee by half to fifteen shillings. La Trobe announced the increase on 1 December 1851, which would apply from the new year. Immediately, the temperature of the diggings rose to dangerous levels.

The following week, a large placard appeared beside the creek at Mount Alexander, near what became the town of Castlemaine. 'Fellow diggers,' it asked, 'will you tamely submit to the imposition or assert your rights like men? Is it fair, is it just, that the gold-seeker should pay as much as the gold-finder?'

The agitator who wrote it did not see himself as an Australian, or a Victorian. He identified as a radical of the mother country. 'Ye are Britons! Will you submit to oppression and injustice? Meet – agitate – be unanimous; and if there is justice in the land they will – they must – abolish the imposition.'

A series of protests followed, culminating in the 'monster meeting' of fourteen thousand diggers at Mount Alexander on 15 December. La Trobe had already backed down. His note advising that the old fee would remain in place was dated 13 December and carried in the press on the day of the protest.

La Trobe had single-handedly united the diggers against authority. It was at this point, with the settlement already in uproar, that Victoria would receive its greatest injection of migrant talent yet.

Assisted passage, and the windfall of wool, had given Victoria an economic base on which gold could build an ever grander settlement. The mother country was willing to encourage her sons to chase this dream. Charles Dickens used his weekly *Household Words* to encourage emigration to Australia. 'How fortunate that the free institutions, the abolition of transportation [in 1850], the diffusion of gospel truths, have had time to do their work,' he wrote in January 1852. 'Suppose a purely penal colony had found this gold? The result would have been something to shudder.'

Even the sceptics were pleased to talk up the colonies. *Punch* urged fee-hungry lawyers and doctors to follow the money. 'What a blessing it will be to have all the sordid and selfish members of every profession at the Antipodes: self-transported. What a clearance of the system by the Gold Fever: what an extremely good riddance of bad rubbish.'

The dash to the migration boats began as soon as the first ships carrying gold back to England docked in April 1852. By year's end a record eighty-eight thousand people had left the mother country for the colonies, and nine out of ten went straight to Victoria. More ships sailed to Melbourne in 1852 than to any other port in the world. And that year Australians officially became the richest people in the world, overtaking the British and the Dutch on the measure of GDP per person.

Another sixty-one thousand Anglo-Celtic prospectors followed in 1853, then a further eighty-three thousand in 1854. In these first three years of the rush, Australia received more free migrants from the United Kingdom than in the previous three decades of settlement. They landed as the new majority, replacing the assisted-passage migrants of the 1830s and 1840s, and most remained to create the most affluent society the world had known to that date.

What set the golden intake apart from the previous wave was its independence. Two out of three migrants from the United Kingdom paid their own fare, marking them as the first significant group to choose Australia over the United States without a government subsidy, and despite the temptation of California.

In the thirty years before gold, Australia attracted just 8 per cent of the free migrants from Britain and Ireland. In the first three years of the rush, the share was 23 per cent – a 15 percentage-point increase in Australia's favour, at the expense of the United States.

'Where is the village that has not contributed its emigrants to the gold-fields,' *The Economist* magazine wrote in 1854, 'or the equally profitable labour markets of Australia, and who in their turn have induced relations or friends to embark in ventures, small or large, to so profitable a market?' By the time those words were written, all the world had heard of Victoria. The colony had a thousand French-born residents, two thousand Chinese, three thousand Americans and four thousand Germans. Each person had paid their own fare.

The migrants who choose Australia at their own expense are likely to be less deferential to authority than the migrants who are recruited through assisted passage. The onus is on authority to turn the prospector into a permanent settler. Yet La Trobe was slow to grasp this simple fact because he was governing on the run.

The challenge of keeping the migrant started with the rush itself. Gold-digging is squatting in miniature form, with the relationships between people and land turned upside down. Tens of thousands of fortune seekers crowd onto the same site, burrowing, sifting and exhausting their respective piece of nature's lottery. The land doesn't belong to any one person, and it has virtually no use once emptied. But the gold is seen as common wealth, to be taken as easily as the squatters grabbed the grazing lands of Port Phillip in the 1830s and 1840s. In the early years of the rush the gold was so close to the surface that it could be lifted out of the ground, as simply as a pickpocket helping himself to a rich man's purse. Former servants or convicts had as much claim to the colonial bounty as the men who might have been their masters in the old country, or their jailers in the new. But once they had claimed their share, they were met by a system that did not recognise their achievement with the basic economic right of property.

The colonial ethos of egalitarianism had been tested during the wool boom, as the grazing land had been monopolised by fewer than one thousand squatters. Officials had been unable to reform land policy to reduce their power before the gold rush began, leaving two very large flaws in the system: the successful digger could not easily acquire his own land to settle, because most of it had been taken before he arrived; and without property, he could not vote. These omissions would likely have led to a confrontation on the goldfields even without the provocation of the mining tax.

La Trobe did not resolve these critical matters of public policy before he retired in 1854. But he did make one notable contribution to attracting and keeping migrants. From his harassed vantage point in Melbourne, he could see that the capital was being trampled by a double stampede. The town was losing more workers to the diggings than it could afford, and receiving more migrants than it could accommodate, who were also bound for the goldfields. Tent settlements, providing a level of discomfort exceeded only by the huts of the First Fleeters, were improvised to house the new arrivals while they planned their own treks to Ballarat and Bendigo. They became an instant eyesore and health hazard due to the lack of basic drainage for Melbourne's streets.

'I am a lately arrived Immigrant, and have the distinguished privilege of being a citizen of Canvass Town,' one resident had written to *The Argus* in 1853. 'I occupy a few square feet of ground, for which I pay 5 shillings a week, for which sum I could rent a very comfortable house in England. God knows it is hard enough to live in a tent in such a place, choked with dust, stifled with heat, and drenched with rain alternately. But the government who could extort this sum from us, their fellow countrymen, must, to say the least, have very little humanity in their hearts.'

Once La Trobe resigned himself to the durability of the rush, he became, by necessity, a nation-builder. He borrowed from Lachlan Macquarie's public works handbook to transform Melbourne into a modern metropolis, capable of servicing the needs of a rapidly growing population, from sewers to a gleaming house of parliament. It was a belated but valuable intervention, and it ensured social cohesion in the city even as the goldfields were seething. In 1854, La Trobe doubled the number of buildings in the city, and opened the country's first train line from Flinders Street to Sandridge, and the first electrical telegraph line between Melbourne and Williamstown. Work started that year on the state parliament and library, buildings La Trobe insisted be made of stone. They stand to this day. He also set aside space for parklands and gardens.

Inevitably, public funds would be mismanaged. However, the spending may well be one of the most timely government interventions in Australian history. It facilitated the movement of people and gold to and from the diggings through the building of roads and bridges, and it created a parallel economy to employ the men who remained in Melbourne. The migrants who were drawn to the capital, not the goldfields, were more likely to be professionals. They included some of the colony's most influential reforming politicians, including George Higinbotham, who became chief justice of the Supreme Court, and Sir Charles Gavan Duffy, a future premier. Melbourne 'contains a greater number than is usual of well educated men' from Britain, *The Times* wrote in an assessment of the city at the height of the influx.

Melbourne was roughly the same distance from the Victorian goldfields as San Francisco was from California's; the proximity provided both with a nation-building advantage that was not available when gold was discovered in New Zealand, Queensland and Western Australia. Having the diggings close to an urban settlement made it easier to eventually convert the prospector into a resident, and drive a second phase of growth through a building boom.

There was no contest as far as the international media was concerned at the time. Reports from San Francisco emphasised not just the crime waves, but the fragility of the settlement itself. Six great fires had consumed the town between December 1849 and May 1851. In contrast, the city La Trobe helped build from scratch inspired *The Times* and others to give it a new name, 'Marvellous Melbourne'. 'The American journals abound with incidents of lawless violence and tales of savage customs with which the condition of the Australian colonies favourably contrasts,' *The Times* declared. The measure of Melbourne's success was its civility. 'In Melbourne we find a large average attendance of readers in the public library, a Mechanics' Institution, and a university, with a staff of well-paid teachers.'

Despite his many blunders, La Trobe had planted the seed for Melbourne as the cosmopolitan capital of the world, an idea that would be powerful enough to resolve the coming crisis he helped create at Eureka.

The critical part of the nation-building equation that Charles La Trobe miscalculated on the goldfields was law and order. The lieutenant governor took some of the revenue from the mining licence fee to fund a special police force for the diggings. The troops were supposed to maintain the peace, but were inexperienced and easily corrupted. The miners refused to accept their authority, seeing them as traitors to their class. The men in uniform took the ridicule personally – as their tormentors had intended – and were heavy-handed in their responses. This cycle of mutual loathing was barely contained while the diggers could afford to pay the tax. When the economy turned, as it inevitably would – it couldn't just grow forever – and London issued foolish orders to reduce government spending, those resentments eventually ignited into an armed uprising.

The story of what became known as the Eureka rebellion is primarily economic. Some of the raw statistics that demonstrate this crucial but often overlooked point confirm a peculiar rhythm to the gold rush that made the masculine Australian society more combustible in the 1850s than it had been in the previous decades of the wool boom. A comparison of Victoria's and California's influence on their respective national economies helps to clarify the nature of the problem.

California's gold made no appreciable difference to living standards across the United States in the first three years of its rush, from 1848 to 1851, during which GDP per person rose by just 2 per cent. The rush was more domestic than is commonly assumed: three out of four people who moved to California were from other American states, so gold essentially transferred activity from east to west coast without lifting national productivity in the short term.

In contrast, Australia's GDP per person jumped by 13 per cent in the first three years of the Victorian gold rush, from 1851 to 1854. Gold replicated the experience of wool, with export income and migration rising in tandem. Two out of three people who came to Victoria in that period were from overseas, adding to the national economy even as Victoria was cannibalising the local economies of South Australia and Van Diemen's Land. The male populations of both colonies fell in absolute terms in 1852, slating both for long-term decline. But the national improvement comprised two outrageously good years in 1852 and 1853 and a crash in 1854, which was associated with a global depression. GDP per person collapsed by 12 per cent in that third year, the year of Eureka.

La Trobe's public works program was simply not large enough to offset the full effects of the global depression. Unfortunately, his 1854 splurge left the budget with an alarming deficit of one million pounds, with revenues of 2.476 million exceeded by expenditures of 3.562 million pounds. Modern economists would praise the timeliness of the government stimulus, as it filled some of the hole left by a retreating private sector. But this was the fundamentalist age of economics, before social safety nets. Budgets were supposed to always be in balance.

London did not believe that a prudent administration would ever get itself in this position. It saw the deficit in moral terms, as evidence of Victoria's depravity. The official view was reflected in a patronising editorial written by *The Economist* later in 1854. 'The world has been occasionally amused by the extravagance of the diggers in wasting their hard earnings in dressing out their wives, or in tumultuous wassail [drinking and singing],' the magazine wrote. But even the 'wildest' indulgence of the diggers 'falls short of the extravagant freaks which the local Legislature and the Government have calmly and quietly resolved to engage in.'

Victoria was spending twice as much on public works than the American state of Massachusetts, which had three times as many people. *The Economist* could not fathom why Victoria needed 'to make roads, docks, quays, barracks, Government houses, customs houses, botanic gardens, Government stables etc.' so quickly. 'There is no extravagance in history, from the time of Pharaohs downwards, which equals this.'

In ordinary times they might have been correct. Yet La Trobe was building to keep the peace. He was also operating on the assumption that the land and mining tax revenues he had received the previous year would continue flowing. No one in Victoria at the time could have expected a double-digit fall in national income, which would slash those revenues in 1854. In any case, Victoria was hardly broke. The deficit for that year could be covered with the spare cash from the land fund that was meant for assisted passage, but not required for that purpose while migrants were coming at their own expense.

A perfect storm of misunderstanding between London and Melbourne was now brewing. La Trobe had already tendered his resignation in December 1852, and his successor Charles Hotham, a naval officer and diplomat, was appointed twelve months later. But Hotham was reluctant to take up his post. He wanted instead to fight the Russians in the Crimean War and lobbied for command of a ship. It is a pity that he wasn't allowed to follow those military instincts. But the Duke of Newcastle, the secretary for war and the colonies, advised Hotham he had a duty to repair Victoria's finances. Unwittingly, he sent Hotham to war in the colony, where the officer would incite Australia's only armed free-migrant rebellion.

When Hotham took up his post in June 1854 he saw Victoria as any other arrival of the time: as a land of opportunity. His first trip to the goldfields reassured him that the boom had not stalled. Successful prospectors made themselves known, while those who were struggling kept their distance. Hotham was told that out of the seventy-seven thousand people on the goldfields, less than forty-four thousand paid the licence fee. But what he did not appreciate was that many miners did not pay up because they could no longer afford to.

The newly arrived Hotham had no knowledge of the disruptive business cycle of gold, with its rollercoaster surges and crashes in income. He only knew that Victoria was wealthier than the mother country, and his instructions were to tighten the colonial belt. The new lieutenant governor demanded a crackdown on the diggers to help close the deficit. His advisers begged him to reconsider. Even the chief commissioner of police argued against his plan. Hotham would not be swayed. In September, he unleashed twice-weekly licence hunts, which were met with predictable outrage.

The diggers had tolerated the excesses of taxation and officialdom in 1852 and 1853 because the economy was strong, and the gold easy to find. These preconditions for stability disappeared in 1854. The economy was in depression, and mining had become less rewarding for individual prospectors. Avoiding the tax was a matter of survival.

The diggers had become embittered by their losses, Italian-born digger Raffaello Carboni wrote. 'Hence desperate and must do something desperate, and can not afford to pay any more "Licence" for sinking to try their luck, many of them working night and day . . . a Nuggety El Dorado for the few, a ruinous field of hard labour for many, a profound ditch of Perdition for Body and Soul to all.'

Eureka is Greek for 'I found it' and Australian for betrayal. Hotham could have killed the first Australian moment in its infancy with his mistimed program of austerity.

6

LEADING THE WORLD: THE RUSH TO DEMOCRACY

On 6 October 1854, two inebriated Scots went looking for another round of drinks. The publican at the Eureka Hotel, James Bentley, turned them away with rougher than usual force, killing one of his would-be customers, James Scobie. Bentley, a former convict from Van Diemen's Land, was arrested along with two associates but all were given bail. At their committal hearing on 12 October, they had the benefit of a friendly bench. One of the magistrates was a business associate of Bentley's. Another was Robert Rede, the English-born official in charge of Ballarat. By a majority of two to one, they decided the accused had no case to answer.

Enraged, the digger friends of the two Scots called a mass meeting on 17 October. They appointed a committee to work for the retrial of Bentley. Later that evening, some of them took matters into their own hands and torched his pub. Even the conservative *Argus* applauded their initiative. 'When all the property of the obnoxious Bentley had been destroyed, the cool, determined spirit of vengeance which had hitherto marked the proceedings gave way to the drunken revelry of the rabble. The hot ashes were ransacked for bottles of ale and spirits.'

Charles Hotham sent in the troops. He had Bentley, his associates and three diggers arrested. The lieutenant governor thought he was showing no fear or favour, but the miners saw it as further evidence of injustice. Thousands gathered at rallies to call for the release of their colleagues. They placed two further demands on the agenda: the abolition of the hated mining tax and the right to vote. The death of one poor drunk digger became the rallying point for a democratic revolution that followed no previous British, American or European script. Within a year, the colonies would be drafting legislation that served as a role model for rich nations for the remainder of the nineteenth century.

The immediate economic setting for Eureka was a global depression. The deeper social and political settings were masculine and oppressive. By 1854, two out of three Victorians were male – a ratio that past experience said would lead to trouble. The troops that provoked the diggers, and were to put down their rebellion, were as corrupt as the Rum Corps; and the lieutenant governor was the least popular colonial ruler since William Bligh. Confrontation seemed inevitable.

The miners set up the Ballarat Reform League and called for a meeting with Hotham, which he accepted. One of the three men he met was the Welsh-born John Humffray. A quintessential middle-class prospector, Humffray had abandoned a legal career in the mother country for the goldfields in 1853. He was drawn into the reform movement within a year, but didn't have the same urge for revolt as his fellow miners. He believed the authorities would yield to moral persuasion.

But Hotham was in a supercilious mood when he talked with Humffray and his colleagues in Melbourne on 27 November. They quibbled over the word 'demand'. Hotham said he wouldn't respond to threats. Yet he was favourably disposed to democratic reform, and told them a dispatch had already been sent to London asking for the diggers to be given the vote. He had also appointed a royal commission of inquiry into the goldfields, which would consider the case for the abolition of the licence. But Hotham could not interfere in the legal process. The men would just have to be patient.

On 29 November, a rally of four thousand miners was told of Hotham's inquiry, and his refusal to release their fellow miners. The men sent a clear message of dissent back to Melbourne: 'That this meeting, being convinced that the obnoxious license-fee is an imposition and an unjustifiable tax on free labor, pledges itself to take immediate steps to abolish the same by at once burning all their licenses. That in the event of any parties being arrested for having no licenses, that the united people will, under all circumstances, defend and protect them.'

Hotham answered the following day with a new licence hunt. One of the diggers approached by his troops ran away and was fired upon. This prompted a smaller rally at Bakery Hill. With other Reform League officials absent, the Irish-born Peter Lalor reluctantly took charge.

Lalor had been one of five brothers to leave Ireland because of the famine. In any other decade, when the colonies favoured British men and Irish women for assisted passage, all five might have gone to the United States. But Peter and Richard Lalor chose Victoria in 1852. They didn't head straight for the diggings. Peter, a civil engineer by training, first found work on the construction of the Melbourne–Geelong railway. Then he teamed up with Richard and another Irish man to sell wine, spirits and other provisions. Richard returned to Ireland for a career in politics, while Peter took up prospecting. He moved to the goldfields in the Ovens region in 1853 and then to Ballarat in early 1854, where he worked with a Scot, Duncan Gillies, a future premier of Victoria.

Unlike his brother, Peter had shown no interest in politics at home. In assuming the leadership at Eureka, he reversed the Irish experience in Australia by becoming radicalised in the new country. He asked for volunteers to organise for the coming fight, and led about fifteen hundred diggers armed with rifles and pikes to the so-called Eureka lead at Ballarat, where they would erect a stockade and wait for the troops to make the next move. If Hotham had wanted to resolve this standoff peacefully, he would have been better off waiting: the troops soon had a numerical superiority.

But Hotham wanted to win, on his terms. The official in charge of the troops, Robert Rede, told Hotham that the five hundred men remaining in the stockade were 'the greatest scoundrels in the Colony'. One-third were French, Swedes and Germans, he advised. The rest were either Irish or Van Diemonians. 'I am convinced that the future welfare of this Colony depends on the crushing of this movement in such a manner as it may act as a warning,' Rede advised. 'I should be sorry to see them return to their work.'

Nine out of ten of Lalor's original group had left the camp when the military launched its assault at dawn on 3 December 1854. Up to 400 troops took on about 150 mainly Irish-born men, and it was over in ten minutes. The exact toll will never be known. The official report at the time from the troop commander, Captain Thomas, said at least thirty were 'killed on the spot' and 'that many since died of their wounds'. Another 114 were taken prisoner. The rebels killed five troops in return.

Lalor received a musket ball to the left shoulder and was carried away by a colleague. He was hidden in a pile of slabs outside the enclosure for an hour then smuggled out before the troops could arrest him or finish him off. He waited in the bush, and the following day friends arranged for a surgeon to amputate his arm.

British authorities at the time routinely called on troops to quell protests at home. Earlier that year the military had broken up the bread riots at Exeter without casualties. In 1848, soldiers had been deployed on the streets of London to prevent the largest reform movement of the era from marching to Westminster to present a petition for democracy. The Chartists, as they called themselves, had a six-point plan for democracy: one vote for each man; electoral districts of equal size; payment for members of parliament; a secret ballot for voting; the removal of property qualifications for people running for parliament; and annual elections. The last time the troops had massacred their own people was in 1839, when twenty-two Chartists were shot dead at the Newport riot.

The colonial experience had been mixed. Troops had defused Melbourne's Orange riots in 1846, while the convict uprising at Castle Hill in 1804 was met with force. Eureka was in another category, as the only governor-sanctioned slaughter of free migrants in Australia. It had more in common with the early massacres of the Indigenous populations but with one crucial difference: the diggers would enjoy the final word.

By the time of Eureka, Australia looked like no other country in the world. Its three largest colonies had three distinctive ethnic faces. Eight out of ten Victorians were migrants. In South Australia two-thirds of the population was born overseas, while in New South Wales almost half the people were born in Australia. China, Germany and the United States provided almost 10 per cent of the diggers on the Victorian goldfields. In South Australia, the Germans alone were almost 10 per cent of the entire colony and larger in number than the Scots. In New South Wales, the Anglo and Celtic populations split fifty-fifty, with the English intake overwhelmingly male and the Irish intake majority female.

Out of this diversity, a remarkable consensus emerged for political and social reforms. The colonies competed with one another to be the first to grant the vote to all men, to develop a secret ballot and to grant an eight-hour day to the workers. The changes came in a rapid, seemingly preordained succession.

At the vanguard of this movement was the golden intake of migrants, which mixed British, Irish, European and American influences to produce breakthroughs in political and social thought. Other nations, most notably France, had already granted universal suffrage for men aged twenty-one and over. But the combination of the vote for all men and the eight-hour day was not thought possible in the nineteenth century without armed conflict between the worker and the state, and between labour and capital. Yet the colonies of south-eastern Australia, representing the wealthiest people on earth, secured these changes peacefully. The reforms were conceived from a position of material strength – one so far removed from the precarious convict settlement of seventy years earlier that they describe not just a different country, but a different people. This Australia had consciously taken a global leadership role. It wished to be seen as a role model, in direct competition with the United States.

The perspective of these people was subtly different to the assisted-passage wave from Britain and Ireland in the 1830s and 1840s. Most of the migrants who joined the gold trail to Ballarat or Bendigo, or the cosmopolitan trail to Melbourne, Sydney or Adelaide had a recent memory of a reform or revolutionary movement that was crushed in their home country. The assisted-passage wave that came before the critical year of European upheaval in 1848 was, almost by definition, less political, as they had not borne direct witness to the tumult. But although the golden intake was more radicalised, it was not predisposed to take up arms.

Just three days after Eureka, on 6 December 1854 a mass rally was held in Melbourne that signalled the determined but moderate tone of the movement. The general public was out in force to express their support for the diggers and the motion agreed demanded the troops be brought to justice for their murderous actions. Charles Hotham became aware that his attempt to cast the rebels at Eureka as enemies of the empire had misfired. Tellingly, no one would ever come forward to claim the reward of two hundred pounds offered for the capture of Peter Lalor; a colony in which the single largest migrant group was English had given shelter to an Irish rebel. The migrant unity between digger and urban dweller is explained by their common background. As historian Geoffrey Serle wrote, most who went to Victoria paid their own fare. '[They] were drawn from the middle class and the higher ranges of the working class, rather than the poverty-stricken.'

The political establishment also sympathised with the diggers, and it turned openly against Hotham before the year had closed. Those appointed to the royal commission into the goldfields refused his order to stick to their original terms of reference, drafted before Eureka. They would look into Eureka as well, they told him. In January 1855, they recommended a general amnesty for the diggers, but Hotham refused. The protest movement, which had moved seamlessly from the public to the political sphere, now attracted the finest legal minds in the colony. They gave their services for free to the thirteen diggers sent for trial for high treason. One by one, the men were cleared by a jury of their peers; each acquittal was a further blow to the credibility of the lieutenant governor.

Hotham was chastened, and began a belated program to restore his authority. A century before opinion polling, Victorians witnessed the spectacle of a leader begging forgiveness. He revoked the warrant for Lalor's arrest in March and prepared to fast-track his response to the royal commission report into the goldfields, due in May 1855.

The report gave the miners everything they asked for. The commissioners were scathing of the mining tax and its administration. They condemned the twice-weekly licence hunts and the 'prematurely violent procedure' authorities took before Eureka, although stopped short of blaming any official for the carnage on 3 December. They recommended the immediate abolition of the licence fee and its replacement with a new miners' right, costing one pound per year. The main source of mining revenue for the administration would come from a new tax on exports. The idea for the miners' right, which tied the cheaper tax with the right to vote, came from John O'Shanassy, a politician who had been in the firing line during Melbourne's Orange riots in 1846.

The commissioners also called for reform of land policy, to loosen the grip of the squatters. It was 'most suicidal to the interests to the colony at large' to deny successful miners access to land. In fact, it was 'incredible' that so little land had been made available for sale in the first three years of the gold rush. When a small parcel came on the market, the prices being paid were obscene because the miserly supply could never satisfy the demand of so many well-off migrants. '[This was] distressing to various classes of colonists, and proving highly prejudicial to the reputation of Victoria as a suitable field for emigration.'

The pressure for reform had been building across all the colonies since the wool boom had elevated the incomes of the Australian people. To persist with a political structure that had been shaped during transportation insulted free migrants and raised two potential outcomes: that these settlers overthrow the establishment, or give up asking nicely and leave for the United States.

Elections for the legislative council, the parliamentary body that advised the colonial governor and vetted his legislation, had only recently been introduced, first in New South Wales in 1843, and then in Victoria, South Australia and Van Diemen's Land in 1850. Each colony had slightly different balances between elected and appointed members. The vote was available to those with property worth at least one hundred pounds, or those paying rent of at least ten pounds a year. Yet even after the gold rush had inflated rents and made more men eligible for the vote, their franchise was not worth that much because power still resided with the governor and appointed members of parliament – usually conservative squatters. This arrangement could not satisfy the ambition of the world's richest people yet it persisted for almost a decade longer than was wise. Earl Grey, who ran the Colonial Office in Lord

Russell's government from 1846 to 1852, was not interested in granting self-government to the colonies, under which the people could
make their own laws. He had given this right to Canada in 1848,
but would not extend it to Australia because he couldn't see past
the country's convict origins.

Earl Grey's retirement as secretary of state in 1852 unlatched the
door to reform at London's end. His successor, John Pakington,
encouraged the colonies to draft their own constitutions, with a
view to granting them self-government. This process was underway before Eureka, but the rebellion almost certainly accelerated
it. Self-government reversed the roles of governor and the colonial parliaments. The elected members would draft the legislation
and the governor would review it. The governor held the power of
veto, and the British parliament could also make laws for the colonies, and could overrule colonial legislation. There would be two
chambers – a new, fully elected legislative assembly from which the
government was formed, and a partly elected House of Lords–style
legislative council.

The constitutions were approved in July 1855, just seven months
after Eureka, and the colonies used their new freedom to pursue
the most radical ideals of the nineteenth century: full voting rights
for all men, and a secret ballot for elections. Unwittingly they
replicated the circumstances of the Phillip and Macquarie gover-
norships, where the Australian culture defined itself as a negation
of the class divisions of Britain.

Democracy was a terrifying concept for the old world of Europe,
and even the new world of North America, where income inequality was rife. The finest minds of the nineteenth century warned
against giving the vote to the workingman, for fear of mob rule
or the tyranny of the majority. But the argument had virtually no
currency in Australia because the convict's upward mobility, and
the country's rapid climb up the global income ladder with free
migration, had allowed the colonies to develop without the large

underclasses that were familiar elsewhere.

Elections under the new system commenced from 1856. Van Diemen's Land marked its transition to self-government by changing its name to Tasmania, signifying the end of transportation and the birth of a free colony. Victoria included seats in its new parliament for the rebels of Eureka, in keeping with the recommendation of the goldfields royal commissioners. Peter Lalor and John Humffray were elected unopposed to the new goldfields electorates.

The ambition for a secret ballot originated in the two most liberal colonies, Victoria and South Australia, where the politicians were more likely to be recently arrived professionals from Britain, Ireland and Germany. The South Australians moved first with a proposal introduced into parliament in November 1855. The Victorians entered the debate a month later, but the Victorian parliament passed its legislation on 19 March 1856, a fortnight before South Australia.

In Britain those who were lucky enough to be able to vote had to include their own name on a ballot supplied by the candidate. Landowners would threaten voters with the loss of work or eviction if they supported a rival candidate. (This voting system had a peculiar application in Australia. With fewer public buildings available, elections were held in pubs, and voters were given grog to help them select the right candidate.) Opponents of the secret ballot thought it was cowardly. A British man had nothing to hide, they huffed. But advocates believed it would allow the people to express their will without fear or favour.

The original Australian model for the secret ballot required voters to strike out the names of candidates they did not prefer, leaving untouched the man they were voting for. If the voter couldn't read, they could ask a returning officer for assistance. The ballot paper would be supplied by the government. It could not be taken out of the ballot room or polling booth. Once the voting was completed, the ballot paper would be dropped into a sealed box. The reform was perfected in 1858 under the inspired hand of London-born migrant William Boothby. It was in his role as South Australia's electoral commissioner that Boothby came up with the idea to include a box beside the name of each candidate. A simple X next to the preferred candidate was all that was required.

South Australia beat Victoria to the next democratic milestone by granting the vote to every male aged twenty-one and over in June 1856. Victoria followed in 1857, and the recalcitrant New South Wales joined in 1858 with both the vote and the secret ballot. Women were excluded, and later the Chinese, so it was not full democracy as it is understood today.

The lag between self-government and universal male suffrage seemed to depend on the composition of migration. The free colonies of South Australia and Victoria were the quickest to reform; the convict settlements of New South Wales, Tasmania, Queensland and Western Australia were the slowest. Tasmania was the last colony to allow all men the vote in 1896, although it had had the secret ballot since 1856.

The Argus saw the passage of the secret ballot as proof that Victoria had become the 'model colony'. 'Somewhere between the systems of Great Britain and America seems to lie the grand secret of the most free and effective Government,' the newspaper wrote in July 1856. 'America cannot control her mobs; England cannot shake herself free from the incubus of her governing classes.' The British eventually followed the Australian precedent for a secret ballot in 1872, while universal male suffrage had to wait until 1914. Massachusetts was the first US state to adopt the secret ballot in 1888, and gave credit where it was due, dubbing it 'the Australian ballot'. The first president to be elected under the Boothby method was Grover Cleveland in 1892.

Eureka holds two incompatible positions in the national psyche: as the fulcrum for democracy and an unfinished revolution. It is neither, because democracy was coming without it, although it might have brought forward change and once authorities yielded to public opinion after Eureka, a wider insurrection was simply not necessary. The more inspiring side of Eureka is the behaviour of the golden intake. The migrants did not lose their heads in reprisal against the state. They had their revenge by securing the defining political and economic reforms of the age. The common bond between the Melbourne professional and the prospector at Ballarat extended to other questions of reform. Coming close behind universal male suffrage was the eight-hour day – another global first. Here, once again, change was achieved without a fight because the old argument between labour and capital did not seem to apply in Australia.

The migrant labourers who avoided the goldfields and settled instead in Melbourne had the same eye for Australia's potential and the same impatience with colonial government as the diggers. Their grievance with the mother country had been the miserable pay and the long hours of backbreaking work, and many had fought a running battle with the establishment for a shorter working day, but were beaten, physically, into submission. Troops were often sent to break up strikes in the industrial districts of Britain in the 1840s and 1850s, but more often the grinding poverty created its own discipline. In an overpopulated Britain and starving Ireland, just having a job could be the difference between life and death.

The normal rules of class struggle in Britain, Europe and the United States dictated a low-paid workforce squaring off against wealthy capitalists backed by the state. In Australia, the gap between worker and employer was not that great. Australia had given the labourer a master's wage, and this enhanced both his bargaining power and his ability to build alliances across the community.

The Australian labourer had been earning at least twice or three times that of his comrades elsewhere since the 1830s. Even in 1855, when the global economy was weak, a labourer in Sydney was still getting at least double what the equivalent worker would get in New York. A plasterer could earn twenty-five shillings a day in Sydney against ten in New York, the *Sydney Morning Herald* assured its readers. A mason was three times more valuable – twenty-one shillings to six shillings. So too was a builder's labourer – thirteen shillings to four shillings. Even a common labourer could live well in Sydney – his daily rate of seven shillings was double the three and a half shillings his brother received in New York.

Yet the replication of British working hours still left the Australian labourer feeling oppressed. Ten hours a day, Monday to Friday, and eight hours on Saturday in the Australian climate was unbearable. He adapted to this confronting environment by refighting the campaign for a shorter working day with the same righteous certainty that had driven the digger at Eureka. Stonemasons working on two churches in Sydney had achieved the eight-hour day in October 1855, but they had swapped it for lower pay. The history-making campaign in Melbourne the following year was for an industry-wide reduction, covering all trades, without the pay cut. But the timing was fraught: the global depression had not yet passed and the Australian economy went backwards for a second year in 1855.

The leader of the movement was the Welsh-born James Stephens. A stonemason by trade, he was both a Chartist and trade union activist. He arrived in Victoria in July 1853, eight months after the Lalor brothers, and took a job on one of the many building sites around Melbourne. There he became involved with the Operative Masons Society. Stephens helped form a local branch of the union in Collingwood and was an active participant at a public meeting in Melbourne's Queen's Theatre on 26 March 1856, which issued the demand to the town's employers for an eight-hour day. The resolution said, 'The laborious nature of the trade, and the continual exposure to the excessive heat of the climate loudly calls for such a reformation.'

Some employers were outraged, and their view was represented by *The Argus*, which framed the campaign as a test of national character. 'A man of Yankee temperament [would prefer] more wages for more work,' the newspaper said. '[But] an Italian believer in dulce far niente [pleasant idleness] would most likely think an hour's continuous work with stonemason's tools much more sufficient for any reasonable man'. Go on, *The Argus* taunted, be 'less Yankee and more Italian in their habits and desires'. But the newspaper forecast that the worker would soon tire of living on less money and once again seek 'more work for equal money'.

Other unions offered their support in meetings across Melbourne. The mechanical trades attracted seven hundred people to the Queen's Theatre on 11 April. Professional men shared the floor with workers, reflecting the popularity of the stonemasons' call, and repeating the experience just over a year earlier when the general public took the side of the diggers over Charles Hotham. A Dr Embling said no one in Calcutta worked in the middle of the day, 'whereas here it seemed as if they were all fools together – no fool being greater than the Englishman who carried with him his English notions wherever he went.' Mr Burt, a Chartist, told the meeting the campaign had failed in England because 'masters and journeymen had been too much separated'. The employer made too much money, while the worker was paid too little. Those economic divisions did not exist in Australia.

On the appointed day for action, 21 April 1856, Stephens led a group of stonemasons off the job at the Melbourne University site. They collected comrades working at the nearby Eastern Markets, and moved on to the most symbolic construction site at Parliament House, where their demand would be put to the colonial government. 'It was a burning hot day and I thought the occasion a good one, so I called the men to follow me,' he recalled. 'I marched them to a new building then being erected in Madeleine Street, thence to Temple Court and on to Parliament House, the men at all these works immediately dropping their tools and joining the procession.'

The Melbourne *Herald* newspaper condemned the workers for putting their livelihoods at risk. 'Wages were recovering themselves, provisions, clothing, fuel and rent were becoming cheaper, and the working classes had a fair chance of getting on again and keeping it all to themselves, when some stupid, mischievous blockhead, the worst enemy they ever had in the colony, set this agitation going.'

The paternalism was explicit. Stonemasons did not appreciate their own interests because they couldn't be expected to know how the economy worked. That was the business of grown-ups, men of means. And yet the workingman was to be trusted with the vote. Why shouldn't he have a say in the conditions of his employment? It made no more sense than telling the digger they could help themselves to a nugget, but couldn't use it to buy land.

The government quickly agreed to the stonemasons' request for an eight-hour day on the old ten-hour wage, and the most daring of the 1850s reforms had been secured without resort to violence. On 12 May workers and their families celebrated their historic achievement with a procession though the Melbourne's streets.

The eight-hour day became the norm in the Victorian building trade by 1858, and by 1870 had extended to all work on government contracts. Interestingly, only women, children and miners had specific legislation passed in the 1870s to confirm their right to an eight-hour day. Most trades relied on agreements with employers. Meanwhile, progress in the other colonies was patchy. In Queensland, stonemasons won their eight-hour day in 1865. In New South Wales, the eight-hour day became the standard across the building trade in 1871, and in South Australia two years later.

Fears that a shorter working day would make men lazy and ruin the economy proved to be unfounded. In a happy coincidence, Australia's GDP per capita rebounded by 22 per cent in 1856, which made up for the losses of the previous two years. Without a crash to associate with the introduction of the shorter hours, Victoria gave the movement more credibility than a thousand eloquent treatises.

The rush to democracy tempted the rest of the world to project onto Australia's thinly populated continent the dream of a model society. In this moment, Australia was catapulted from the former prison of a rising empire to an example more powerful than the empire itself. The Australians of the 1850s pursued these reforms from a position of material strength, from the very top of the global income ladder. This, in itself, was unusual because the lesson since ancient times was that rapidly acquired wealth was captured by elites, creating large gaps between rich and poor, and civil strife. The first part of that equation did play out with the squatters, who had dispossessed the original occupants of the land and then shut out their fellow colonists. But the squatters could not translate their temporary advantage into a permanent landed gentry because the Australian settlement was ultimately metropolitan in character. This compelled the political system to respect the rights of the newest arrival over the established population. To retain the working and middle class migrants who came in the gold rush, authorities had to guarantee both economic and democratic freedom. Australia's established egalitarian tradition and the recent memory of its isolation created two overlapping reasons for why reform made perfect sense.

Australia was in many ways a beneficiary of its late development. It joined the nineteenth century global economy as its richest member, with the two big exports of wool and gold, and a population drawn from some of the world's most advanced nations. Australia was settled late enough to avoid the American blight of slavery. In 1860, on the eve of the American civil war, the US had as many slaves and free migrants – four million each out of a total population of more than 31 million. In the 15 slave-owning states, there was one slave for every two 'whites'. Slavery helped make America rich, but divided it between races, and between north and south. Its absence in Australia reduced the risks of inequality once prosperity came to the colonies.

The free migrants from Britain, Ireland and Europe carried their own version of egalitarianism because they were leaving hunger and unemployment. But it was in Australia where that ideal could be achieved in the 1850s. The wealth came easily – first the wool and then the gold – but the social cohesion was hard-earned. It began with groundbreaking policies of religious freedom that helped secure an Anglo-Celtic union. On this relatively tolerant field, free migrants from Britain, Ireland and Europe mixed more easily than their equivalents in the United States, where sectarian conflict was more pronounced.

The concept of Australia as a fair-minded citizen of the world bore fruit in the 1850s, but the seeds were planted decades earlier. The ideal survives to this day in the notion of the fair go, and the Australian enthusiasm for policy experimentation has been a constant of political life in the century and a half since the gold rush.

Wool and then gold internationalised the colonial economy, which in turn fed the national self-image as a people of the world. This is perhaps the most crucial thing to understand about the Australian personality until the mid-point of the nineteenth century: the isolated and open selves shared the same bedrock value. But it was the open self that prospered economically and socially, and had the confidence to reform ahead of the world. The isolated self could maintain social cohesion, but it could not grow.

Affluent egalitarianism would be hard to live up to. But in the 1850s, the lure of this role-model society was strong enough to measure through migration. Victoria and California had commenced the decade with populations of 76 000 and 93 000 respectively. By 1860, Victoria had 40 per cent more people than California – 540 000 versus 380 000. The advantage was due entirely to migration – Victoria attracted twice as many new arrivals from overseas than California in that ten-year period.

Australia had not even reached the peak of its earning power. The greatest decades of prosperity were still to come. But there was an early warning that future generations would not be as welcoming of migrants. The first clue was back on the goldfields. After Eureka, a new bogeyman emerged to replace the detested troops: the industrious Chinese.

PART TWO

THE FALL

7

THE TIDE TURNS:
THE CHINESE ON
THE GOLDFIELDS

Australia realised its potential as a migrant settlement in the mid-nineteenth century, without the class and sectarian divisions of the nations from which it drew its people. It had only a mild case of xenophobia when compared with the United States. As early as the 1840s, the American-born were organising political movements to call for the restriction of Irish migration. The only free migrants Australians objected to up to this point were the Irish orphan girls. Given that Irish men would soon become the heroes of Eureka, that earlier controversy suggested the colonial hang-up had more to do with sex than race or religion.

But something changed once Australians became the world's richest people. They began to worry that the next arrival would reduce their standard of living. This anxiety would turn a migrant society against its own origins by fooling the Australian worker into equating his income with the colour of his skin. He saw future waves of migration from Asia, and later Europe and even Britain, as a threat to the classless utopia he had imagined for himself. The fatal flaw of nineteenth-century egalitarianism was the fear of foreign competition.

This xenophobia was peculiar to Australia at the time because it sprang from the insecurity of instant economic success. The Australian worker didn't make his own wealth, as an American entrepreneur might. He took it from the ground, or clipped it from the back of the sheep which roamed the land. What he created with his bounty was an idealised settlement that placed him at the top of the social order. He had a high wage and the vote, but he did not have the confidence that the next wave of migration would help him create even more wealth, because to his mind, the windfall had already been extracted. He couldn't share it, he assumed, without sacrificing his position. As his political power grew with his income, the Australian worker became the first in the world to use democracy as a deliberate tool of exclusion. The first victims were a few thousand Chinese who walked onto the goldfields in 1854.

The Chinese joined the rush a little later than the Europeans, but they had an explicit right to come to Victoria. Under the treaty of Nanking, which had ended the first Opium War in 1842 in London's favour, the Chinese were granted the same freedom to migrate and trade throughout the British Empire as the British had given themselves in China. When the agreement was signed the Australian colonies had yet to find gold.

Most of the Chinese prospectors were peasants from the southern provinces, where a tragic combination of local uprisings, imperial interventions, floods and famines were killing the people at the same rate as in Ireland. The scale, however, was much greater: while Ireland saw one million people die, and two million emigrate due to famine between 1841 and 1855, the Chinese would lose almost fifty million lives and another five million to migration between 1850 and 1870, reducing the total population from 412 million to 358 million. It was the greatest single shock to China's population since the Mongols had brought mass murder and the bubonic plague to the country half a millennium earlier.

Yet Australia only ever saw the smallest part of the Chinese wave. When tensions first arose on the Victoria goldfields in 1854, the Chinese numbered just 2341 people across the entire colony, or one per cent of the population. Yet their unity intimidated the European diggers, and in the depressed economic setting that coincided with their arrival, a misunderstanding between the two groups was almost inevitable. The Chinese prospectors worked in gangs on ground that had already been abandoned. Every piece of overlooked gold that they found through their collective effort wounded the pride of the Europeans. The Chinese prospectors kept their distance as a show of respect, but the diggers saw an aloof, conniving people. Even their indulgences differed: the Chinese preferred opium to grog, which reduced the opportunities for a social truce on Australian terms, in the pub.

The diggers were individuals to a man. The subsequent association of the digger with the trenches of Gallipoli obscures this conflicted aspect of gold rush egalitarianism. The diggers wanted to strike it rich alone, or with a mate, rather than pour the winnings into a communal pot, to be divided equally at the end of the day; this distinction only became apparent when the Chinese brought their alternate method of labour to the goldfields.

The Chinese came to the goldfields for the same reason as anyone else: to strike it rich. But unlike the Europeans, most did not pay their own fare. Typically, they came from rural villages. They borrowed for, or were given a credit for the trip from Hong Kong to Melbourne, which they would repay out of the gold they found. They were greeted by members of the Chinese community in Melbourne and, once on the goldfields, they would have stayed with their group. There is nothing unusual in this. Contemporary statistics show that about eight in ten of all migrants will settle, initially, in an area where there is an established community from their home country.

The diggers feared they would be outclassed and overrun by this regimented people. But Australia's proximity to China also played a role in the European anxiety. The colonists were keenly aware that the world's most populous nation was between them and their own home countries in the North Atlantic, and once Australia achieved a global reputation as a land of plenty, then the hungry Chinese would want to come just as surely as the hungry British and Irish.

The campaign against the Chinese was led by the most influential newspaper in Victoria, *The Argus*, which used the same language it had previous deployed against the Irish orphan girls and the English convicts. 'The presence among us of even 20 000 Chinese is a social evil of no ordinary magnitude. These men are aliens in language, customs, and religion,' the newspaper warned in April 1855. 'They are regarded by the mass of the colonial population as inferiors; and they tacitly admit their inferiority.' The 'lying, gambling, thieving' Chinese could not be redeemed. 'They would continue to constitute a lower stratum of society, into which the most degraded of the superior race would sink.'

The growth in the Chinese population must have seemed alarming. By early 1855, their ranks had trebled to more than six thousand. They poured off the boats in Melbourne and headed straight to the goldfields, passing disappointed diggers on their way back to the capital. Yet even this number was only a fraction of the fifty thousand-plus new British and Irish migrants who would arrive in the colonies in 1855.

The Chinese had only a few people willing to speak on their behalf. One man who called himself Quang Chew wrote an open letter to plead for understanding. He detailed the skills of Chinese migrants, including those who were carpenters who could work fine wood, and farmers who could manage 'the worst as well as the best soils. Not only do the people of England come here, but the people of India, and Japan, and America, and also from French lands and other places.' He asked why all the people of the world should be welcome except the Chinese.

The *Freeman's Journal* in New South Wales published the plea under the headline 'The Chinese Invasion of Australia'. A note to readers explained it was important to know one's enemy: 'This speech will be found well worthy [of] perusal, exhibiting, as it does, consummate shrewdness, with that grovelling servility which the Orientals so well know how to assume when they feel themselves in a state of weakness and dependence, and for which they never fail to indemnify themselves by the boundless extent of their arrogance when in possession of power.'

The *South Australian Register* hedged its bets after some of its readers claimed the statement was a hoax. 'If it is a fiction,' the newspaper replied on 8 May, 'all we can say was that it was cleverly written'. This prompted London-born poet and goldfields official Richard Horne to claim credit for the work, which he said he wrote on behalf of the Chinese. 'It seemed to me that there was a louder outcry against these people than justified by reason or right feeling, and I thought a speech from one of themselves would be the most advantageous means of calling and obtaining attention to the other side of the question. The Chinese are very ingenious and industrious, and their presence among us, if properly regulated, may be for rather a good than an evil.'

The Chinese also received support from the Victorian chamber of commerce. At a meeting in Melbourne in late April, speaker after speaker praised their work ethic. A Mr Bowden said the Chinese were an obedient people, 'expert at agriculture and the artificial irrigation of land'. He said: 'These, then, were exactly the men who were wanted in this colony.' Mr Sichel said the feeling against the Chinese sprang from the jealousies of the working man. 'These people found the Chinese interfering with their labors. They said, "we are Englishmen; these are strangers; away with them". This agitation had not been got up by the general class of the community.' He predicted that once the workingman acquired a 'little capital' he would be the loudest supporter of Chinese migration.

But most political forces in the colony were lining up against the

Chinese. The diggers had used the royal commission inquiry into the goldfields, established in the wake of Eureka, to vent against their unfamiliar rivals. The royal commissioners did not accept everything the diggers claimed, noting the Chinese were less prone to crime than the Europeans. Nonetheless they did agree with the diggers that restrictions should be placed on the Chinese. 'Even if the Chinese were considered desirable colonists, they are unaccompanied by their wives and families, under which circumstances no immigration can prove of real advantage to any society,' they declared in their report, released in April 1855. 'Nor is the economical argument of their utility as servants available, as they all seem to proceed to the mines. [Their] presence in such large masses must certainly tend to demoralise colonial society.' The commissioners had no interest in calling for 'the absolute exclusion from this colony of this or any other branch of the great human family'. But it was self-evident, they said, 'that some step is here necessary, if not to prohibit, at least to check and diminish this influx'.

Later, in a petition to the Victorian parliament, the Chinese explained why they did not bring their wives or children to the goldfields: 'We wish to leave some of the family to look after our aged parents as the climate there is very rough'. They wrote that Chinese women 'are not like English women, when they go into ships they cannot walk or stand, and we cannot afford the passage money'. They had unconsciously recited the argument that the early governors had made against the female convicts: Chinese women had no immediate economic value in this new settlement.

The goldfields report foreshadowed the argument the colonies would have with London for the remainder of the century. London wanted the colonies open to all, to further its interests in trade. The British, Irish and Europeans in Australia wanted the colonies to themselves, without the Chinese. *The Argus* made this argument plainly. 'What we mainly wish to guard against is a Chinese inundation. We wish to keep them from coming here in sufficient numbers to swamp our population, to constitute a large slave class amongst us, or to enable them to defy our laws and regulations,' the newspaper said. 'The last evil has in part arisen already, hundreds of Chinese came in a body, and marched upon the diggings together like a small army; ignorant of our speech and of our customs – "aliens in blood, aliens in language, and aliens in religion," as Lord Lyndhurst said of the Irish – knowing little about us except our general toleration of all foreigners, on which toleration they presumed.' There was no sense that *The Argus* appreciated the irony in their quoting an attack on the previous victims of xenophobia, the Irish.

Charles Hotham wanted no more trouble on the goldfields, and in May 1855 released 'a Bill to make provisions for certain immigrants'. It applied a ten-pound tax to all Chinese, payable within twenty-four hours of arriving at any port. The measure appears to have been inspired by the earlier Californian tax on foreign miners. Leading the argument for the anti-Chinese tax was the Irish-born John O'Shanassy, the royal commissioner who had designed the miners' right.

O'Shanassy's personal story is one of the most symbolic of the nineteenth century: a previous victim of colonial bigotry who rose to become a respected member of the community and Victoria's first Catholic premier. O'Shanassy dismissed critics, most notably from the chamber of commerce, who said the colony had no authority to impose a selective migration policy. Victoria had every right to act against 'whatever intended to overthrow its moral or political status'. He explained, 'The immense influx of Chinese, by swamping the European population, was calculated to produce such a result; and the Legislature were perfectly justified in taking steps for preventing it.'

The bill was passed without amendment, and the measure had an immediate effect. The Chinese intake fell by almost a third in 1856. But the Hong Kong–based agents who arranged the trips to

Victoria responded by changing the route. The ships ignored Melbourne and deposited their Chinese passengers in South Australia, from where they made the duty-free trek of more than four hundred kilometres to the goldfields. Authorities conceded that almost fifteen thousand Chinese arrived through the back door in the first six months of 1857, which was still only half the number of British and Irish migrants in that period. The Victorian census taken at the end of March 1857 recorded just over twenty-five thousand Chinese-born men and three women; a tenfold increase since 1854. That year, 1857, also found the global economy in another depression, and Victoria with self-government. That combination would prove lethal for the Chinese.

As reports of rising anger on the goldfields filtered back to Melbourne, the convict sons in the parliament began pressing for an outright ban of Chinese migration, reflecting the eternal Australian paradox that the last intake slams the door on the next. Among them was Horatio Wills, a well-known squatter. He took up the cause in parliament in May 1857, calling for measures 'to arrest the inpouring of Chinese from the neighbouring colonies, to prevent the eventual expulsion of our countrymen and race from the gold-fields of Victoria'. John Pascoe Fawkner followed in June by establishing a seven-member committee to draft new anti-Chinese legislation. The bill would aim to 'control the flood of Chinese immigration setting into this colony, and effectually prevent the gold-fields of Australia Felix from becoming the property of the Emperor of China and of the Mongolian and Tartar hordes of Asia'.

The aggression in parliament was a dress rehearsal for one of the most shocking episodes on the goldfields, at the Buckland River diggings, in north-eastern Victoria. Here the European miners felt they were losing ground to the Chinese and, after weeks of mutual suspicion, the Europeans decided to force the issue. On the morning of 4 July 1857, they organised a meeting to consider 'what measures should be adopted to protect the body of the white miners from the incursions of the Chinese'. The Europeans resolved to evict their rivals, and the diggers marched on to the Chinese camp at Louden's Flat, with some chanting, 'Come and let us drive the long-tail devils off at once'. The Chinese began packing their belongings, ignoring the sole policeman on duty who advised them to stand their ground. Once they had abandoned the camp, the vigilantes entered, grabbed whatever items were left behind and set fire to the tents. The mob went from camp to camp, extending the nominal courtesy of allowing the Chinese time to clear out. But as the crowd swelled, a darker urge took hold. A massacre threatened as the Chinese were pushed to the river's edge. If they had rushed across the water, many would have drowned. But a number of European diggers intervened on their behalf, holding back the mob to ensure an orderly passage. Nonetheless, three Chinese were said to have died from exposure.

At first the press blamed the victim. The *Ovens and Murray Advocate* said, 'Exasperated by the perpetual interference of the Celestials with their mining pursuits, and alarmed at the overwhelming numbers continually pouring in upon them, the Buckland diggers of European origin have taken the law into their own hands.' The article made clear the racial nature of this eviction. 'The whole white population, even to their very domestic animals the dogs, have manifested such a deadly hatred towards the Chinese that, had they been wise, they would have taken themselves out of the way long ago.'

But once the extent of the violence had been understood, colonial opinion shifted against the diggers. After a second disturbance at Forest Creek, *The Argus* said it was 'perfectly ashamed of the tone adopted by those who insist upon the expulsion and exclusion of the Chinese from Victoria'. The newspaper wrote a mea culpa, retracting its earlier attacks on the Chinese. 'There is a systematic suppression of everything calculated to tell in favor of this people, and a deliberate exaggeration of everything that can be urged against them, whether founded upon credible testimony or merely based upon hearsay.' These people were 'neither better nor worse than their neighbors'.

Buckland River contained some of the aspects of squatting, and others of frontier war. The European diggers had moved ahead of the law to assert control over land that was not theirs to claim. They considered the Chinese an inferior people who did not deserve the same rights that they had fought for at Eureka less than three years earlier. Much like during the frontier wars, authorities were not impressed, yet showed more sympathy for the aggressor than the victim. Police arrested fifteen diggers, but only four men were convicted – three for unlawful assembly and one for riot. Justice Noel told the guilty their crimes would normally attract many years of hard labour, but he took account of their good character and gave them a 'generous' sentence of nine months each in Melbourne's jail.

The two thousand five hundred Chinese who fled Buckland River had an estimated fifty thousand pounds in gold and possessions taken from them. The government did provide compensation and an escort for those who wanted to return, though few did. But it also saw the riot as a warning, and decided to avert future violence with even tougher legislation to discourage the Chinese from the diggings.

By the time of the riot, there were 170 000 people on the Victorian goldfields, of which 126 000 were male. The English were the largest group, accounting for forty-five thousand, or 36 per cent, of the total male population on the goldfields, while the Chinese came in second at twenty-four thousand, or 19 per cent, of the total. The Chinese numbers had increased tenfold in three years, and the government shared the concern of the diggers that, left unchecked, this trend would see the Chinese replace the English as the largest group of miners. Yet the Chinese were still only 6 per cent of the wider colonial population. The compressed setting of the goldfields exacerbated this fear of foreign competition and invasion, and the political overreaction formed the bedrock of what would become the White Australia policy. That attempt to control would undermine the Australian economy into the twentieth century.

There were two strands to the defence of Chinese migration that emerged in the wake of the Buckland River riot, and the first was an economic argument. The danger to Australia from restricting migration was understood even in the 1850s. Sir Henry Barkly, the governor of Victoria under the new system of representative democracy, warned politicians that 'the withdrawal of thirty or forty thousand industrious labourers and great consumers would, at any rate of time, affect very much the prosperity of the colony'. Whatever the parliament decided, he urged that it not succumb to the passions of the moment. 'We owe it not merely to our social welfare, but to our national repute, that we should let the counsels of moderation prevail,' he said in August 1857.

The second defence of Chinese migration was moral, and it came from the most surprising part of the Victorian settlement: the goldfields themselves. One of the few politicians to defend the Chinese unconditionally was Peter Lalor, the hero of Eureka. In September 1857, when William Haines, the first colonial premier, proposed to tax the Chinese ten shillings per month to help pay for their security on the goldfields, Lalor argued passionately against it. The bill was a form of slavery, he said. He had always opposed the system of mining licence fees, regardless of creed or country. He would claim for the Chinese the same right he had sought for himself.

Yet Haines went further with his bill, demanding that 'every Chinaman' show that he had paid the ten-pound landing tax. This amounted to a retrospective tax on those who had come lawfully through South Australia. Haines conceded 'that in a free country it was unfair to subject any particular race of persons to a tax'. But the circumstances of this case were unusual: the Chinese were 'a barbarous race' and had come in large numbers 'unaccompanied by their wives'.

The legislation was passed by twenty-three votes to three. Yet the three politicians who voted against the tax – Peter Lalor, Butler Aspinall and John Wood – were those who served goldfields electorates. They appeared to be shocked by the escalation of politics, which had taken the material grievances of the diggers against their Chinese competitors into the realm of racial exclusion. The detail of this debate is long forgotten, but it provides an important lesson about the inherent danger in the politics of race. Leaders are prone to overcompensate on behalf of the established population, thus perpetuating xenophobia, when the community can in fact be trusted to reach an accommodation with the newcomer.

'The diggers were not unjust,' Aspinall told parliament. 'Nor did they wish to see digger-hunting revived.' The Chinese had just as much right to a fair hearing as the Christians did in earlier times, said Wood. 'Look again at the charges against the Jews in the Middle Ages, and how unfounded they seemed now.' Wood was the member for the Ovens electorate, which included the Buckland River diggings.

The diggers appeared to be the catalyst for the anti-Chinese sentiment and legislation, but the votes of Lalor, Aspinall and Wood suggest the view on the Victorian goldfields was more nuanced than in the rest of the community. The Chinese did not live among the politicians or the media who sat in judgement of them. This meant they could not easily counter the toxic scare campaigns with the antidote of human contact. On the goldfields, the Chinese were 19 per cent of the male population. But in the rural districts, they were less than 2 per cent of the total population, and in the towns, less than 1 per cent. The physical and cultural separation of 'white'- and 'yellow'-skinned miners, and the lack of any noticeable Chinese population elsewhere, created an empathy gap from the mines to the steps of Parliament House.

When the diggers left Victoria for the less promising goldfields of New South Wales, the riots became bloodier, and the legislative response more punitive. Here the Chinese were the largest ethnic group on the diggings, accounting for 28 per cent of the male population, followed by the Australian-born (24 per cent) and the English-born (23 per cent). At Lambing Flat, between Sydney and what is now Canberra, the European diggers were so brazen that they defied repeated government warnings to leave the Chinese alone. Even after troops were dispatched to the goldfields in early 1861, the diggers would not be deterred. On 30 June they unleashed an even deadlier eviction than Buckland River.

Miner George Preshaw wrote that two thousand men, led by a brass band and carrying a banner that read 'Roll-up – no Chinese', assembled in the town at 10.30 a.m. and marched on the first camp. 'The poor fellows ran in all directions, leaving behind their tents and all belonging to them. The mob set fire to the tents, and those of them that were on horseback rounded up the Chinese, and commenced cutting their tails off – cutting, you could not call it cutting – they pulled them out by the roots, chopped off with hatchets, this they did by taking them by the tails and dragging them to the nearest log. I myself saw one man, an Irishman, in his hurry to cut off a tail, cut all the skin off the back of the poor fellow's head.'

In November 1861 the New South Wales parliament passed legislation placing a ten-pound landing tax on the Chinese and a limit on the number of new arrivals per vessel. These were bold moves not just because of their patent unfairness: the colonies were challenging London's own preferred model for open borders. London had signed two further treaties with China in 1858 and 1860 that extended the rights of the Chinese to migrate and trade through the British Empire.

London was now losing patience with the colonists. The Duke of Newcastle sent a letter of protest to the New South Wales government in 1861, but he did not exercise the power of veto over the legislation. Much as Earl Grey had backed down after the protests against the *Hashemy* convict ship, the calculation in this instance was probably the same: the mother country, mindful of the American precedent in 1776, did not want to lose its arrogant sons on the question of migration. Yet London's view would prevail, at least in the medium term. Victoria would remove its restrictions in 1865, followed by New South Wales in 1867, allowing the Chinese who remained to live in the colonies without official harassment, although they were tellingly denied the right to vote.

The economic and social damage of racial exclusion was not immediately apparent while Australia sat on top of the global income ladder, and there were still new frontiers to develop. The decision to restrict the Chinese came when the colonies were receiving record numbers of migrants from the United Kingdom, and there was no thought given to what would happen if those familiar intakes slowed. Migration was inexorably linked to prosperity, but the Australians of the mid-nineteenth century thought they could afford to be choosy. This version of egalitarianism, geared to protecting the Australian worker, was, in fact, elitist. It trip-wired the economy for failure in the long run by removing the two things that had brought Australia its success – open migration and markets.

8

THE QUEENSLAND
DESCENT

Before the Australian settlement expanded northwards in the 1860s, the country could claim with some confidence that it was more cohesive and progressive than any society on earth. Admittedly, the bar was low. The United Kingdom remained divided by class, and still treated the Irish as outcasts; the United States had not yet rid itself of slavery; and Europe was in perpetual conflict along the fault lines of class and nationality.

Australia's ethical balance sheet had, on one side, the abuse of the Indigenous and Chinese populations, and to a lesser extent the Irish, as debits, and, on the other side, world-leading political reforms as credits. But Queensland altered Australia's moral trajectory by importing the most toxic aspects of contemporary British, American and European life to the world's richest settlement, and reviving the darker side of early colonial history.

Queensland ran against the very grain of egalitarianism. The southern colonies had secured an alliance between labour and capital. In Queensland, the two sides fought a class war that culminated in the great strikes of the 1890s. The southern colonies were pioneers for democracy. In Queensland, it was delayed for a generation. Without these foundations of social and economic equality, material progress in the northernmost colony proved unsustainable and ultimately presaged Australia's decline.

The first Queensland-inspired setback for the egalitarian model came when the *Don Juan* docked in Moreton Bay on 14 August 1863. On board were seventy-four young Pacific Islander men dressed in matching pants and shirts. They were neither migrants nor tourists, but indentured labourers under contract to Robert Towns, one of the richest men in all the colonies. The American Civil War meant cotton supplies from the American south had been disrupted, and Towns saw an opportunity to crack the British market with Australian-grown cotton. He could not make the venture pay with European labour, and so had hired Pacific Islanders to work on his cotton plantation on the Darling Downs, on pay and conditions well below what a white labourer would accept. The men would receive up to ten shillings per month, be housed in 'comfortable huts' and provided 'regular rations of rice, meat, pumpkins, potatoes, and yams – if they will grow'. After twelve months, they would be sent home, and replaced by a new workforce. Towns had told agent Ross Lewin to look for 'young lads from 14 to 18 years of age', with a few older hands required to act as guides. On no account was force to be used in their recruitment.

Brisbane's *Courier* noted the arrival of three vessels that day. The German migrants who came on the *Alster* and *La Rochelle* 'were all of a first class description', the newspaper enthused, 'principally agricultural laborers and mechanics from all parts of the Fatherland. There has been little or no difficulty in obtaining employment for the large number of these new arrivals, as there is a demand for steady good workmen; and it is well known that the Germans are steady, careful, and very industrious.' But the *Don Juan* had 'excited the suspicion of many persons'. It was feared some of the young men had been 'kidnapped'.

American Civil War buffs may recognise the pathos of the

Don Juan's expedition. The Pacific Islanders were being recruited as General Robert E. Lee's Confederate troops commenced their retreat to Virginia following their defeat at Gettysburg on 4 July 1863. Abraham Lincoln's campaign to abolish slavery in the United States was now assured.

Brisbane's *Courier* did not believe any good could come from Towns' scheme. On 22 August, it published an article under the heading 'The Slave Trade in Queensland'. The government was 'winking at the disgraceful transaction' when it should be doing everything it could 'to suppress this traffic in its infancy'. 'It is a crying disgrace upon the colony, and can only bring a curse with it; no reason can be urged for such an unnatural proceeding when hundreds of thousands of our fellow countrymen are starving at home [in Britain] – seeking employment and cannot find it.'

The Sydney newspapers joined the chorus of condemnation. *The Empire*, founded by Henry Parkes, saw the trade as a threat to Australia's very being. 'We do not believe that the people which has struggled so long and so earnestly to rid itself of the blessings of convict labour will tamely submit to encumber itself with the still more objectionable blessings of savage labour. We do not see that we shall have gained much by our rejection of the convict system, if we have only exchanged it for the Chinese system, the Coolie system, or the South Sea Island system. For the scum of our own countrymen would at all events be preferable to the scum of humanity.' This view was reflected widely throughout the colonies.

Towns wrote to the Queensland premier to defend himself. He had tried to develop a cotton industry with German labour, but they asked for too much money. 'My agent was glad to give up all claim to the fellows, whose laziness, combined with their large ration-consuming and useless family – for your laws do not seem to reach the wives and children – would have soon ruined the whole enterprise.' Other businessmen were suffering the same problems, he said. 'I came to the conclusion that cotton growing upon a large scale either must be abandoned in Queensland, or be carried out by cheaper labour.'

The question of how someone like Towns, a Sydney-based entrepreneur, single-handedly defied the will of the Australia people on such a sensitive issue can be answered with one of the missing pieces in the Queensland settlement – democracy. The colony achieved self-government from New South Wales in 1859, but did not grant universal male suffrage until 1872. The early parliaments were compromised by an unusual voting system, which allowed those with substantial holdings of property to vote more than once. Inevitably, government would fall into the hands of the pastoralists.

The kinship that politicians in Victorian felt with labourers was missing here. The first Queensland premier, Robert Herbert, 'invested heavily, though not profitably, in cotton-planting and a large sheep station'. As a grandson of the Earl of Carnarvon, he was drawn from London's political class, but his pastoral interests made him the antithesis of the reform-minded professionals who ruled in the southern colonies. Most Queensland politicians had little or no political experience, historian Raymond Evans has written. 'A civil servant, who arrived in 1862, found the small governing class imbued with "great ignorance" and "strange ideas" that "would astonish those who think and read".' They saw the colony through the narrow prism of profit and were happy to support businessmen like Towns, who asked for and received generous government subsidies to establish his cotton planation. But he could not turn a profit, even with the handout and the indentured labour. The experiment should have ended there, but the unrepresentative Queensland parliament was willing to entertain other forms of tropical agriculture on the same terms. It was in the year that slavery ended in the United States – 1865 – that Queensland grazier and politician Louis Hope imported Pacific Islanders to work on his sugar plantation at Ormiston. With the government's encouragement, others followed, and by 1871, there were 2255 Pacific Islander men and 81 women living in Queensland.

Australians had ended the 1850s on top of the global income ladder. National income contracted slightly in all but one year between 1860 and 1865, in the hiatus between the end of the Victorian gold rush and the start of Queensland's. But the damage was mild, and when the economic good times resumed with Queensland's expansion, Australia kicked clear of the pack. It was during this period that Australia had no peer – from the second half of the 1860s until the end of the 1880s. It was not unusual for Australia's GDP per capita to be at least 20 per cent larger than the next ranked nation, which was often the United Kingdom. By the late 1870s, Australia's advantage over the United States, which was still recovering from the civil war, had extended to more than 60 per cent.

This part of the winning streak cannot be explained by gold because total production was falling despite the entry of Queensland into the export market. The new boom in national income was due to technology. Australia as a rich people had, in effect, first-mover rights on the great advances in transport and communication of the age. Adelaide, Melbourne, Sydney and Brisbane were connected by the telegraph cable in late 1861, just in time for the people in each capital to receive the results of the first Melbourne Cup horse race on the day it was run. The colonies were becoming more accessible for trade through the steam engine, as the development of railways brought people and goods together across the continent. New machines increased the productivity of the worker, so living standards continued to grow as the population expanded.

There was also a conscious effort to educate the people. School became compulsory for children, and all colonies recorded dramatic improvements in literacy. In 1861, less than half the Victorian children aged five to fifteen years (49 per cent) could read and write. By 1881, 80 per cent could do so. South Australia was second with a literacy rate of 70 per cent, followed by Queensland at 67 cent, New South Wales at 65 per cent, Tasmania at 62 per cent and Western Australia at 61 per cent. Note how closely the ladder correlates with convict foundation, or in the case of Western Australia, its late entry into transportation.

Prosperity did not come easily for Queensland. It had been established as a convict settlement in 1824, following the recommendations of the Bigge report to create new, more rigorous prisons away from the main colonies. Queensland remained a part of New South Wales for the next thirty-five years, and in that time it missed the early pastoral boom and the first gold rushes because its focus on transportation limited the settlement to the Brisbane area. When it finally separated from Sydney's rule in December 1859, Queensland had a base of just 23 520 settlers, still living mainly around Brisbane. They were outnumbered more than two to one by the sixty thousand Indigenous people living throughout the colony, where the colony's natural resources were waiting to be exploited.

Self-government coincided with the good fortune of gold. A small find at Canoona, near Rockhampton, was followed by a bigger one at Gympie. The colonial population exploded, passing a hundred thousand in 1868, 150 000 in 1874 and 200 000 by the twentieth anniversary of separation in 1879. But this growth was less impressive than it seemed. In those first twenty years, the national population grew by one million, and Queensland only accounted for 17 per cent of that total. New South Wales was responsible for 36 per cent of the increase and Victoria another 30 per cent. Nevertheless, Queensland had sufficient momentum to consolidate the eastern coastline at the expense of the south and west, overtaking Tasmania's population in 1867 and then South Australia's in 1885 to become the third-largest colony.

The early colonial records show that Queensland followed, at least initially, the same cultural development as the other colonies, with an excess of men from overseas. In 1871, the registrar-general, Henry Scott, was pleased that Queensland was receiving a decent standard of foreigner. 'It is true that occasionally people in authority [in the mother country] take advantage of emigration to relieve themselves from the burden of paupers and lunatics; but, as a general rule, our immigrants have not been of this class.'

Yet he did not address the most interesting part of the colony's ethnic face, which was drawn from three corners of the globe: the United Kingdom and Europe; Asia; and the Pacific. Queensland was the most diverse Australian settlement of the nineteenth century. The British and Irish were never in danger of being eclipsed in the earlier colonial settlements. In Queensland, the risk was ever present. By 1871, the state had three significant non-English-speaking groups of men – the Germans (7 per cent), Chinese (5 per cent) and Pacific Islanders (3 per cent). Individually each tribe was no larger than the Germans in South Australia, or the Chinese in Victoria and New South Wales. But no other colony had Germans and Chinese together on this scale, let alone a third non-English-speaking group, the Pacific Islanders. The combined total of 15 per cent would rise to 19 per cent by 1881, which was one percentage point larger than the English- and Welsh-born male population at the time. Migrants from Ireland and Scotland outnumbered the English in the censuses of 1864, 1868 and 1871, and would do so again in 1881. New South Wales and Victoria had seen more Celts than Anglos before their gold rushes, but not after them.

On paper, it reads like a pointer to modern multicultural Australia, but this mix was not sustainable. The Pacific Islanders, imported against their own wishes, and of those of the wider colonial population, were not intended as permanent settlers. The Chinese, on the other hand, were prepared to settle. But this unnerved the pastoralists, who feared the Chinese could claim the northern part of the colony on their own. This created one of the many contradictions in Queensland's settlement: parliament tolerated indentured Pacific Island labour, but would move to restrict the Chinese. The only way to reconcile this double standard is from the perspective of capital. To Queensland's business interests, the Chinese were seen as potential rivals in agriculture, with their own numerically superior workforce. The Pacific Islanders posed no such threat because they were the property of the pastoralists.

Queensland's land mass was twice the size of New South Wales, and almost eight times that of Victoria. Its topography and climate unnerved the Europeans, but proved no barrier to the Chinese, who would, in the 1870s, prove the most successful diggers on the goldfields at Palmer River. In addition, the north of Queensland was more easily accessible to the Chinese than to the Europeans. The journey by ship from Hong Kong to nearby Cooktown and the trek to the goldfields, or perhaps to a sugar plantation, was quicker than coming overland from the Queensland capital, or further afield from New South Wales or Victoria.

The earlier free migrants who gave Victoria, New South Wales and South Australia their creativity were drawn from a mother country that had abolished slavery and was taking the first tentative steps towards genuine democracy. The governing class that came with assisted passage and gold were liberal capitalists, influenced by Adam Smith and John Stuart Mill. They consciously sought to make Australia better than the United Kingdom and the United States, using the law to avoid the creation of an underclass. Queensland received the next generation of British migrants, who were inspired by Charles Darwin. They saw the white race as the fittest of the species. Their narrowness of mind was manifest, and it predated the arrival of the *Don Juan* in the attitude of the settlers to the Indigenous population.

———————

The frontier wars in Queensland were more deadly, for both sides, than in the other colonies. The severity of the settler response was shaped by the harshness of the environment and the greater resistance of the locals, but that does not excuse the violence. The cycle of revenge was closer to the barbaric outcome on the Hawkesbury than the more enlightened, although flawed, attempt to negotiate a treaty at the foundation of Melbourne.

The most infamous example was the Nogoa massacre, which set the tone for future conflict between the settlers and the much larger Indigenous population. Horatio Wills, the anti-Chinese politician from Victoria, led a party of twenty-five stockmen, shepherds, servants and their respective families into the heart of central Queensland in 1861. The locals seemed unfussed by their arrival in October, and looked on as the newcomers established their camp. Horatio, an experienced pioneer, evidently felt no threat, because he had taken no precautions to secure the site. On 17 October the locals staged a bloody eviction, striking when Horatio was resting. Although he managed to fire a shot with his pistol, he was promptly clubbed to death. Nine other men, two women and seven children, including an eight-month-old baby, were also killed, in the largest massacre of settlers in Australia history. The murders were said to be payback for the earlier shooting of two locals.

The settlers unleashed their first reprisal on 23 October. 'Several blacks lay dead where they had been peacefully sleeping only a short time before,' according to one eyewitness account. The native police took over the next day. 'The punishment meted out to the murderers was very severe, and of the many who took an active part in the massacre very few lived to tell that tale.'

The *Queensland Times* pronounced the guilt of the whole tribe, while the *Sydney Morning Herald* informed readers that 'sixty or seventy' locals were executed in one round-up – the shooting ending only 'when their ammunition was expended'.

On Queensland's goldfields, a similar pattern asserted itself. Death stalked this rush. At Palmer River, in Cape York, prospectors and locals engaged in armed combat. 'The darkies are very numerous, and on several occasions very troublesome,' according to a detailed account published in *The Queenslander* in December 1873. The census collector for the Palmer district estimated 'over five hundred unregistered deaths' between 1871 and 1876 – although he confessed the true figure was probably higher.

Palmer River reveals another aspect of Queensland's curse that would have long-lasting effects. None of the northern goldfields were located close enough to major population centres to recreate the Victorian experience, where gold helped build a global city in Melbourne, which was a people and investment magnet long after the rush had ended. Palmer River was two thousand kilometres from Brisbane. Without a strong capital in these formative years, Queensland took a decidedly parochial turn, away from the cosmopolitanism of the southern cities.

Perhaps the story of Palmer River and Queensland would have been different if the colonial parliament had taken a more liberal view of the Chinese. At the 1876 census, almost three out of every four diggers at Palmer River were Chinese-born – 6672 out of 9712. The following year, the Queensland parliament unilaterally moved to expel them from the goldfields. A punitive tax on 'Asiatic or African' migrants only was legislated, and the measure was so offensive that London refused to ratify it. The secretary of state for the colonies, Earl Carnarvon, reminded the young colony that Victoria and New South Wales had repealed their poll taxes on the Chinese in the previous decade. 'I cannot but regret, therefore, that the Legislature of Queensland should now have thought it necessary to enact a measure of this character,' he wrote. London may not have been immune from the social Darwinism that infected the colony, but its interests in China dictated a more open view of migration than the colonists'.

A wound was reopened, but without a riot to justify it. The lack of widespread agitation against the Chinese suggests this policy was designed for the benefit of the pastoralists. The new Queensland premier, the London-born John Douglas, wrote a letter to his fellow premiers asking for their support to assert the colonial right to decide migration policy. He rehashed the arguments first made a generation earlier by the diggers of Victoria. 'We are now threatened with a large and unrestricted Chinese immigration, and I do not hesitate to assure you that the consequences of this immigration are contemplated with serious misgivings by all classes,' Douglas wrote. 'Industrious, frugal, and, law-abiding as the Chinese people may be, they are not colonists in the best sense of the term. They do not bring their women with them or, if they do, the women who immigrate belong for the most part to an immoral class.' The Chinese, if allowed to arrive in large numbers, would 'entirely supplant European labour'.

Although Earl Carnarvon was sent a copy of the letter, the implied threat of a colonial revolt was not followed through. Douglas made a tactical retreat by modifying the legislation, imposing a lower ten-pound entry tax on the Chinese that would be refunded if they left Queensland within three years. Restrictions were also placed on the number of Chinese people each ship could carry. The governor gave these measures his assent in October, and London did not object.

These restrictions were specifically designed to discourage Chinese settlement. The Chinese could come for the gold, but not stay to develop the north – the inverse of the old Victorian and New South Wales objection that the Chinese were only interested in the diggings. Once Queensland had shown the southern colonies that London could be defied, albeit without policy logic, the other colonies revived their restrictions. In 1881, Victoria followed Queensland's lead by limiting the number of Chinese that could be carried on each ship.

Yet Queensland's colour line was blurred by the presence of the Pacific Island labourers, who were treated no better than slaves. Their abuse was Queensland's greatest curse, and marked the turning point in Australia's nineteenth-century history, from a progressive settlement to a belligerent one.

The case that attracted most attention in the early years involved the *Carl*, a vessel that left Melbourne in 1871. The ship's owner, Dr James Patrick Murray, ran a smallpox sanatorium in Bendigo. As he later conceded, the purpose of the trip was to 'capture' natives in the Pacific and take them to Fiji, where they would work on colonial plantations. They caught 140 men in total, and kept them in the hold below. When some of the men protested, the order was given to fire into the hold. 'A great number were shot during the night, and more in the morning,' Murray said. The final toll was about fifty dead and another twenty wounded. The dead and the wounded – all 'seventy souls' – were thrown overboard together.

The captain and crew were rounded up and two trials were conducted in Sydney and Melbourne in the second half of 1872. No one could listen to the evidence without being moved, Mr Justice Faucett said. 'These unfortunate men were shot down in the dark hold of the *Carl* by scores; the hold being transformed, in one dreadful night, into a human slaughter-house full of victims; and then the ship was cleared. The murdered dead were first thrown overboard, and then the wounded and dying men are brought up on dock. These living outraged men are thrown overboard too, flung into the deep water, one by one, with the life blood still flowing in their veins – the living as well as the dead. There could be no possible pretense for this cruel deed.' The judge sentenced both men to death, later commuted to life in prison.

While the abuses remained offshore, Australians could pretend that the continent had not been tarnished by this brutal trade. But that changed when a British-flagged ship, the *Hopeful*, left Townsville for New Guinea on 28 April 1884 to collect labourers to work in Queensland. Impatient with the results of early talks with the islanders, the ship's second mate and recruiting agent, Neil McNeil, suggested they ram the canoes as they came out to greet them and drag the men on board, the same tactic used by the *Carl*.

On 13 June, near a little island in the d'Entrecasteaux group, several canoes approached the *Hopeful* as it looked for a spot to drop anchor. The locals were carrying yams and coconuts for barter. McNeil, armed with a Winchester rifle, called from the deck, 'Let's round them up.' He joined two European and two Pacific Islander seamen in the port boat, which was lowered into the water to begin the chase. They targeted a canoe with fifteen or twenty people on board. McNeil ordered one of the Pacific Islanders to grab the canoe. He did, but one of the locals started whacking his hand with a paddle. McNeil yelled to a colleague, 'Shoot the . . .' The shot missed, so McNeil decided to finish the job himself. He took careful aim at a young boy and shot him through the heart.

Rumours of the atrocity soon spread to the mainland, and authorities had little difficulty encouraging witnesses to come forward. A trial took place in November 1884, and in summing up the evidence for the jury, the chief justice Charles Lilley addressed the question of colour: 'It was very frequently said that the life of a black man was of little importance; but under the English law all lives were protected, and if an English subject took a life, whether that of a white, black, or yellow man, he was answerable for it.'

The jury deliberated for an hour and five minutes and found McNeil guilty. The chief justice sentenced him to death. 'I will not say anything that can possibly give you more pain than you probably experience at the present moment. Unhappily, it is to be feared that yours is not the only case of outrage in the South Sea Islands.' The boatswain Barney Williams was also sentenced to death for murder. The ship's master Lewis Shaw and the government agent Harry Scholefield, the latter of whom was meant to protect the New Guineans but had been too drunk to intervene, were given life for aiding murder. Three other crew received lengthy terms for kidnapping.

But the verdict offended Queenslanders. Petitions were drawn up across the colony pleading for clemency for the two condemned men. At a mass public rally in the centre of Brisbane in December 1884, attended by politicians and clergy, the first resolution for mercy was greeted with 'a perfect forest of hands in favour'. No one voted against it. Archibald Meston, a journalist and former politician, moved a second resolution to ban the 'demoralising traffic'. He believed the men were sentenced to death to please the mother country. 'It might be asked "What will be said in Great Britain if we don't hang these men?" But it would be a far greater reflection upon the colony if they hanged two white men on the evidence of cannibals than if they did not.'

Public opinion proved too strong for the politicians, and the death sentences of McNeil and Williams were reluctantly commuted to life in jail. But the wheels of justice kept spinning in reverse. In February 1890, all but one of the original party were released. Scholefield had already died in prison, just thirteen months into his sentence.

The case was more shocking than the court had heard. In subsequent evidence to a royal commission, it emerged that McNeil had led a rampage through a number of islands. On one stop, he set fire to a village, shooting people as they fled. 'The history of the cruise of the *Hopeful* is one long record of deceit, cruel treachery, kidnapping and cold-blooded murder,' the commission said in its report. The final toll was 38 people killed. Only 9 of the 480 'recruits' had understood what they had agreed to.

Queensland's political and business establishment could not cope with the demons they had unleashed. Although the lower house of parliament was by now democratically elected, and there was widespread support for abolishing the trade, the system struggled to close this sorry chapter. Samuel Griffith had taken power in 1883 on a popular platform of ending the trade by excluding 'servile or coloured labour' from the colony. By 1884 he had banned the importation of 'Indian coolies' before a single boat had arrived. In 1885, he took advantage of the royal commission findings to end the practice altogether. But the prohibition was delayed until 1 January 1891 – eleven months after McNeil would walk out of prison. And then, in one of the most extraordinary backflips in any democracy, a Griffith-led coalition government allowed the plantation owners to begin importing cheap labour again in February 1892. He explained the change of heart was because the sugar industry had fallen on hard times, but assured Queenslanders he would still keep out the Chinese. 'My objections to Polynesian [Pacific Islander] labour were from the first, less strong than to the introduction of Asiatics. The people of the Pacific Islands are not so numerous as to be a permanent danger to our social or political institutions, and I have always regarded their employment as a temporary and transitional expedient,' he said.

Griffith protected an industry at the expense of his own and the colony's dignity, and condemned the Pacific Islanders to a humiliating eviction when the program was finally abolished after federation.

Any industry that relies on a form of slave labour does not pass the simplest test of civilisation. Australia held this as a self-evident truth before Queensland. But in Queensland, the very meaning of Australia was perverted. The balance had swung so far to capital that every relationship in the colony became more fractious – between boss and worker, between migrant groups, and between the people and parliament. Without a clear moral purpose that was superior to Britain's or America's, Australia damaged not just its international reputation; it imperilled its very prosperity.

Every other settlement in Australia to this point had been established for the benefit of the workingman, from the convict given land with their freedom to the free migrant who secured the eight-hour day. Queensland tampered with this golden rule by becoming the first colony with an active policy to reduce wages. The Pacific Islanders were just one part of a relentless campaign that culminated in class war between the pastoralists and the shearers in 1891. Parliament sided with the pastoralists, and the military was deployed to crush the strike. From this defeat, a new political movement was formed, the Labor Party, which sought to restore the position of the worker. But the terms for reconciling labour and capital after the rupture in Queensland were onerous. This was Queensland's final curse: it made the White Australia policy inevitable, with its self-defeating program of racial, industry and wage protection.

ABOVE By 1803, Sydney was a bustling port with its own newspaper, *The Gazette*. The front page of the first edition announced that Governor Philip Gidley King had authorised the importation of '4000 Gallons of Spirits', or just over half a gallon (1.9 litres) for each colonist. State Library of New South Wales

BELOW Arthur Phillip took his friend Bennelong to London in 1792, but Australia's first emigrant did not enjoy his time away and returned home in 1795.

State Library of New South Wales

BELOW On the eve of the Rum Rebellion, in 1808, Sydney had become little more than a garrison town. It would take Lachlan Macquarie to turn it into a capital. James Meehan, State Library of New South Wales

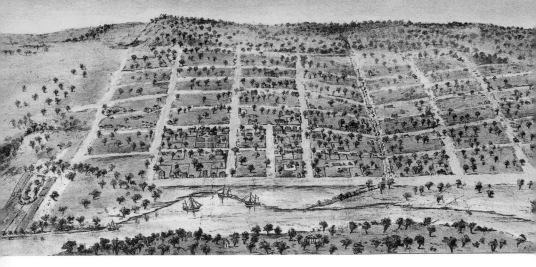

ABOVE The speed of colonial development accelerated with the founding in 1835 of a village at the southern tip of the mainland. Melbourne suffered none of the early hardships of the Sydney settlement and within twenty years was the richest metropolis on earth. State Library of Victoria

LEFT Wool made Australia viable. By 1837, the New South Wales governor Richard Bourke was sending urgent calls to London for 'shepherds, stockmen [and] agricultural labourers' to maintain the industry's success. State Library of Victoria

BELOW The difference between the misery in the old country and the opportunity in the new was starkest in the hungry decade of the 1840s. While the Irish would eventually lose one million lives to famine, Australians enjoyed the fastest rise in living standards of any nation. National Library of Ireland

Alfred Deakin, prime minister 1903–4, 1905–8, 1909–10 National Library of Australia

Stanley Bruce, prime minister 1923–9 National Library of Australia

Robert Menzies, prime minister, 1939–41, 1949–66 National Library of Australia

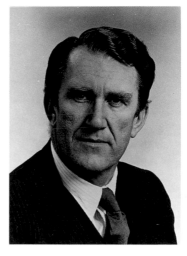

Malcolm Fraser, prime minister 1975–83 National Library of Australia

The golden intake of migrants to Australia in the 1850s included the parents and grandparents of the four most significant conservative leaders of the twentieth century. Deakin's English father and Welsh mother arrived just before the gold rush in 1850. Bruce's Irish father migrated to Melbourne in 1858, where he thrived in business. He happened to be a supporter of Deakin's first significant foray into Victorian colonial politics in the 1880s. Menzies had grandparents on both sides who migrated from Scotland and Cornwall during the gold rush and settled in Ballarat. Fraser's Canadian grandfather arrived in 1853, and after two years in Bendigo went into business in Melbourne. He was a senator in the first federal parliament.

ABOVE The anti-Chinese riots on the Lambing Flat diggings, in the south-west of New South Wales, might well have ended in a massacre if it weren't for the intervention of local man James Roberts. He provided shelter for 1276 Chinese on his property at Currawang. Here, Roberts and his family tend to the wounds of one of the men.

National Museum of Australia

LEFT The Chinese arrive at Cooktown, Queensland en route to the goldfields and sugar plantations.

National Archives of Australia

LEFT From the moment the first boatload of Pacific Islander labourers docked in Queensland on 14 August 1863 to work on a cotton farm, the venture was condemned as slavery. But the trade survived for another forty years.

State Library of Queensland

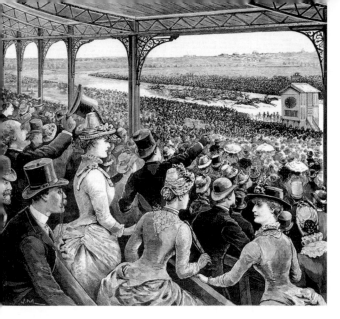

LEFT The Melbourne Cup horse race went from modest event to mass celebration in record time. The four thousand spectators at the track for the first meeting in 1861 were at least seventy-five thousand by 1877, and well over a hundred thousand in the early 1880s, when Melbourne's population was approaching three hundred thousand.

State Library of Victoria

LEFT After the diggers had left the Victorian goldfields in the 1860s, agriculture became once again the top employer across all the colonies. Sheep shearing was one of the most prestigious labouring jobs, and men competed to see who could have the most sheep shorn in a day.

State Library of Victoria

LEFT Sydney's business community embraced the world, and even after the long boom ended with the land bust of 1891 it continued to support free trade. The Melbourne business establishment went the other way, demanding and receiving protection from foreign competition.

State Library of Victoria

ABOVE Australia's demise at the end of the nineteenth century was felt hardest in Melbourne's inner suburbs. By the 1890s Collingwood was a slum, a state that would not change until the postwar boom of the 1950s. State Library of Victoria

BELOW The 1956 Olympics, dubbed the 'Friendly Games', helped restore Melbourne's confidence after more than half a century of economic decline.

State Library of Victoria

BELOW Arthur Calwell used the media to create the misleading impression that the British dominated the intakes of postwar migrants. Here he is pictured in 1949 with the hundred thousandth British migrant to Australia.

National Library of Australia

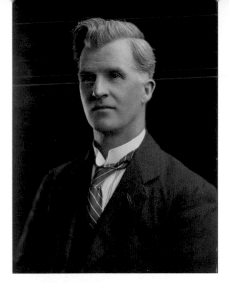

James Scullin, prime minister 1929–32
National Library of Australia

Joe Lyons, prime minister 1932–9
National Library of Australia

John Curtin, prime minister 1941–5
National Library of Australia

Ben Chifley, prime minister 1945–9
National Library of Australia

The local-born children of migrants have traditionally been Australia's overachievers, outperforming all others in their peer group for education and income. The Irish migration wave of the nineteenth century demonstrated this trend with a remarkable sequence of prime ministers on both sides of politics from 1929 to 1949. All were born in the final quarter of the nineteenth century, when their Irish parents represented almost 10 per cent of the Australian population. All had humble starts. Scullin's father was a railway platelayer; Lyons' father lost the family savings at the Melbourne Cup; Curtin's father was a prison warder at Pentridge; and Chifley had a local-born blacksmith father and an Irish mother.

BELOW Two sides of Australian migration: asylum seekers; and those coming from China and Hong Kong, now the biggest overseas community in Sydney. *The Australian*, 22 June 2012

ABOVE Today, if an asylum seeker tries to come to Australia by boat, they are greeted by the navy, which will either push them back into Indonesian waters or escort them to an Australian detention facility on a tiny Pacific Island. If they are found to be a genuine refugee, they won't be allowed to settle in Australia. Yet in the 1970s and '80s the Fraser government flew refugees from South-East Asia directly to Australia.

James Brickwood/Fairfax, National Archives of Australia

THE AUSTRALIAN

WWW.THEAUSTRALIAN.COM.AU | THE HEART OF THE NATION

RESCUE MISSION LAUNCHED AFTER BOAT CAPSIZES WITH UP TO 200 ON BOARD

Mass asylum drownings feared

Moving in, moving west, moving up: a nation going places

Senator resigns after new offence

Chinese, Kiwis surge past Poms

Indigenous identity rises with 'apology effect'

9

CENTENNIAL TANTRUM: CLOSING THE DOORS

The nineteenth century was kind to Australians, gifting them an economic winning streak that lasted longer than a lifetime. Someone born at the founding of Melbourne in 1835 could have expected to live until the end of the 1870s and still missed the top of the boom which peaked in 1891. Australia's GDP per person quadrupled over those five and half decades. Its nearest rival, the United States, could only double theirs. No other settler society had flown as high, or been less prepared for a fall.

The colonies seemed to defy the global business cycle by surging when the British and American economies were either stagnant or growing at a noticeably slower rate. There were two particular phases to this overachievement. The first, from 1842 to 1853, was the familiar story of wool, gold and free migration at a time of hunger in the old country. The second, from 1871 to 1878, had a more suburban explanation. Australia had found a temporary internal driver of growth through housing, at a time when the United States had not yet recovered from its civil war.

Victoria led this transformation, hitting a demographic sweet spot in which the migrants of the wool and gold booms had settled

down to raise children, while another wave of migration was adding to the population. The colony remained ahead of its time in this
second phase, predicting economic trends many decades before they
were normalised in the rest of the world. The transition from gold
to property was completed in a generation, as men moved from the
diggings to new jobs in manufacturing and construction, or to their
former work in the agricultural sectors. Women also reflected the
switch to manufacturing, with clothesmaking replacing domestic
service as the main female occupation. The development of rail,
tram and telephone lines created a further impetus for growth by
encouraging families to move into larger dwellings in new suburbs.

The advance of the world's first middle-class economy could be
measured in the size of the houses that the Victorians lived in. At
the end of the gold rush in 1861, almost six in ten dwellings (59
per cent) contained one or two rooms only. The middle-class home
of the day, with three or four rooms, represented 28 per cent of
the total, while the elite houses, with five or more rooms, had the
remaining 13 per cent. That housing stock was completely renovated
over the next twenty years. By 1881, elite houses with five or more
rooms were 36 per cent of a much larger number of properties in the
colony, while the middle-class home with three or four rooms now
accounted for 42 per cent of the total. This left the dwelling with
one or two rooms at 22 per cent.

The shift to the suburbs accelerated in the 1880s as Melbourne's
population soared by more than 70 per cent over that heady decade,
from 283 000 in 1881 to 491 000 in 1891. From this vantage point
at the top of a half-century-long boom, it appeared that Australia
was poised to become the new America, with Melbourne as its
capital. Henry Hayter, the Victorian colonial statistician, calculated the 'probable' population of Australia and New Zealand at
ten-year intervals and could barely contain himself. From almost
four million in 1891, he drew what he thought was a conservative
trend line to show the population roaring past a hundred million

within another century. The precision of his confidence was a thing of wonder. He wrote, 'The population in 1991 would be 133 288 495, and in 2001 it would be 189 269 663.' Although 'such large numbers naturally excites thought' about Australasia's future, he did concede that 'such speculations are more curious than practically useful'.

The sense of unlimited possibility was written into the celebration of the hundredth anniversary of Arthur Phillip's landing in 1888. Australians were convinced greatness was at hand, and their confidence even had a physical dimension. 'The typical Anglo Australian [male] is taller and slenderer than his British forefather, with less breadth of chest and greater length of limb, wiry rather than muscular,' *The Argus* explained, which reflected the advantages of a higher income and better diet. He was 'capable, in certain emergencies, of considerable endurance, with more élan and impetuosity than patient tenacity of purpose'. The Anglo Australian woman was described in similar elongated terms. 'She is slight and frequently tall, supple in figure, shallow in the chest, elastic in movement, and early of development. Her complexion is clear, but with little colour, except in Tasmania and New Zealand.' A child born in Australia in the 1880s could expect to live five years longer than a child born in the United Kingdom or the United States.

The popular press marked the centenary with odes to Australian exceptionalism. The *Sydney Morning Herald* marvelled that a people of such humble origins could become so rich. 'We do not pretend to falsify history, or conceal the key of the closet that contains the skeleton. We own up to the truth that Australia began as a convenience to Great Britain, as a distant prison. It was no band of adventurous colonisers, no fugitives from tyranny, no persecuted saints that sought to plant the flag of commerce and of liberty upon these shores. A hundred years ago, the Union Jack when unfurled for the first time on Australian shore was waved only over an unwalled jail. What we pride ourselves on is the fact that the settlement outgrew its origin, and completely effaced the traces of it. Thanks to the physical resources of the country itself, and the enterprise of the population that was drawn hither, a penal settlement, after a few early struggles, passed into a free and prosperous community.'

The original inhabitants were mentioned only in passing. *The Argus* said Australia had been 'home to a few prowling blacks' before European settlement. *The Queenslander* was more circumspect. The newspaper wrote that in Sydney, 'there is scarcely a trace of the dark-skinned thousands whose dances and songs enlivened the forest' in 1788. 'They have gone away to the happy hunting grounds where they can be no more disturbed by modern civilisation or by modern vice! They have their graves in the land, but no man has marked the spot.'

This centennial optimism was tainted by an aggressive nationalism. It was fed, in part, by the Australian-born children of migrants who were now the majority of the population across the country, and in every colony except Queensland. These Australian sons and daughters approached adulthood with perhaps the first sense of entitlement of any colonial generation. The boom they grew up in was all they knew, and they presented a conflicted face to the world: they demanded its admiration, but warned it not to spoil their paradise with its imperfections. This attitude was articulated most forcefully by *The Bulletin*, which adopted the slogan 'Australia for the White Man' in 1888 as part of its campaign to unite the colonies into an independent nation. On the eve of the centenary, it defined Australia with sharply drawn lines of class and colour. 'All white men who come to these shores – with a clean record – and who leave behind them the memory of class distinctions and the religious differences of the old world [are] Australian.' The people who did not belong to Australia's egalitarian family were the Africans, Asians and the Pacific Islanders, and their employers. 'No nigger, no Chinaman, no lascar, no kanaka, no purveyor of cheap coloured labour is an Australian.' The experience in the north had

clarified White Australia as an industrial as well as a racial issue for
The Bulletin. But this misguided assumption of Australian superiority was about to be tested by a series of international shocks.

By 1888, Australia had accumulated the excesses for a financial
crisis. That year, the property markets of Melbourne and Sydney
were reaching their peaks after an extraordinary decade of growth,
in which prices more than doubled in each city. To support those
prices, demand for housing had to endure into the next decade and
beyond, into the twentieth century. The colonies also had to rely on
forces beyond their control to maintain the line of overseas credit
that had helped to underwrite the boom.

Foreign money had been flowing freely across the globe since
the 1870s, when the British began directing half their investments
overseas. Australia received the lion's share of those funds in the
1880s for projects such as new railways, cable tram lines, and some
of the world's first tall buildings.

But the international financial system was inherently volatile. In
this era of free trade, shocks were frequent. The United States, for
instance, had suffered a long depression between 1873 and 1879 and
two relatively shorter depressions between 1882 and 1885 and again
between 1887 and 1888. It was reckless for colonial governments
to assume the good times would last forever. Yet that was how
they conducted their affairs, trusting that the flow of investment
from Britain reflected some basic truth about Australia's boundless
potential.

The colonies had been encouraged by the freedom of self-
government to ease the old controls on lending that had been put
in place by London. One decision in particular by the Victorian
parliament in 1876 would have serious consequences for the housing
market. This naive piece of deregulation allowed Victoria's financial
institutions to buy and sell property themselves, effectively turning

them into gamblers. There was no prudential supervision in those days: no central bank or financial regulator to monitor credit growth or to encourage banks to maintain adequate buffers to cover for loans that went bad. The so-called land banks and building societies that were created in this footloose age took on the established trading banks in a fierce contest for a share of the booming housing market. The number of bank branch offices almost doubled in the 1880s, bringing inexperienced managers face-to-face with gullible borrowers. Every family was told by the moneymen who financed the boom that they could afford to borrow, build and repay their own home through good and bad times. The ordinary investors who provided the deposits used to invest in property were promised high rates of interest. As Michael Cannon wrote, the mania swept across every section of society. 'Clergymen, labourers, widows, schoolmasters – all grasped at the chance of quick wealth and invested their savings.'

Many members of parliament were caught up in the boom as gentlemen investors. Some used their position to lobby for infrastructure to be built in pet suburbs, trusting that houses would follow the new train or tram line. Duncan Gillies, the old gold-digging partner of Peter Lalor, was one of the few politicians who didn't speculate personally, but he was arguably the one most responsible for the policy errors that helped inflate the property market, as minister for the railways in the early 1880s, and from 1886 to 1890, premier, treasurer and minister for railways. 'An inexpert treasurer, for some years he swam with the tide of the boom, building and borrowing freely in response to demands from all sides of the House,' according to *The Australian Dictionary of Biography*. He had the dubious honour of producing the budget before the bust, which in 1889 projected a large surplus, never to be realised, and approved eight hundred miles (1287 kilometres) of new rail lines to suburbs where houses would not be built.

The deputy premier, the young Alfred Deakin, was an active

participant in the commercial side of the boom. He borrowed his father's life savings, which he later lost, and was a chairman or director of many of the dubious companies, including those associated with the colony's most notorious land boomer James Munro, the founder of the Federal Bank and the Federal Building Society. Munro himself later became Victorian premier. Even the colonial statistician Henry Hayter bought into the boom, becoming a director of the Metropolitan Bank and the Metropolitan Building Society in 1887.

No one dreamed that property prices could collapse, even though it had happened before in Victoria in the late 1830s. But the Australians of the 1880s had no collective memory of hardship, nor any experience with debt. Bank credit more than doubled over the course of the 1880s, from about 35 per cent of GDP to more than 70 per cent. Borrowing by colonial governments to pay for infrastructure increased by a similar amount.

The financial system couldn't raise deposits fast enough to meet the demand it was stoking, so both the banks and the colonial governments sought funds from overseas to cover the difference. Most of the public debt was borrowed from British investors, making Australia suddenly dependent on London. That vulnerability can be seen in the economic cost of servicing those debts. The best measure is the share of export income required to meet the annual interest and dividend repayments on overseas loans and investments. Australia's foreign debt burden quadrupled over two decades from about 10 per cent in 1870 to about 40 per cent in 1890, a figure at least double the rate that history shows is sustainable for any country.

Australia had already had its share of booms and busts, most notably in the exaggerated cycles of the gold rush. But bubbles, in which prices inflate well beyond reasonable value and suddenly crash, are rarer events. They are marked by a long period of economic stability beforehand and the introduction of new technology.

Growth in the early years involves genuine activity, but a collective mania takes hold at some point and what was once carefully assessed investment becomes reckless speculation. The Melbourne and Sydney land booms had become bubbles by 1888. Prices were rising solely due to speculation; and because the speculators included the banks themselves, with obligations to foreign investors, any global shock could bring down the entire economy.

One of the factors that had been driving the long boom was migration, but it slowed sharply over the course of the 1880s, removing one of the props for the housing market. Australia had received 210 000 people from overseas between 1880 and 1884, but only 170 000 between 1885 and 1889. This was due to conscious decisions taken in the two largest colonies to limit migration from the mother country. Victorian had been winding back assisted passage since 1874 and stopped it completely by 1880. In the same year, New South Wales premier Henry Parkes declared his intention to stop the Irish-born from overtaking the English-born population. 'I would advance every opposition in my power to the bringing here of a majority of people from Ireland. I hope I may be able to express this opinion boldly and without reserve, without being charged with bigotry or with a dislike to the Irish people.' These policies undermined the economy by leaving the property sector with more houses than buyers – the precondition for a crash.

The politicians were egged on by the trade unions to slow migration, and this call for protection from foreign labour became more insistent over the course of the 1880s. In the lead-up to the centenary, the Trades and Labour Council of New South Wales sent John Norton, a recently arrived migrant from England, as a delegate to international union congresses in London and Paris to issue the warning that Australia was full. He said Europe's workers would be better off staying at home and agitating for change, rather than risking unemployment in the colonies.

The irony of a newly arrived migrant deterring his fellow workers was not lost on *The Argus*, which reminded readers that 'tens of thousands of the wage earners of Australia must have belonged to the very classes to which Mr. Norton now appeals to remain in England, in order to carry out "the much needed social revolution".'

What no man appreciated, be he banker, politician, trade unionists or contributor to *The Bulletin*, was that Australia's prosperity depended on openness. To close the door at the top of a boom was to guarantee Australia's decline, because once the cycle turned, all migration stopped, and there was no easy way to restore growth without new arrivals.

Two impulses collided at the centenary of settlement – one open, the other closed. There was understandable pride in the colonial achievement, and a gathering confidence that Australia was ready for nationhood. But there was an unmistakable insecurity in the air. The political economy, like the real economy, seemed ready to explode in 1888 as the colonies picked a fight with the mother country on the question of Chinese migration. It was at this moment that the premiers made the fateful decision that had loomed for decades – to officially declare Australia 'white', and deny the country to the very people who might have helped it avoid a deep and prolonged depression in the 1890s.

The premiers were suspicious of London's improving diplomatic relationship with China. The Chinese for their part had felt assured enough of their standing with London to send a two-person commission of inquiry to the Australian colonies to see how their people were faring. This visit lit the fuse for the diplomatic crisis of 1888, when the premiers told London that the Chinese were no longer welcome in any form. The tour had run for twelve weeks, from late April to early August 1887. The Chinese commissioners found their reception became more hostile the further north they travelled. By the time the commissioners reached Brisbane, the premier Samuel

Griffith 'went out of his way to tell them that Chinese were not wanted in that colony'.

The *Sydney Morning Herald* sided with the upfront Queenslanders and declared the visit an insult to Australia's identity. 'The Commissioners, there is every reason to believe, came to Australia, not only to discover how the Chinese who are already here are getting on, but with the object of paving the way for the arrival of others.'

The Chinese had been returning to the colonies in the 1880s, encouraged by shipping agents in Hong Kong who told them they could enter Australia for free if they had papers showing they were naturalised British subjects. The numbers weren't significant in themselves, and it was surprising that any came at all without the lure of gold. The combined Chinese populations of Victoria and New South Wales had fallen by almost half in the twenty years since the gold rush ended, from thirty-eight thousand in 1861 to twenty-two thousand in 1881. What the politicians did not seem to appreciate was that many of the new arrivals were actually former diggers returning to the world's richest settlement.

In November 1887, Victorian premier Duncan Gillies and New South Wales premier Henry Parkes began discussing how to restrict the inflow of the Chinese. Parkes then invited all fellow premiers to establish uniform legislation across the colonies. By early 1888, Gillies and Parkes had changed tactics, believing that it would be more effective if London renegotiated her treaty with China to limit migration to the colonies. But they returned to their earlier, more confrontational strategy following the arrival in Melbourne on 27 April 1888 of a steamer named the *Afghan*, carrying 268 Chinese migrants bound for various parts of Australia and New Zealand. The diplomatic crisis that Gillies and Parkes provoked in response to this boat borrowed from the script of the convict ship the *Hashemy*.

Under Victoria's anti-Chinese restrictions, reintroduced in 1881, a vessel of the *Afghan*'s size would be able to land fourteen migrants. But the secretary of customs and trade, Mr Musgrove, was startled to learn that sixty-seven people wanted to disembark, and fifty-eight of them produced naturalisation papers. Musgrove claimed that every document was bogus, placed the boat in quarantine and told the Chinese they would not be allowed to land.

A public meeting was held in the town hall on 1 May to call on the government to 'prevent any further influx' of Chinese. The lord mayor chaired proceedings, and the first person to speak was a local politician, Mr Roberts. 'If they allowed the unlimited influx of Chinese,' he said, 'the result would be that British labourers must succumb and take a lower rate of wages. At the present time they were in a very prosperous condition, which had only been achieved after a great struggle, and surely they were not going to allow a blight to come over the colony in the shape of Chinese immigration.' He offered the example of the furniture trade, in which 'the Chinese were able to work on Sundays and holidays, to live upon rice, and to compete with the honest labourers who spent their money in the colony, while the Chinese took their money out of it'.

Here was the crux of the problem. The Chinese had been living peacefully in Victoria for a generation, and on the available statistics were actually well off. The 1881 census found that the Chinese in Melbourne were housed in relative comfort. The typical Chinese dwelling was, in fact, less crowded than the typical European dwelling. But instead of being embraced as ideal migrants who would enhance Australia's prosperity, they were seen as threats to that prosperity.

The government had already decided to expel the *Afghan*. The ship was sent to Sydney on 2 May, while another vessel carrying Chinese migrants, the *Burrumbeet*, remained in quarantine in Melbourne. The Colonial Office in London telegraphed the New South Wales government to demand that the Chinese be allowed to land.

On 3 May, thousands gathered at the Sydney Town Hall to

demand the *Afghan* be turned away. 'The Chinese were a very undesirable class to be introduced here,' the lord mayor, John Harris,
told the audience. 'He did not want to harm them, but he did not
wish to see them in Australia.' These resolutions from the meeting did not even pretend to respect the rule of law. The first said:
'That this meeting emphatically condemns the continuing influx of
the Chinese, whether they be provided with English naturalisation
papers or not, as being fraught with peril to the rights and liberties
of the Australian people.' The second called on all colonial governments to 'totally prohibit Chinese immigration, regardless of
England's treaty relations with China, and, if need be, without the
sanction of the English Government'.

A deputation led by Harris was authorised to present the resolutions to the premier. By the time they reached parliament, a crowd
of five thousand had gathered. Some of the chants recorded by the
Sydney Morning Herald that evening threatened violence: 'The Chinese must be stopped'; 'We will pitch them overboard'; 'We must
see the Premier tonight, or the *Afghan* will be here at daylight'.

The premier, Henry Parkes, leader of the protest against the
Hashemy four decades earlier, refused to see the delegation that
evening although he gave an assurance, via a note read to the crowd,
that the passengers of the *Afghan* would not be allowed to land.
Another boat, the *Tsinan*, with 148 Chinese migrants on board,
was due in Sydney the next morning. Parkes had a police guard
waiting to meet them to assure the mob that no people would be
allowed to disembark.

The *Afghan* arrived on 6 May. To the embarrassment of the Victorians, the New South Wales inspector did not detect widespread
fraud in the naturalisation papers. He found forty-two migrants had
valid exemption certificates. Another thirteen on the *Tsinan* were
also deemed to be genuine migrants. But Parkes took the law into
his own hands and refused their entry, while hurrying legislation
through the parliament to indemnify the government for its actions.

The Chinese played the most reasonable card available: they got in touch with a lawyer, who advised them they had been illegally detained. One of the passengers was selected to act as a test case to go before the Supreme Court. His name was Lo Pak, a former resident of New South Wales, who was returning to the colony. Justice William Charles Windeyer, a former political colleague of the premier, found in the returning migrant's favour. 'To my mind it is clear beyond all doubt that his detention on board the ship, where he now is, is perfectly illegal,' he said in his judgement on 18 May. Lo Pak and his countrymen with valid papers were free to disembark, but their victory proved pyrrhic for their people.

Parkes had pre-empted the court verdict with the harshest anti-Chinese legislation to date, introduced with an incendiary speech. The premier said he had nothing against the Chinese. They were a 'law-abiding, industrious, thrifty, and peaceable' people. His opposition to the entry of more Chinese was rational, not racial. It was his job to respond to the 'legitimate agitation [of] all classes' and defend the 'social fabric'. To those who had taken him to court, he gave what reads like the dictator's defence: that stability trumps liberty. 'You tell me about obedience to the law; you tell me that because I occupy the great place which I am permitted to occupy in this country that I am to set an example of obedience to the law. I say in reply that there is one law which overrides all others, and that is the law of preserving the peace and welfare of civil society. Would you talk about the technical observance of the law if a plague was stalking in your midst, if a pestilence was sweeping off population, if famine were reducing the members of your household to skeletons? Why, a Government that stood in fear of a technical observance of the law in such a case as that would be swept away and deserve castigation.'

The legislation Parkes rushed through the lower house on that day, 16 May, imposed a hundred-pound landing tax, and a twenty-pound residential tax – the same levies called for at the Melbourne

Town Hall meeting earlier in the month. He also restricted all Chinese arrivals to the five largest towns in New South Wales, mirroring controls that existed for the British in China itself. Those Chinese already settled in New South Wales were free to go wherever they pleased, with one proviso – they had to carry an identity card. The legislation was backdated to 1 May, to protect the government against any legal action for false imprisonment. The upper house moved some amendments, but they did not alter the substance of the crackdown.

Parkes required a united front to discourage London from vetoing this legislation. The premier knew it was in breach of London's free-trade treaty with China. He promptly convened a special meeting of colonial premiers in Sydney over 12–14 June 1888, and it was here that the first draft of the White Australia policy was written. Victoria, New South Wales, Queensland and South Australia agreed to limit the number of Chinese who could come off each boat. Only one migrant would be allowed to land for each five hundred tons of a ship's burden (during the gold rush, the limit had been one person for every ten tons), and a fine of five hundred pounds would apply for each passenger over the new limit. The Chinese already in Australia would need to seek permission to move from colony to colony. With these restrictions there was no need for Parkes to apply his rushed legislation. Western Australia did not sign up immediately, but joined the club the following year. Only Tasmania, where the Chinese population was the lowest of the colonies, stayed out.

Chinese-Australians lodged a number of petitions, calling for the premiers to honour the treaties between Britain and China. One, signed by residents from South Australia, Victoria, New South Wales, Queensland and Tasmania, emphasised peace and mutual commerce. Another from Victoria correctly predicted that the country would come to regret the White Australia policy. 'The cry of a great influx of Chinese [is] one of those poor hollow things that time and reflection will cause the generous British mind to feel heartily ashamed of, but at the same time the cruel injustice inflicted under it may be far-reaching.'

There was something more than xenophobia at play. It was fear of foreign competition. This Australia no longer wished to set an example: it was issuing demands. Its political economy, like its real economy, had made the dangerous assumption that the world owed it a living. Parkes said it himself: he did not care for the rule of law if it did not suit his view of the national interest. He saw a white Australia as a declaration of independence from Britain; the first step to nationhood. This was a meaner country than the one he had landed in half a century earlier. The old Australia wanted to be seen as a role model. This new Australia was bloated with self-importance.

10

THE LONGEST
DEPRESSION

After eclipsing their British, American and European peers for the best part of the nineteenth century, Australians lost the habit of prosperity in the 1890s and the role model suddenly became a global basket case. Once the property bubble burst, the entire swaggering edifice of the world's richest settlement collapsed with it. As the setbacks accumulated, Australians reverted to something closer to their sullen former convict selves, separated from the world, and overly reliant on an inattentive mother country. Australia could only define itself to the world by what it wanted to exclude. The White Australia policy, drafted at the top of the boom, became the wrong answer to almost every problem the colonies confronted once growth ended, and then the wrong message to send the world when they finally formed a federation in 1901.

Australians entered the final decade of the nineteenth century unaware that their property bubble was about to burst, or that the global economy was about to fall into a deep depression.

In the autumn of 1891, the six colonies and New Zealand met in Sydney to draft a constitution to create a new independent nation, the Commonwealth of Australia. The air was thick with hubris as the two largest colonies debated whose house was worth more. The New South Wales premier Henry Parkes took the stage to declare his own people number one. 'In point of private wealth, which was the most subtle and the most convincing test of a nation's happiness; New South Wales stood ahead of the civilised world,' he declared.

The boast offended Victoria's statistician Henry Hayter, who penned an open letter to Parkes to advise that his statement was 'entirely wrong'. 'The private wealth of the people of Victoria [is] so far as I am able to judge, considerably greater than that of the people of New South Wales,' he wrote in March 1891.

They were like two landowners in Pompeii arguing over who had the better view of Vesuvius. The previous November, the London finance house Baring Brothers and Co. had almost gone broke after the collapse of its investments in Argentina and Uruguay. Although the institution was saved by a bailout arranged by the Bank of England, the episode still caused a global financial panic. British lenders began to reassess their overseas investments, worrying whether there was another potentially insolvent country in their portfolios. Australia may not have been drawn into the crisis if its financial and political institutions had been more prudent. But these institutions had borrowed and spent on the assumption that property prices would keep rising, and were about to find out that much of the activity in the 1880s was based on a confidence trick the colonies had pulled on themselves. As credit became scarce, the property market stalled, and the bubble burst. Prices collapsed by as much as half from their boom-time highs in Melbourne and by about 25 per cent in Sydney. Now Australia would write a new chapter for global economic history, as one of the first nations to fall into depression and the last one to climb out of it.

Once property prices crashed, depositors and investors in Australia and Britain made a run for the banks to retrieve money that wasn't there. One by one, Australian financial institutions closed their doors. Between 1891 and 1893, fifty-four land banks and building societies suspended their operations. Two out of three went into liquidation, while the remainder reopened their doors carrying heavy losses.

Among those that went under permanently were Henry Hayter's Metropolitan Bank and Metropolitan Building Society. Hayter had borrowed from the bank to invest in the building society, a double-or-nothing bet typical of the 1880s. The final amount he owed, comprising the principal of the loan and the interest, was thirty-six thousand pounds, or more than five million in today's dollars. He offered to resign his post, but the Victorian government persuaded him to stay on to collect the 1891 census. In one of the most outrageously symbolic deals of the bust, Hayter was put through the Insolvency Court in secret. He agreed to repay his creditors just three pennies in the pound, or 1.3 per cent of his total debt.

The financial panic reached the trading banks in January 1893 with the collapse of the Federal Bank of Australia, the bank set up by the former Victorian premier James Munro. Three months later, the Commercial Bank of Australia suspended its payments. By May, thirteen of the twenty-three trading banks had also closed their doors, although twelve reopened in August carrying heavy losses. But the crisis was far from over. The banks returned to business with a defensive mindset. They were reluctant to lend for new ventures, thus choking off the recovery before it could begin. Depositors had been granted immediate access to small amounts of cash, but the majority of savings were held back while the banks restructured their operations. Receipts were issued to depositors with a promise to repay with interest at a later date, with some claims dragged out until 1918.

In 1893, the global economy fell into its most damaging depression of the era, extending Australia's crisis. The international factors mirrored the local: financial panics in the United Kingdom, Europe and the United States pulled down the world's major economies.

Each had enjoyed long growth runs, facilitated by the expansion of railroads that connected goods and people. But that development hit an inevitable dead end in the 1890s when supply exceeded demand. The fallout from the depression was felt throughout the decade. In the United States, for instance, the economy took five years to recover, and the unemployment rate remained above 10 per cent between 1894 and 1898.

But as the major economies pulled themselves out of depression in the second half of 1890s, Australia, recovering from larger losses, was left behind. Nature then turned against the colonies with a long drought between 1895 and 1902 that retarded the agricultural sector. Not even the discovery of Australia's last big gold deposit could revive the economy this time.

The final rush of the nineteenth century was in the forgotten colony of the west. Like Queensland before it, Western Australia could not find a growth driver before gold. In its first seventy years of existence to 1889, the colony added just 652 settlers per year – one hundred fewer than the convict intake of the First Fleet. London did not believe this tiny settlement was ready for self-government until 1890.

With the Chinese effectively banned from the goldfields, the diggers in Western Australia were free to make their fortune without the excuse of ethnic competition. Gold made the west viable, quadrupling the settler population in a decade, from just over fifty thousand in 1891 to almost two hundred thousand in 1901. But like Queensland, the deposits in Western Australia were too far removed from the main population centre of Perth to generate a Melbourne- or San Francisco–style cycle of growth that could multiply the benefits of mining.

Western Australia's gilded trail snaked inland, from the north-west in the Kimberleys to the south. The jackpot was struck in Coolgardie in 1892 and nearby Kalgoorlie the following year. These two goldfields would prove to be the richest since Bendigo and

Ballarat. But there was something missing: large-scale migration.

In all previous rushes, the majority of the new arrivals to a colony had come from overseas. But more than half the increase in Western Australia's population was due to internal migration – the local-born from other colonies. The Victorians alone eclipsed the migrants from the United Kingdom. Add those who came from South Australia, New South Wales and Queensland, and the influx of local-born was more than double the intake from the United Kingdom. The British and Irish had accounted for more than half the gold rush populations of Victoria and Queensland, but they were less than a quarter of the Western Australian gold rush population in 1901.

In the past, high levels of unemployment in Britain and Europe had coincided with increased migration to Australia, and the gold rushes in the eastern colonies had made the country an appealing destination. This time, migrants stayed at home. Migration across the world slowed in the 1890s due to the weaker global economy, and the depression in Australia was an additional deterrent.

This is the moment when Australia and the United States moved in opposite directions. As Australia turned inward, the United States reclaimed the title it had previously ceded to Victoria as the world's most desirable place to migrate.

Both nations had received comparable numbers in the 1880s, adjusting for population size. The United States welcomed half a million per year, while Australia had almost four hundred thousand new arrivals over the decade. In the 1890s, net migration to the United States slowed to less than three hundred thousand per year during the worst years of the depression, between 1894 and 1898, before rebounding to one million per year in the first decade of the twentieth century. Australia, by contrast, did not return to its former migrant self. People were not prepared to come at their own expense while the economy remained depressed, and the country lost more people to overseas than it received between 1892 and 1908. Assisted passage might have mitigated the damage, but the colonies, which became states at federation, were reluctant to actively recruit migrants while the economy was weak.

Without new arrivals from overseas to replace those who had left, Victoria – the golden economy of the nineteenth century – dropped behind the older, more resilient New South Wales economy. The two had been equals before the depression. Each had reached populations of one million in 1887, with Victoria taking half the time of New South Wales to achieve that benchmark. But the immediate effects of the depression were so stunning in Victoria that New South Wales passed Victoria in 1892, and at federation in 1901 New South Wales was 14 per cent larger. By the time the depression finally ended in 1909, New South Wales had almost doubled its advantage and was now 26 per cent larger, with a total population of 1.61 million to Victoria's 1.28 million.

Melbourne's population fell from 490 000 in 1891 to 458 000 in 1897; and this was yet another factor that delayed the national recovery. Victoria's decline set up the terms for the insular federation, with a colour line to keep out Asian migrants and later, a tariff wall to protect local businesses from foreign imports. This closed Australia would be anchored in Sydney, not Melbourne, and without New Zealand, which had withdrawn from the federation process. New Zealand had no immediate economic reason to join. It had a much shorter depression, and by 1901 could boast a GDP per person that was 10 per cent larger than Australia's.

To this day the 1890s depression remains the worst economic crisis in Australia's history. National income collapsed by a quarter between 1891 and 1897, and it took another twelve years to recover those losses. At the bottom of the depression Australia dropped to sixth on the global income ladder, behind Switzerland, the United States, the United Kingdom, New Zealand and Belgium. The data from this period is sketchy, but the unemployment rate certainly crossed 10 per cent in the 1890s and was still as high as 9 per cent by

1905. Destitution on this scale and for this long had not been known by any generation since the earliest years of the convict settlement.

Australia was the worst performing economy in the world for the twenty years between 1889 and 1909, which includes both the global depression of the 1890s, and the global recovery of the 1900s. Australia's national income was virtually stagnant, improving by just 5 per cent over that twenty-year period. By contrast, it grew by 12 per cent in the United Kingdom, 28 per cent across Western Europe, 29 per cent in New Zealand, 47 per cent in the United States and 72 per cent in Canada. Even Japan bettered Australia, growing by 39 per cent.

The 1890s depression had many of the characteristics of the global financial crisis of 2008: a long period of stability had seen banks and other financial institutions across the world take risks that ultimately undermined the entire system. After the bust, the defensive behaviour of banks and the reluctance of consumers and business to resume taking risks compounded the problem. Australia's position in the 1890s was comparable to that of nations that boomed spectacularly leading up to 2008, such as Greece, Ireland and Spain, and who were still deep in recession many years after the main crisis had passed. The debts that had been run up in the boom took many years to clear, and the length of the depression affected the national reputation. Australia was no longer a role model: it was a small country at the other end of the world.

Most significantly, the extended depression meant that Australia did not immediately catch the next wave of large-scale global migration – this time from Europe. The continent had already replaced the United Kingdom as the main source of migrants to the United States in the 1870s, an early demographic warning for Australia that the mother country was coming to the end of her great century of emigration. By the 1880s, the Germans were supplying three times as many new arrivals as Britain and Ireland to the United States. The Swedes also exceeded the UK intake. The depression had stopped migration from the United Kingdom to the United States – reflecting the high unemployment in both economies – but not from Europe, where the motivation to leave was stronger. Russian and Polish Jews were fleeing persecution; Italians were escaping poverty and the United States continued to add to its melting pot even in its weakest decade for new arrivals. Tellingly, the Statue of Liberty had just been installed in New York, and American poet Emma Lazarus wrote her clarion call to the world's tired, poor, huddled masses; her poem was drafted in virtually the same breath that *The Bulletin* was calling for a White Australia. By 'white' *The Bulletin* did mean European. But without a booming economy to attract these Europeans in the 1890s, Australia could not divert some of the flow that was going to the United States. By 1910, 87 per cent of America's foreign-born population was from Europe. In Australia, the British were 57 per cent of a diminished migrant community.

To attract European migration, Australia would have needed to actively recruit. But from the defensive crouch of depression, no one in Australia could see the opportunity. The Europeans who went to the United States in this period helped build great American industries and were crucial to the development of its coming cultural power through Hollywood. When small numbers of European prospectors did turn up in Western Australia during the gold rush, they were told to go back to where they came from. Early in 1902, the arrival of just fifty people from Italy and Austria was marked by a local newspaper with the headline: 'Undesirable Aliens – A Deluge of Dagoes'.

The resourceful, cocky people Australians had been for the best part of the nineteenth century approached the new century cowed and resentful. It was a timid position from which to claim independence from Britain.

The achievement of federation on 1 January 1901 was, in itself, magnificent. The people of six bickering colonies created a new nation,
covering an entire continent, without bloodshed. But the occasion
will forever be associated with the first major piece of legislation
for the new nation: the introduction of the White Australia policy.
It was a stunning act of self-harm; there was no practical reason to
restrict migration at a time when more people were leaving Australia than arriving. It was just the easiest thing that the politicians
could agree on, a common resentment they could dress up as a
declaration of Australian values. It quickly grew into a political
defence mechanism that united labour and capital by extending
the principle of racial purity to industry protection, so the cheap
foreign worker and the cheap foreign import were treated as a common enemy.

The lost opportunity extended well beyond the migrants that
Australia missed out on. This new nation denied itself the chance
to make a confident statement to the world. The inaugural federal
parliament, elected on March 29 and 30 that year, was, in fact,
imbued with a progressive spirit. There was bipartisan support for
female suffrage and the age pension, and either reform would have
demonstrated Australia's policy ingenuity, especially when those
measures were still some years away from being adopted in the
United Kingdom. Yet the politicians placed a higher priority on
restricting migration. It was a wrong-headed choice, but for the
fathers of the federation it seemed perfectly reasonable. They
equated White Australia with equality.

The members of parliament who had the greatest interest in the
White Australia policy represented the workingman. The Labor
Party achieved the balance of power in the first federal election, and
told the two parties of capital – the Protectionist Party and the Free
Trade Party – it would support whichever could guarantee the prohibition of 'coloured labour'. There were two aspects to Labor's call: to
deny entry to 'any person who is an aboriginal native of Asia, Africa,

or of the islands thereof', and to remove the original Queensland curse through the deportation of the Pacific Islanders. The restriction was not aimed at European migration – at least not yet.

The Labor caucus finalised its position at a meeting on 20 May 1901, eleven days after the parliament was formally opened. It placed White Australia first on a five-point policy platform, ahead of compulsory arbitration for the settlement of disputes between bosses and workers, and female suffrage.

The existence of a Labor Party itself was one of the distinguishing features of federation. Formed a decade before the nation itself, first in Queensland and New South Wales in 1891 and then in the other colonies, the trade-union-based party saw parliament as an effective means to pursue better wages and conditions for workers after the defeat of the great strikes of the 1890s. But that ambition was never just about industrial matters. From the gold rush onwards, workers had expected to shape the very character of the Australian settlement around notions of fairness. In 1901, with the economy in its tenth year of depression, the White Australia policy offered what Labor thought was a failsafe mechanism to restore and defend a high-wage society.

The fallout from the depression was written in every ballot box in that first federal election. Edmund Barton's Protectionist Party dominated in Victoria, where the economy was weakest, while George Reid's Free Trade Party was ascendant in New South Wales, South Australia and Tasmania. Labor achieved its best returns in its states of origin, Queensland and New South Wales, and won the most seats of any party in Queensland.

Labor was also split on the issue that divided the conservatives – whether Australia would remain a free-trade economy. Some members believed that using tariffs to penalise imports would help maintain high wages by encouraging local industry to flourish. Others thought that high tariffs would lead to high prices for consumers. But ultimately White Australia was the pressing issue for Labor. Where the tariff fitted into that scheme was a question for business to resolve.

Labor gave the Protectionist Party its support, but the two were almost immediately at odds on the detail of the White Australia policy. Labor demanded an explicit ban – a literal black list of races that would be prohibited from migrating to Australia. Edmund Barton, the nation's first prime minister, would not accept this condition for fear of reviving the old argument with London over the anti-Chinese legislation.

Although federation had given Australia the right to make its own laws and set its own foreign policy, the Australian Constitution was an act of the British parliament, and, in theory, could be amended by Westminster. The secretary of the colonies in London, Joseph Chamberlain, had pre-empted the White Australia debate by repeating the warning, first made to the New South Wales colonial parliament in 1861, not to damage Britain's own treaty arrangements. 'Any attempt,' Chamberlain wrote of an explicit racial ban, 'is contrary to the general conceptions of equality which have been the guiding principle of British rule throughout the empire.'

Barton offered the compromise of a dictation test, which would vet prospective migrants according to education, not race. London accepted, and so did Labor when its own amendment failed.

Hope duelled with anxiety when the men of the foundation legislature debated the policy they agreed would define their new nation to the people, and the world. Their dream was to guarantee an egalitarian society, without the contamination of class and racial inequality. Their stated fear was that the Chinese would return to take the jobs of hardworking Australians. Their unstated fear was that Japan would eye the sparsely populated Australian continent with the same imperial hunger as the European powers had the continents of Asia and Africa.

The nation's first seven prime ministers were in that parliament. A sample of both conservative and Labor views demonstrates that

Australia's political class was born thinking small. That defensive mindset has never really left the system, even if the White Australia policy has long since been abandoned.

Barton set the tone by saying that a coloured man could not be brought up to the same level of development as a white man; a coloured man could not become a true Australian. 'The doctrine of the equality of man was never intended to apply to the equality of the Englishman and the Chinaman,' the prime minister said. 'There is a deep-set difference, and we see no prospect and no promise of its ever being effaced. Nothing in this world can put these two races upon an equality. Nothing we can do by cultivation, by refinement, or by anything else will make some races equal to others.'

The author of the White Australia legislation was the attorney-general, Alfred Deakin. He would succeed Barton as prime minister and become the most significant political figure of the first decade of federation. Deakin marvelled that the constitution gave Australia's politicians more power than 'our cousins across the Atlantic . . . to deal with this difficulty in all aspects'.

'We have power to deal with people of any and every race within our borders, except the aboriginal inhabitants of the continent, who remain under the custody of the States. There is that single exception of a dying race; and if they be a dying race, let us hope that in their last hours they will be able to recognise not simply the justice, but the generosity of the treatment which the white race, who are dispossessing them and entering into their heritage, are according them.'

Deakin wanted to distinguish the Chinese from the Japanese. Both would be kept out, but there would be no offence intended to the latter. He did not see the Japanese in the same category as the 'many uneducated races of Asia and untutored savages who visit our shores'. The Japanese should be kept out 'because of their higher abilities'. Deakin said, 'It is not the bad qualities, but the good qualities of these alien races that make them dangerous to us.

It is their inexhaustible energy, their power of applying themselves to new tasks, their endurance, and low standard of living that make them such competitors.'

The Labor leader Chris Watson, who would become the party's first prime minister for sixteen unfulfilling weeks in 1904, said the issue was one of colour. 'As far as I am concerned, the objection I have to the mixing of these coloured people with the white people of Australia – although I admit it is to a large extent tinged with considerations of an industrial nature – lies in the main in the possibility and probability of racial contamination,' he said.

Labor's Billy Hughes, who would be Australia's seventh prime minister in 1915, agreed with Deakin in saying the real menace was the intelligent Asian. 'There is no conceivable method by which the Japanese, if they once got a fair hold in competition with our own people, could be coped with. There is no social legislation by which we could sufficiently handicap them. We must face this matter whilst there is yet time.'

There were two more history-makers in that first parliament, the Labor-friendly Henry Higgins and the protectionist Isaac Isaacs. Both were destined for the High Court, and to further promotions. Higgins became president of the Commonwealth Court of Arbitration in 1907 and in his first case he laid the foundation for a fair minimum wage. Isaacs, the son of Jewish migrants from what is now Poland, became Australia's first local-born governor-general in 1930.

'I prefer to state outright that we do not want yellow and black faces in Australia,' Higgins said. Isaacs did not try to lighten the mood. 'It is a white man's war that we must face, and I would not suffer any black or tinted man to come in and block the path of progress. I would resist to the utmost, if it were necessary, any murky stream from disturbing the current of Australian life.'

The views were sincerely held, even if the arguments were overblown. A sole contrarian in the parliament accused his colleagues of playing politics. Bruce Smith, a free-trade politician from New South Wales, a lawyer, writer and business representative, believed the legislation was being pursued because it was popular, not because it was necessary. 'The public have been told over and over again that the purity and whiteness of the Australian Commonwealth is being endangered by the incursion of these hordes of Asiatics. I say that it is a fable; that it is altogether a fairy story.' He meant what none would admit to, that Australia was not receiving migrants from Asia at the time. The *Afghan* incident in 1888 had discouraged any further migrants from China. Almost one in five Chinese had left Australia or passed away between 1891 and 1901, although thirty thousand still remained at federation. Meanwhile, the fear of the Japanese was certainly exaggerated. They were 0.1 per cent of Australian population at the 1901 census – just over 3500 people, of which two-thirds lived in Queensland.

The White Australia policy had three essential elements. The first was the Pacific Island Labourers Act, which became law on 17 December 1901. It dealt with Queensland's problem in stages by allowing the sugar industry to continue importing indentured labour until 30 March 1904. After that point, there would be a mass deportation of 'time expired' labourers to their former homes; the phrase was taken straight from the convict nomenclature. No 'kanaka' would be allowed to work in Queensland after 31 December 1906.

Edmund Barton placed on the record his view that the trade had been a form of slavery. 'The traffic, we say, is bad, both for the kanaka and for the white man. It is bad for the kanaka, because it is not inaptly described . . . as limited slavery. In some aspects it must be slavery. The difference in intellectual level, and the difference in knowledge of the ways of the world between the white man and the Pacific Islander, is one which cannot be bridged by acts or regulations.'

The second strand, the Immigration Restriction Act, became law two days before Christmas 1901. Barton had told his private secretary Atlee Hunt that the dictation test should apply to 'all aboriginal inhabitants of Africa, Asia and Polynesia', effectively enacting Labor's explicit racial ban through the back door. The plan was to test them in a language they did not speak, thereby denying them entry. 'In the case of White Races, the test will be applied only under special circumstances . . . if in your opinion the immigrant would, for reasons which you would be prepared to state, be an undesirable immigrant, it may be better to substitute for the English test a passage from some other language.'

Eager to please, Hunt wrote to the prime minister on 28 May 1902 with an assurance that the Asians were being kept out. 'We continue to eject the monstrous Jap and the wily Chow with persistence. The I.R. Act has not exhausted its possibilities yet. I have four matters now with the A-G for opinion. The April returns show that no coloured aliens passed the test, over 40 were rejected, mostly chows who tried to enter Queensland on false papers.' He had reversed Deakin's epithets of the competitive Japanese and the uneducated Chinese.

When the time came to deport the Pacific Islanders, officials enforced the order with excessive zeal. In December 1906, the Burns Philp Shipping Company's *Malaita* took 271 boys back to their native Solomon Islands. On board was a reporter from the *Brisbane Courier*. After an incident-free landing, many of the boys refused to go to their old villages. 'At the present time, fighting among the various villages is taking place from one end of this island to the other, and, in fact, is said to be worse than at any previous period known to white men.'

The observation that most touched readers back home was confirmation that Queensland-born children of Pacific Islander fathers and Australian mothers had been removed unlawfully. '[What] appears to have been overlooked by those in authority is the cruelty of sending away children born in Queensland, some of whom have been taught in schools and brought up under Australian conditions. They have not been informed, they say, whether they are exempt from deportation or not, but just told to get out.'

The deportations occurred despite the recommendations of a royal commission that returning long-term residents of Queensland, the frail, or families where parents were not from the same island 'would be inconsistent with humanity'.

Alfred Deakin, who was prime minister at this time, conceded some children were deported without their parents being advised of the option to stay in Queensland. He ducked responsibility by questioning the victims. 'No doubt, the Kanakas said they had not been asked, but they are not always trustworthy,' Deakin said. Nonetheless, he would 'strain the Act to the utmost to avoid the slightest inhumanity'.

About seven thousand Pacific Islanders were removed from Queensland between 1904 and 1908. The population was reduced to less than two thousand, or 0.3 per cent of the state total, by 1911.

The final part of White Australia was, in fact, universal female suffrage. The Commonwealth Franchise Act, passed on 12 June 1902, gave women the vote from the next federal election. Australia was just the second nation after New Zealand to give women the vote. This ideal of equality for women could co-exist with racial exclusion, in part because women did not pose a threat to men in work. Labor was more enthusiastic about this reform than the conservatives. Barton had said during the 1901 election campaign that he was never personally in favour of female suffrage, but would support it to avoid confusion because it already applied in some states and not others.

The vote for women should have gone some way towards restoring Australia's reputation as a pioneer for democracy. Yet it was tarnished by its association with the White Australia policy. The all-male parliament took the opportunity to sully this reform by clarifying who could not vote. 'No aboriginal native of Australia Asia Africa or the Islands of the Pacific except New Zealand shall be entitled to have his name placed on an Electoral Roll unless so entitled under section forty-one of the Constitution,' the legislation said, without punctuation. It was the same petty drafting used in section 127 of the Constitution, which declared the Indigenous population should not be counted in the census. The final insult to the original Australians was in the exception for New Zealanders. Under all these laws, Maoris were considered 'white'.

At every step on its journey into the twentieth century, Australia took the low road. The vote for women should never have been a coda to the White Australia policy. But Barton and Deakin, egged on by the Labor Party, defined Australia by the people it would keep out. Capital and labour were walking arm in arm towards a little Australia.

11

DISUNITY
ON THE
HOME FRONT

Wars are positive shocks in the impersonal data of economics. They tend to reduce unemployment and boost national production as men move into uniform and women into the armament factories. And if they are fought overseas, and there is no political opposition to the deployment, the home front is generally more cohesive than in peacetime.

Australia broke every one of those rules in the First World War. The economy went backwards in every year of the conflict, unemployment remained a persistent problem, and the illusion of national unity was shattered by outbreaks of tribalism across the home front, from the highest office in the land to the churches and the trade unions. By the war's end, Australian living standards were still below their colonial peak of thirty years earlier.

Gallipoli overwhelms discussion of this period because the futility of the landing and the bravery of the soldiers fits neatly into preferred narratives of Australian victimhood and stoicism. But the deeper legacy comes from the conflicts within Australian society itself, which entrenched the cycles of poor economic performance and parochialism.

Yet the Australia that approached the war was finally emerging from that two-decade-long depression with a political system that had discovered bipartisanship. The conservatives had resolved their argument over industry policy when the protectionists prevailed over the free traders in 1905. Alfred Deakin's Protectionist Party was returned at the 1906 election with Labor's assistance, and capital and labour struck their grand bargain, which dictated the nation's economic policies for the next seven decades. Tariffs would be used to defend local industry by penalising foreign imports. In return for this government support, business would maintain high wages for its workers. Industrial disputes would be resolved by a conciliation and arbitration commission, which would have the power to set wage rates across the economy.

Deakin eventually brought together the disparate conservative factions to form the first Liberal Party. With a platform of industry protection and social benefits, it was to the left of the establishment Tories in Britain, who remained free traders. Yet at their first election contest in 1910, the Liberals were deemed too conservative by the Australian people. The voters gave Andrew Fisher's Labor Party forty-three of the seventy-five seats in the House of Representatives – the first majority government of the young federation, and the first majority government for any labour party in the world. But it lasted just one term.

Writing after Labor's narrow defeat in 1913 to the Joseph Cook–led Liberal Party, Russian revolutionary Vladimir Lenin professed his bewilderment with Australian politics. 'What sort of peculiar capitalist country is this, in which the workers' representative, predominate in the *Upper* house and, till recently, did so in the Lower House as well, and yet the capitalist system is in no danger?' he asked. 'The Australian Labor Party does not even call itself a socialist party. Actually, it is a liberal-bourgeois party, while the so-called Liberals in Australia are really Conservatives.' Lenin wanted workers to overthrow the capitalist state, not become part of its governing class.

On the eve of war, facing an impasse in a Labor-controlled Senate, Joseph Cook called a double-dissolution election for 5 September 1914. Britain declared war on Germany on 4 August, in the first week of the campaign, and the main parties promptly engaged in a duel of loyalty, each pledging to serve the empire. Andrew Fisher argued that only Labor could be trusted to look after the vulnerable at home while prosecuting the war abroad: 'Australians will stand beside [Britain] to help defend her to our last man and our last shilling.' His message clearly resonated with the public, and the party of the workingman was returned to office with forty-two of the seventy-five seats. The primary vote of 50.9 per cent remains its highest ever. Here was an egalitarian nation, ready to fight for the empire under the banner of Labor.

Along with Deakin, Fisher had established a relatively civil quality for domestic debate in federation's first decade. Fisher generously praised his opponent's speeches, while Deakin delivered Labor's platform for the age pension. But war broke Fisher's health, and he resigned as prime minister on 27 October 1915, just weeks after receiving a secret report from journalist Keith Murdoch that detailed the 'continuous and ghastly bungling' of the British command at Gallipoli. In his place, the Labor caucus elected Billy Hughes, the government's most popular member after Fisher.

Hughes created a new model for Australian leadership that was divisive at home and abroad. He was the wrong man for the moment, in charge of a party which cracked under the responsibility of governing in wartime.

As attorney-general in Andrew Fisher's government, Billy Hughes had already demonstrated his propensity for xenophobia. He had ordered the internment of thousands of German-Australians as a wartime precaution, arguing that they could not be trusted to remain loyal to their adopted country. 'If I were in Germany for 100 years, if I could live that long, I should still be British or Australian, and I would not think it wrong to do what I could for Great Britain or Australia,' he told parliament in October 1914. 'I put a German in Australia on exactly the same footing. His sympathy is for Germany in this struggle. Is it not a question of life and death with him and with us?'

In confusing his own prejudices for the common experience of every migrant, he also ignored the quintessential example of the loyal German-Australian. General John Monash, the Melbourne-born son of Prussian Jews, had been in the military for thirty years when the war broke out, and in 1915 served as chief censor before assuming the command of the 4th Infantry Brigade of the Australian Imperial Forces, where he served in Gallipoli.

The Germans had been co-founders of South Australia alongside the British, with the first intake of 517 arriving in 1838. At the 1911 census, they were the largest migrant group in Australia after the United Kingdom, at thirty-three thousand – almost three times the size of Billy Hughes' own Welsh community. Many German-Australians volunteered to fight for Australia yet ultimately one in three German males living in Australia – seven thousand out of the twenty-one thousand – were interned under the War Precautions Bill. The two in three who were not interned were testament to a relative degree of pragmatism by authorities, who knew that most Germans were in fact more valuable to the war effort as workers. The measures nonetheless had popular support, and at town hall meetings across the country Germans were urged to give themselves up.

There was nothing in Hughes' career to this point to suggest that the next target of his suspicion would be Australia's Irish community. He was typical of the late nineteenth-century British migrant in embracing Australian nationalism and gravitating towards the labour movement, where British and Irish were equally respected. A teacher by training, he migrated to Queensland in 1884 at the age of twenty-two, working in odd jobs, before settling in the Sydney suburb of Balmain in 1890, where he found his voice in trade union activism. Once in federal parliament, Hughes pitched himself as a man of the people, yet the biggest decisions he made as prime minister fundamentally misjudged public opinion.

One of his first acts as wartime leader was to travel to London to press his case for greater cooperation between the Australians and their British commanders. On his return to Australia that winter, the prime minister was confronted with the issue of conscription. Military planners told him they were running out of volunteers. Fearing that the war could be lost, Hughes decided to act. He had the power to legislate for a call-up, but the Labor Party was formally opposed to conscription, and he knew he couldn't hold the government together if he moved unilaterally. Convinced of success, he put the question to the people by calling a referendum for 28 October 1916. Parliament, he reasoned, would not stand in the way when a majority of voters and states voted for conscription.

Hughes underestimated the community feeling against compulsion. The war was popular, and young men across the country had enlisted in their hundreds of thousands. But voters did not want their government to force them to make an even greater sacrifice. For many Labor people, conscription violated their rights as free men; it reduced them to subordinates of the state.

The Queensland Labor government of Tom Ryan accused Hughes of being a class traitor. Deputy premier and treasurer Ted Theodore penned an incendiary pamphlet that was as vicious as any wartime propaganda that Australia had aimed at the Hun. 'At the instigation of an erstwhile leader of democracy; drunk with the lust of power and flattered to insanity by the patronage of the historic enemies of the common people, Australia stands threatened with that greatest of all industrial and social curses – Conscription,' Theodore wrote.

In anticipation of victory at the ballot box Hughes had ordered a call-up of men, and one of those who refused was the organiser of the 'no' campaign for the trade unions, the journalist John Curtin, a future prime minister. He was sentenced to three months' jail, but was released after three days inside. The referendum was narrowly defeated with a national vote of 51.6 per cent to 48.4 per cent. Of the four states with Labor governments, three voted no – Queensland, New South Wales and South Australia – while Western Australia voted yes. The two states with Liberal governments – Victoria and Tasmania – both voted yes.

The position of Hughes as Labor leader was now untenable. But his opponents did not count on his political cunning. At the caucus meeting to decide his fate on 14 November 1916, Hughes simply walked out on his party before a vote of no confidence could be put. He took twenty-three members of the government with him, including Labor's first prime minister, Chris Watson, splitting the party in two. With Liberal opposition support, Hughes retained the prime ministership as leader of the newly formed National Labor Party, comprised of his fellow defectors and some ex-Liberals.

At the next election on 5 May 1917, he combined his rebels and the Liberals to form the conservative Nationalist Party and won in a landslide. Hughes promised voters he would not introduce conscription without another referendum, and would only call one if 'the tide of battle which flows strongly for the Allies turns against them'.

While Hughes had been in Britain early in his prime ministership, the troubles between Britain and Ireland had reignited with the 1916 Easter rebellion, undermining the war effort. This influenced the prime minister's reading of the first conscription vote, the loss of which he blamed on the Irish in Australia. He told British prime minister Lloyd George that Labor was divided between two sections, the Irish and his. The Irish were a quarter of the Australian population, he said, but 80 per cent of the Labor Party. The latter figure seems an exaggeration; the former reflected the proportion of the population that identified as Catholic. 'There is a war to the knife between the old section of the Labor Party and my section,' he wrote in a secret cable. The Irish 'were the keystone of the sectional arch. Cut that away and the whole opposition [to conscription] crumbles'.

Hughes returned to the question of conscription late in 1917 when there were genuine fears that Germany might win the war. He called a second referendum for 20 December 1917, and reached for the race card as part of his campaign by publicly questioning the loyalty of Australia's Irish community. More than a century of good relations between Protestant and Catholic in Australia was put at risk, and at a time of war.

Malcolm Fraser's father was in France when the war started. 'He thought it would be a waste of time to sail back to Australia and sail back again, so he served in the British army,' Fraser told me in one of his last major interviews. Fraser winced at the memory of his father repeating the prejudices of the prime minister. 'What the prime minister said about the treacherous nature of the Irish and Catholics bit into the troops on the western front,' he said. 'He [my father] and his peers, they believed what Billy Hughes said.

'When you have these kinds of arguments, logic goes out the window, reason goes out the window. Billy Hughes, to my mind, because of all of this, was the most wretched, bigoted racist; he wasn't the little digger hero, he was awfully short-sighted.'

The Catholic Church had stayed out of the first referendum, but the policy changed with the second. The Irishman Daniel Mannix had migrated to Melbourne in 1913 to serve under Archbishop Carr, and with Carr's passing in May 1917 he assumed the mantle. He proved radically different to his predecessor; where Carr had been careful to avoid controversy, Mannix courted it. The new archbishop took up the 'no' case with the provocative slogan, 'Put Australia first and the Empire second'. Mannix had reframed the referendum as a question of national sovereignty: Australia wanted to fight as an independent nation, and it should not be told to do so as a colony of Britain.

There was an unambiguous violence in the air at pro- and anti-conscription rallies held across the nation. Rivals accused one another of treachery as the very meaning of what it was to be an Australian was being contested. As the debate degenerated in November 1917, leaders on all sides lost the sense of shared purpose that had defined the Deakin–Fisher era before the war and took the nation to the precipice of mob violence.

Mannix antagonised fellow Catholics for blurring the line between church and state. One prominent critic was Charles Heydon, the president of the New South Wales Court of Arbitration, who wrote a letter to the press in late November: 'In proclaiming his sympathy with Sinn Fein, in urging us to put Australia first and Empire second, the Catholic Archbishop of Melbourne has shown himself to be not only disloyal as a man but – I say it, emphatically, archbishop though he be, and simple layman though I be – untrue to the teaching of the Church of which, by his office, he should be the guardian . . . For a Catholic Archbishop to lead his flock along the paths of sedition is to disobey the clearest teachings of the Catholic Church.'

Speaking at a rally in Croxton Park the following day, Mannix ridiculed the judge before turning to his real target – Hughes. The archbishop urged the women of Australia to deny him their husbands and sons. 'The Prime Minister had appealed to the ladies on the previous referendum, and he (Dr Mannix) was afraid that they had given him more votes than he had been entitled to, but he hoped that the ladies would not be led astray by Mr. Hughes, who had designs too deep to be penetrated by any lady,' according to reports of his speech. That attempt at humour was greeted with cheers from the audience.

At a pro-conscription rally in Melbourne on 27 November, chaired by the Reverend D Daly, the president of the local Protestant

Federation, accusations of treachery were directed at the Catholic Church. The motion agreed to that day made the anti-Chinese resolutions of 1888 appear almost welcoming by comparison.

'That this meeting of loyal citizens views with grave concern the disloyal and seditious utterances of prelates of the Roman Catholic Church, especially at a time when the whole of the liberties of our Empire are at stake. It believes that this disloyalty has been encouraged, and has grown because the responsible authorities have not punished the authors of disloyal utterances through mistaken clemency, which has been regarded as weakness, and it urges the Commonwealth Government to remember its responsibilities to the honor of our flag and to prosecute all traitors and rebels in our midst.'

Hughes did not take the advice to lock up his political opponents, but his manner might indicate that he was tempted. On 29 November, he made a campaign stop at Warwick, in Queensland. As the prime minister stepped off the train, 'he was surrounded by a howling mob', according to an animated account in the *Brisbane Courier*. Eggs were thrown and the perpetrator was set upon by a returned serviceman, after which Hughes entered the fray, throwing punches at those who remonstrated with him. 'Mr. Hughes was hustled and jostled by men twice his size, but when he emerged it was his hand, and not his face that was bleeding. One of the men in the crowd carried a hammer, and another a heavy spanner, but the Prime Minister was daunted by nothing.'

He demanded the police arrest the egg thrower but the officer at the scene, Senior Sergeant Kenny, declined, saying he recognised the laws of Queensland only. Hughes exploded, claiming the men who had attacked him were unworthy of retaining their liberty. 'The law shall be obeyed by every man in this country, police or not. Here, in this great crisis in the history of Australia and the Empire, when the citizens are asked to decide a question upon which the safety and liberty of Australia depends, the Prime Minister is assaulted and denied the opportunity of free speech.'

That evening back in Melbourne, Mannix addressed a rally of twenty thousand people. He called the prime minister the 'little Czar of Australia' and said, to cheers, that his performance in Queensland 'was the effort of a desperate man trying to retrieve his failing fortune'.

The second referendum, on 20 December 1917, was lost by a larger margin than the first – 53.8 per cent to 46.2 per cent, with Victoria swinging to the no camp, which suggests that the intervention of Mannix had an effect. Hughes resigned, but he was immediately recommissioned as prime minister because no one else had the numbers to form government.

One of the first intuitive rules of settlement saw governors treat the Protestant and Catholic faiths equally. That policy was codified at federation with section 116 of the Constitution, which prohibited the government from favouring any religion in particular. Mannix may not have appreciated the historic influences that led to this policy of neutrality, most notably Richard Bourke's Church Act of 1836 and the response of the New South Wales parliament to Melbourne's Orange Riot a decade later. If he had, he might have tempered his language and saved his own followers decades of recrimination. But Hughes understood well the context for section 116 of the Constitution. Leaders determine the quality of the national conversation, and the debate the prime minister indulged in during wartime was reckless. It created a rift between the Protestant and Catholic communities that would take the next half century to heal.

Discrimination against Catholics became commonplace after the war, as Malcolm Fraser explained to me, reflecting on his memories growing up in Australia. It is clear that the bigotry he observed in his youth informed his determination as prime minister to promote multiculturalism.

'[Masonic] Lodges were set up trying to prevent Catholics from getting into positions of authority. There were many professions that would not register Catholics. There were advertisements in newspapers saying Catholics need not apply.

'As a result of the professions shutting the door on the Catholics, many more than one would have normally thought joined the Commonwealth public service. But this became a papal plot to take over the Commonwealth from the back door.'

Billy Hughes' letter to Lloyd George, which spelled out the proportion of Australians who were Catholic, suggested that he thought a majority yes vote could be achieved in the referendums simply by appealing to his own Protestant tribe. Yet in moving the debate from the issue of conscription to religion and race, the political calculation Australia's wartime leader made was flawed. At least one in three Protestants did not support him, and along with the Catholics who voted no, they combined to form a majority; bigotry could not secure an electoral win. Hughes was wrong in thinking the country would divide along strict sectarian lines, but it fractured nonetheless.

'Billy Hughes thought, If I turn this into an anti-Catholic, anti-Irish referendum I'll win it. He lost it twice,' Malcolm Fraser said.

Paul Keating was born in the second half of White Australia, in 1944. When he first went to work as a fifteen-year-old in the Sydney City Council, the pall of bigotry had not lifted from his religion. 'I remember reading ads in the [*Sydney Morning*] *Herald*, "Catholics need not apply",' he says. 'They were still being run in newspapers as late as 1959–60. There was another guy I worked with, Frank Keating, who was the local secretary of the Masonic Lodge. And I used to get his correspondence. Sometimes I'd open it because it'd just have "Mr Keating" or something. And I could never quite work out why someone with the name of Keating was tied up in the Masonic Lodge, but he was.'

The New South Wales Labor Party had avoided the split in the mid-1950s when anti-communist Catholics in Victoria formed the breakaway Democratic Labor Party. 'The moderates always kept control of the thing [in New South Wales],' Keating says. 'But nevertheless there was still a big sectarian divide. In the left of the Labor Party, you'd be probably surprised to know that the leaders, certainly in New South Wales, were invariably members of the Masonic Lodge. Try and work that one out.'

John Howard recalls the low rumble of sectarianism as a child of the 1940s. 'I was conscious of the differences as one grew up,' he says. 'Sectarianism in Australia didn't totally disappear, but it all but disappeared between 1960 and 1965.' He credits this to the 'far-sighted' decision of Robert Menzies to provide government funding to Catholic schools, as well as the emergence of a less religious Australia in the 1960s. 'As secular voices became more assertive, Catholics and Protestants suddenly thought, Well, gee, our common beliefs are under attack. Why on earth are we arguing with each other?'

The ill feeling outlasted its protagonists by a generation. Billy Hughes and Daniel Mannix had privately reconciled by the 1940s, exchanging Christmas and birthday cards.

The stated aim of the White Australia policy was to secure social cohesion through racial purity, but the disunity on the home front during the First World War proved this to be wishful thinking. Anglo and Celt were white, but no longer united. An equal division between ethnic groups is not necessarily a prerequisite for social cohesion, but the fifty-fifty Anglo–Celt split that had been a feature of the prosperous nineteenth century had tilted sixty-forty in favour of the English-born by the eve of the conflict. The Irish-born community was reduced from 210 000 before the depression to just 140 000 by 1911 through departures and death. Their share of the total population fell from 10 per cent in 1881 to just 3 per cent in 1911, and this reduction mirrored the shift to a predominately

Australian-born population. The overseas-born had been 37 per cent of the population in 1881; by federation that figure had dropped to 23 per cent and by 1911 it was just 18 per cent. Without migration, paradoxically Australia became more conflicted.

The weak economy exacerbated the divisions. Australia did not have a manufacturing sector ready to drive its war effort, and national income fell in each year of the conflict. By comparison, the war machines of the United States, United Kingdom, France and Germany were each able to raise production during the war.

By 1918, Australia's standard of living was once again below where it had been in 1889. The brief rally on the eve of the war in 1910, when Australia passed the United States for the last time on the measure of GDP per capita, was reversed. The two-decade-long depression bled into a three-decade-long decline.

The unemployment rate was higher throughout the conflict than it had been in the fleeting years of recovery after the depression. This added to the grievances of the labour movement, which had already seen its political wing disintegrate in office. Industrial disputes hit then-record levels during the years of the two conscription debates. In 1917, workers in every state went out in support of their comrades at the Government Railway Workshops in New South Wales over the issue of timecards. Almost four million working days and more than two million pounds in wages were lost in this strike alone.

Even the return of the diggers after the war, the single largest wave of humanity to land on Australia's shores since the gold rush, failed to reunite the nation. They were too damaged to inspire an economic or cultural recovery. Three out of every four people who had enlisted were either killed or physically injured, a casualty rate exceeded only by the fallen empires of Russia and Austria, even though not a shot was fired on Australian soil. A century later, the raw numbers still have the power to shock. Of the almost 332 000 Australians who served overseas 60 000 perished; 159 000 were wounded, gassed or shell-shocked; and 4000 were taken prisoners.

The war left a hole in the young nation's demography. By 1921, there were fewer Australian men aged twenty to twenty-four than there had been in 1911.

In 1919 there were 166 000 net arrivals to Australia. The diggers returned with a deep resentment of the British establishment, which added a fresh layer of animus to the toxic homebrew of sectarianism. When migration resumed after the war, the British who came stepped into a cultural trap. To the parochial Australian media, they became the new Chinese. 'The Worst Yet! Latest Immigrants Described as Crime Recruits,' a headline in Melbourne's the *Sun News-Pictorial* screamed on 9 September 1923. 'What was described by others on board as one of the roughest batches of immigrants yet to reach Australia came by the *Demosthenes*, which berthed at Port Melbourne yesterday,' the article began. There were tales of smashed cabins and nightly fights with razors drawn. 'The scum of Great Britain is certainly being dumped into Australia,' said a British ex-officer travelling on the ship. 'I never knew until they came on to the ship that Great Britain possessed such undersized creatures.'

This was a new form of Australian bigotry, aimed at all British classes. Sectarianism and Pommy-bashing were symptoms of a wounded national pride. The First World War didn't make Australia; it shrank it.

12

MISSED
OPPORTUNITIES:
THE LOST 1920S

The 1920s roared everywhere but Australia. The decade that most rich nations associate with boom times and jazz music was for Australia one of extended economic weakness and a creeping cultural cringe. The former role-model society had the slowest economy of the developed world apart from New Zealand in the 1920s. The United States grew twice as fast as Australia; the continent of Europe grew three times as fast.

The contradictions in the national personality sharpened as the years of underachievement accumulated. Australians were an urban people, still dreaming of a bush life for which they lacked the life skills; a kind-hearted people who didn't want to share the continent; a proud British race that resented Britain. The sons of federation acquired the philistine's certainty that the rest of the world didn't matter.

After the First World War, a conscious national decision was made to preserve homogeneity across all aspects of life. The White Australia policy, originally designed to exclude 'coloured labour', was gradually applied against 'white' people from Europe – in particular, Germans, Italians and Greeks. The tariff wall was raised to further restrict the entry of foreign goods. And in perhaps the ultimate throwback of public policy in Australian history, governments tried to resettle the countryside at the expense of the cities.

The political system had correctly diagnosed the problem: Australia needed more migrants to restore the economy and society. The official statistician had calculated the loss of population growth due to the war at between 240 000 and 600 000 people. To recover those losses, and build large internal markets to create a virtuous cycle of production and employment, migration had to be revived. But a series of epic policy blunders left the nation saddled with debts that would once again make Australia vulnerable to another global shock.

The most symbolic of these mistakes was the soldier settlement scheme, the first systematic attempt to nation-build through migration since assisted passage was introduced in the 1830s and 1840s. It might have yielded the fruits of diversity and creativity if politicians weren't so obsessed with the utopia of a British agrarian identity for Australia.

Billy Hughes looked to the wrong workers and the wrong part of Australia to define the future. He told parliament in November 1921: 'If we cannot create conditions which, of themselves, will insure an influx of the right kind of population – the kind which will enable us to hold as well as to develop this country – we are undone.' By the right kind of people he meant farmers. 'All of us are agreed that it is of no use to call more people into our cities,' he said. 'We have a few great cities strung around the fringe of this continent like glorious, flaming jewels; but, inland, there is an almost barren countryside. There is no way of overcoming the handicap of our empty spaces but by encouraging more and more people to go out upon the land.'

Hughes struck joint agreements with state governments to provide subsidised farms to returning soldiers, including those from the British Army. Later, other migrants from the mother country were encouraged to join them. There were countless precedents to warn against settling the bush by government fiat. The earliest attempts to establish colonies at Swan River and in Adelaide in the 1820s and 1830s were doomed by a basic misunderstanding of the Australian land. But the federation generation of politicians perhaps didn't remember their history, or assumed that their best intentions would help tame the nation's intolerant natural environment.

One in three of the thirty-seven thousand soldiers who took up the offer of country living eventually walked off the land. The program would lose twenty-four million pounds by 1928 (more than 2 billion in 2014 dollars), according to confidential official estimates at the time. The losses were borne by state governments, and they added to the large Commonwealth debts already accrued from fighting the war.

Royal commission after royal commission documented the debacle. Among the most telling was the sharply worded report to the Tasmanian parliament in 1926. 'The soldiers made a rush for farms, and the department had to work at flat speed,' the commissioner said. 'The fact is that every soldier who wanted a farm got it, whether he was fit or not.'

It was hard not to hear echoes of the 1890s crash in this commentary, with its unsustainable mix of land, greed and debt. 'There can be no doubt that hundreds were pushed on to farms by public enthusiasm or by the urgings of those whose motives were less idealistic, and after wearily struggling for a time, short or long, at last found that they were utterly incapable of making a success of their farms, threw them up and drifted back to the cities.'

Hughes, while grasping the link between migration and economic growth, made a fundamental mistake, which was repeated by his successor Stanley Bruce. He thought the British would provide enough migrants to close the demographic holes left by the war, and that the economy could thrive through British markets alone. With these beliefs firmly in mind, Hughes turned the screws of the White Australia policy, starting with the Germans. Those already in Australia and those interned during the war were allowed to return to their old lives. But he did not allow their kin to join them. In 1920, Hughes introduced the Enemy Aliens Act, which prohibited new migrants from all countries that had been opponents in the war – Germany, Austria, Hungary, Bulgaria and Turkey. The ban was lifted in 1925, but by then it was too late to catch the postwar wave of German artists, scientists and shop-keepers. The German-born population halved from thirty-three thousand in 1911 to seventeen thousand in 1933.

The politician most associated with Australia's muted 1920s was Stanley Bruce. He had replaced Billy Hughes after the 1922 election in the most unusual circumstances. Hughes had fallen short of a majority at the ballot box. The Country Party, led by Earle Page, had the balance of power and would not serve in a coalition with Hughes as prime minister, and after six weeks of haggling Bruce became the nation's leader. Born into privilege in Melbourne in 1883, Bruce was educated at Melbourne Grammar, and then Cambridge, and ran his late father's import business. What endeared him to the Australian people was his war record: he was wounded in Gallipoli in June 1915, and on his return to the battlefield risked his life to aid a group of stranded soldiers. That act of bravery earned him the Military Cross. The French also honoured him with the Croix de Guerre avec Palme.

Bruce differed from Hughes in one important area: he wanted to repair the rift with Australian Catholics. But he succumbed to the same failure of imagination on the postwar migration program. He adopted the catch-cry of 'men, money, markets', and struck deals with the mother country to facilitate a two-way trade in which migrants and capital flowed to Australia and goods were sold back to Britain. This cosy arrangement would be propped up by tariffs. The main agreement signed in 1925 was meant to run for ten years, during which London would distribute 3.4 million pounds per year (260 million in 2014 dollars) to the states in low-interest loans. One half of the fund would pay for assisted passage, the other half would be invested in public works. Assisted passage in the nineteenth century had been funded by the revenue from land sales, not debt.

Bruce saw the world through the wrong end of the telescope, confusing race with prosperity and security. He told parliament in 1926 that Australia must remain white. 'Australia is part of the British Empire. Despite what may occasionally be said in the heat of the moment, the majority of our people are proud of our British origin and connexion, and know that our future safety depends upon the British Empire maintaining its position in the world. One factor that will ensure this is the better distribution of the white population of the Empire, and we in Australia could probably do more towards bringing that about than any other part of it.'

Bruce proved to be a disappointing recruiter, with migration averaging just thirty-eight thousand per year on his watch. In the three fleeting years of recovery before the First World War, Andrew Fisher had welcomed twice that figure – 77 000 people per year – without the attendant government borrowing. Net migration under both Hughes and Bruce barely covered half the projected 600 000 in lost population growth between 1914 and 1919. Australia received just 310 000 new arrivals between 1921 and 1930. Were Bruce able to see beyond his British bias, he might have proved a more successful nation-builder, as the example of Canada shows.

Fed up with losing people to the United States, the Canadians embarked on a Richard Bourke–style program of assisted passage at the end of the nineteenth century. It was an openly bigoted program, favouring German, Scandinavian and eastern European farmers over the urban Briton, the southern European, the Asian and the African. Canada had ceded 480 000 of its people to net emigration between 1861 and 1901, at a time when Australia received 780 000 more arrivals than departures. But the new Canadian wave carried 810 000 migrants in the first decade of the twentieth century, and another 310 000 in the 1910s, for a twenty-year total of 1.12 million, at a time when migration to Australia virtually ceased. One natural asset in Canada's favour was fertile, undeveloped agricultural land, whereas the soldier settlement scheme had demonstrated that much of Australia was, in fact, uninhabitable. Canada's investment in migration paid off in the 1920s, with her national income growing twice as fast as Australia's.

There were many layers to Australia's poor migration record in the 1920s. Demography acts like a slow tide, and population shifts are often only visible decades after the fact. The First World War marked the end of the great British and Irish century of emigration, yet from Bruce's position in the mid-1920s he could not see the turn that had occurred many years earlier. The Irish, restricted decades earlier by the likes of Henry Parkes, now had their independence and were staying at home, while in Britain, the birth rate had been falling since the later part of the nineteenth century. The migration wave of the 1920s was coming from Europe, most notably from Italy, and if Bruce had kept the door open he would have received people without needing to borrow money from London.

But Bruce feared an inundation, and took the fateful step early in his term to limit migration from Europe. This saw an already restrictive policy – the White Australia policy – redefined even more narrowly as the British Australia Policy, damaging the very economy that Bruce sought to protect. In the 1901 parliamentary debate on the policy Labor members had insisted the door be kept open to white Europeans, 'so long as immense hordes do not come over'. The first Labor prime minister, Chris Watson, had said of the Europeans: 'We have room for every man who has a standard of living equal to our own, and whose general tone is in no way inferior to that of our own people.'

Although Europeans did migrate to Australia before the war, the intakes were small. Italy had signed a treaty with the United Kingdom in 1883 that guaranteed them access to the empire for trade and settlement, but Italians were discouraged by Australia's long depression. Less than seven thousand had settled before the First World War, of which a third went to Western Australia, chasing gold, while their community numbered 1.6 million in the United States at the time.

Those who had come were greeted with courtesies of the day. At a meeting of the Sydney City Council in May 1907, Alderman Kelly complained that 'the Dagoes' were taking over the local fish market after already conquering the fruit trade. 'So long as the "Dagoes" have control,' he said, 'so long will the public have to pay "through the nose" for what they get [and] Britons and Australians will not be able to live here directly.' Before the war, the word 'dago' was applied loosely, and could mean anyone from an Austrian to a Syrian.

In 1921 there were just eight thousand Italians in Australia, representing 0.1 per cent of the population. By 1933, the community had trebled to almost twenty-seven thousand, or 0.4 per cent of the population, partly filling the void left by the departing Germans. One in three went to Queensland, where the trade unions were quick to call for their restriction, on the grounds that the Italians were undercutting the local worker.

The Italian wave to Australia sprang from an unlikely source. American public opinion had turned sharply against migration from southern and eastern Europe after the First World War. In 1924, the US Congress moved to shut the door by introducing limits on the number of people arriving from each country. The measure was aimed primarily at the Italians who had been coming to the United States at an average of 200 000 per year in the first decade of the twentieth century. The new quota would permit the entry of just 3845 Italians per year. Bruce, fearing they would seek out Australia instead, would soon impose his own quotas on the Italians.

Other Europeans wanted to come to Australia in the 1920s, notably the Greeks and the Maltese, who as subjects of the empire had an explicit right to migrate. Bruce made sure they were not welcome, targeting the Maltese first. He advised the South Australian premier John Gunn in 1924 that an arrangement had been made with the British colony to limit the number of passports being issued to their citizens up to a quota of twenty per month. In the same correspondence he wrote that other Mediterranean migrants who had been paying their own fare to London and then applying for assisted passage to Australia would also be stopped: 'The British Government is being asked to instruct His Majesty's Commissioners to refrain from granting passport facilities to Spanish or Greek intending migrants for Australia unless they possess a certain minimum amount of capital or unless their maintenance is guaranteed.' Britain raised no objections.

Italian migrants became the formal target the following year, after pressure from the trade unions in Queensland led to the establishment of a royal commission into 'alien immigration', the phrase used at the time to describe any non-British or Irish migrant. Like a modern-day John Thomas Bigge, Queensland public servant Thomas Ferry asked the locals to tell him what they didn't like about the Italians. The Australian Workers' Union, one of the foundation organisations of the Labor Party, was only too happy to oblige. The union officials did not 'object to aliens on racial grounds', according to a summary of the report published in the local *Northern Miner* in June 1925. 'Their objection was solely to the crowding of workers into the sugar districts where employment was definitely limited, and the necessary labour for the season was already oversupplied. They would raise the same objections if hundreds of unemployed Queenslanders were dumped down in the district.'

The Ferry report did concede the Italians looked after their children as well as, if not better than locals by sending them to primary school, and, where they could, to secondary school. But the report did not see all Italians equally. 'The population of Italy, however, was divided into two distinct groupings: Northern and Southern Italians. The latter are shorter in stature and more swarthy than the people of Northern Italy.'

Ferry nominated five main reasons for Italian migration in the 1920s, all of which resonate across time. Firstly, the restrictions in the United States encouraged the Italians to look elsewhere. Secondly, Europe's steamship agents, eager to cash in on the assisted-passage scheme, had been promoting Australia as a destination. Thirdly, 'the present political situation in Italy, and the prevailing economic conditions in Europe' – in other words, the dictatorship of Benito Mussolini – caused many Italians to seek a better life elsewhere. Then there was 'the advice and assistance of friends and relatives in Australia', which played a role. And lastly, the impression Australia's well-paid diggers had created during the First World War was not to be discounted.

To Ferry, these were evils to be addressed, not compliments to be gratefully accepted. Queensland's economic future might have been different if the report had advocated the continuation of migration from Italy. But Ferry urged the Commonwealth and state governments to restore social harmony and economic balance by limiting the number of Italians. 'Consideration should be given immediately to the racial stock of immigrants. The number of many of those now arriving should be reduced, and in other cases altogether prohibited. There should be a selection of a type of immigrant that would assist, rather than hinder the building up of superior social and economic conditions in this State.' That was code for maintaining a high-wage White Australia. But Ferry's recommendations meant that Queensland passed up not just another opportunity to develop the north, but counted itself out of the European migration that occurred after the Second World War.

Stanley Bruce responded to the Ferry report by placing further

restrictions on the Italians. The criteria for entry were toughened so
that only those with close relatives or a definite job to go to would
be issued a passport in London. A limit of three thousand Italians
per year was also adopted. The door to a more diverse intake was
slammed shut, even before the Great Depression stopped migration across the world.

Many Australians can point to a page in history when their convict
forefathers were bullied by officialdom. I have the next best thing
in my bloodline: an alien. I had known that some of my ancestors
migrated to Australia before the First World War. But it didn't
occur to me until I found their files in the National Archives that
they help tell a deeper story of how Australia missed the European
wave of the 1920s, leaving a gap in our identity.

My great-grandfather Constantinos Megalogenis was an oyster-
man from the Greek island of Ithaca. He took a number of trips
to Australia, starting in the late nineteenth century. When the
First World War broke out, he was fifty-two years old and living in a boarding house in Little Lonsdale Street, Melbourne. He
was subject to the War Precautions Act because Greece had not
yet committed to the allied cause. Under the legislation, migrants
could be deported without appeal, or forced to live within certain
areas and required to inform police of any change of address, business activity or travel plans.

Constantinos registered 'as an alien of Greek nationality' at the
Russell Street police headquarters on 16 October 1916. The paperwork said he was five foot six and a half inches tall, with grey hair
and brown eyes. My father chuckles at this detail on his record.
'His eyes were green,' Dad tells me. Constantinos remained under
state surveillance after Greece joined the allied side in the fighting,
and even after the war had ended. In July 1919 he reported to police
that was he was moving to another abode.

My great-grandfather had brought his eldest son, Grigorios, with him to Australia on one occasion. Grigorios then moved to America, where he died young. My grandfather George, the middle of Constantinos' three sons, remained at home, breaking the migration chain to Australia for the time being.

Impoverished, Constantinos returned to Ithaca in 1920. He brought back a present for his youngest son, Lukas, then fourteen – a leather bag for his schoolbooks. Lukas found a more practical use for the gift, by reworking the leather to make himself a pair of shoes.

Another federation Megalogenis was the generous Apostolos, the son of Constantinos' brother Spiros. Apostolos was five feet five inches tall, with black hair and chestnut eyes, according to his record. He was born on Christmas Day 1893 and sailed to Australia as a teenager in 1911. He spent a year in Perth and three years in Sydney, before settling in Melbourne during the war. His occupation was listed as a cook at the Megalos Bros Café, also known as the Paris Café, at 199 Bourke Street.

The War Precautions Act was repealed in 1920, and in 1926 Apostolos became a naturalised Australian. This document is as poignant for me as Constantinos' alien registration card. Apostolos could read and write English 'with some difficulty'. He provided no birth certificate, or other evidence of birthplace and nationality. Question nine on the document asked if he had been registered as an alien during the war. He explained that he had done so in Sydney, but the papers were lost. I suspect he had registered under the abbreviated surname of Megalos, which he sometimes used for the sake of simplicity. Under 'general remarks', inspector Roland Browne had a bet each way. 'Applicant is a Cook in a Greek Café in Bourke Street. Nothing can be advanced against him. He is of the negative type of alien who has little real national sentiment in any direction. He seems qualified for naturalization as far as length of residence and character are concerned.'

Apostolos paid my father's fare to Australia in 1950 and was a regular visitor to my childhood home in Melbourne. I remember one such occasion in September 1971. The date is seared in the embarrassment of my childhood because my Aussie Rules team, Richmond, was beaten by St Kilda in the preliminary final that day. I cried; it was the only time I shed a tear over a game of football. Apostolos tried to cheer me up but I kicked him, and my mum dragged me outside. She should have given me the koutala – the wooden spoon she used to threaten me with – but she took pity and shepherded me to the local milk bar to buy me a bag of marbles.

In 1911, the Greeks in Australia numbered less than two thousand, including up to a dozen or more Megalogenises and Megaloses. They doubled their total by 1921, and doubled it again to just over eight thousand by 1933. This put the Greeks in the same bracket as the Chinese, with 0.1 per cent of the total population. Many more would have come if they could, but the sons of federation were too busy looking to the past to see the opportunity for large-scale migration from Greece, Italy or Germany in the 1920s.

The Bruce–Page government was the first politically stable alliance of the federation, combining urban conservatives and agrarian socialists. But its economic management was poor, and its approach to politics was polarising. Stanley Bruce won a second term in November 1925, but could not deliver on his promise of good times. The economy stalled in 1926 and slipped into recession in 1927, two years ahead of the Great Depression. As the unemployment rate climbed, the White Australia policy's consensus between labour and capital collapsed. Bruce wanted to force down wages. The Labor opposition replied by attacking his migration program, declaring that it was no longer prepared to accept any arrivals – not even from the mother country – until the economy recovered. 'We must first find employment for our own people, and then if we could bring a couple of hundred thousand of our brothers and sisters from Great Britain and give employment to them we should all welcome them gladly,' opposition leader Matthew Charlton declared in moving a censure motion against the government in February 1928.

Labor played on the fear of Italian migration, even though the coalition had already restricted it. Francis Forde, the Labor member for the northern Queensland electorate of Capricornia, said, 'The Labour party is not opposed to the Italians as a race. We admit that they make good settlers, and are useful workers. I recognize, too, that they are white men, and that their country is noted for its art, science and learning. Many of them have done good pioneering work in Queensland.' Labor's concern, he said, was that the Italians 'do not understand our arbitration laws and industrial conditions'. Business hoped 'to induce them to work for less than the award rate, and thus break down the conditions of employment operating in Australia'.

It was a vicious circle of unemployment, fear of foreign competition and political and media misinformation. Once Labor chose to present any migration as a threat to national wellbeing, the debate veered to the low road of vilification. Labor provoked the nation's first race-based election in November 1928 by accusing Bruce of putting 'dagoes before heroes'. That election slogan belonged to Ben Chifley, the Labor candidate for the Blue Mountains electorate of Macquarie. '[The government] had allowed so many Dagoes and aliens in Australia that today they are all over the country taking work which rightly belongs to all Australians,' he said.

Chifley won the seat, and Labor had its best result in New South Wales since 1914, claiming fourteen out of the state's twenty-eight seats. But in Queensland, where the presence of Italian labourers was supposed to be contentious, the coalition held its ground, with Labor winning just two seats. This is one of the oldest rules of the politics of race: the anti-migrant vote is weakest in the areas where the migrants actually live. Alternatively, it is easier to harvest votes from xenophobia in places with low rates of migration.

The coalition's majority was reduced to forty-two seats out of the seventy-five, leaving Labor still seven seats short of reclaiming office for the first time since the split over conscription. Bruce soon after made the inexplicable decision to remove the security blanket of the Commonwealth Arbitration Court, which set wages across the country, and hand the power back to the states, which he hoped would deliver less generous verdicts for the trade unions. In other words, workers would lose their protection, but not business, which still had the tariff. Billy Hughes, now an outcast in his own party, moved an amendment to the legislation to prevent it from applying until after the people had their say, at a referendum or a general election. Bruce took the amendment as a vote of no confidence in his government, and when it prevailed by a single vote, he called a snap election for 12 October 1929, less than eleven months after the previous one. He was stunned by the result. The coalition was defeated in a landslide, reduced to twenty-four seats – eighteen fewer than in the previous year's election. Labor gained fifteen seats, to claim a majority of forty-six out of seventy-five, with James Scullin as prime minister.

Labor people today would see the 1929 election as a vindication of the middle ground on industrial relations, in which the interests of workers and bosses were balanced. But the politics of race did play a part. On the Wednesday before polling day, the prime minister addressed three thousand rowdy voters at the Prahran Town Hall in Melbourne. 'When Mr. Bruce rose to speak there were shouts of "Importer of black-fellows" and "The Dagoes' friend",' according to a report in the Hobart *Mercury*.

Yet migration may not have been as potent an issue if the economy had been in better shape. Australia began the decade in arrears, with a large debt from the First World War. The interest bill chewed up 16 per cent of export income. In an ideal world, that ratio would have fallen as the economy recovered. But Australia

went further into debt in search of Billy Hughes' agrarian utopia and Stanley Bruce's British industrial hub. Once the economy
stalled in 1926, the repayment burden increased. On the eve of the
Great Depression, it was 27 per cent of export income, with no
prospect of relief once the price of wool collapsed in 1929.

James Scullin's election as Australia's first Catholic prime minister should have been the occasion for national congratulation, but
it was overshadowed by the catastrophe that followed. Scullin, born
in 1876, had served in the first majority Fisher government in 1910,
but lost his seat after a single term and did not return to parliament
until a by-election in 1922. When he became opposition leader, the
party was in disarray. But the advances made in the general election of November 1928 and the victory in October 1929 marked him
as a potential Labor hero.

Scullin was sworn in as prime minister on Tuesday 24 October. Two days later, the New York Stock Exchange suffered its first
crash. Allowing for the time differences, Scullin technically had
three nights' sleep before the world changed. He had expected to
govern in difficult times, and warned voters during the 1929 election
campaign that he would inherit a 'huge deficit' from the coalition
government. But the political burden of the crash fell unfairly on
him, as the Great Depression overwhelmed all previous understanding of how market-based economies functioned in a crisis.

Australia's credit had actually run out two months before the
Wall Street crash – in August 1929, when the coalition government
was told it could not access any more long-term loans from London.
It did raise some short-term funds through a combination of treasury bills sold to investors in London and a bank overdraft. Those
bills became a debt time bomb for the next government. When the
repayments were due in early 1930, the international economy was
in freefall and the country was short of cash. 'Fundamentally, we
are suffering from the effects of worldwide depression, accentuated
by over-borrowing,' Scullin told parliament on 12 March 1930. He

tried to close the trade deficit by promoting Australian wool and wheat exports, and increasing tariffs on imports. Unfortunately, every nation had the same idea. They protected their own businesses, and punished those of their competitors. Australia was too small to fight a trade war.

Scullin insisted that Australia honour its debts. He invited a Bank of England delegation, led by one of its directors, Otto Niemeyer, to examine Australia's books. As the Greeks can testify in the twenty-first century, nations that enter a global financial crisis with large public debts can expect to be made an example of. The whipping boy for austerity during the Great Depression would be Australia.

Niemeyer arrived in August 1930, armed with the old orthodoxy that the budget must always be in balance. He told a special meeting of Commonwealth and state leaders that they had to reset their expectations downwards. 'There is evidence to show that the standard of living in Australia has reached a point which is economically beyond the capacity of the country to bear without a considerable reduction of costs,' he said. By lower costs, he meant lower wages: the issue on which the last election had been fought. The language was patronising, although the general point was valid. Australians had been living beyond their means. 'Australia must reassure the world as to the direction in which she is going financially and economically and no one else can do that for her.'

Niemeyer's advice for austerity completely destroyed a generation of Australians. The cuts to wages and welfare payments reduced spending power, which undermined the stated objective of restoring the nation's economic viability. Unemployment almost trebled in three years, from 6.7 per cent in 1929 to 19.7 per cent in 1932. The unemployment rate for trade union members jumped from 11.1 per cent to 29 per cent over the same period. At the bottom of the depression in 1932, Australia's GDP per person was below the level it had been at the bottom of the previous depression in 1906, and the debt repayment burden had crossed 40 per cent of export income, breaking the record set in the 1890s.

Australians had had fair warning in the previous depression that a nation's prosperity is the sum of its people, its natural endowment and international confidence. The country would have thrived even after the gold ran out if it had remained open to migrants and markets. But it retreated to the false comfort of White Australia, with its racial selection and industry protection. It takes a certain bloody-mindedness to repeat the mistakes of one's parents, but Billy Hughes, Stanley Bruce and Earle Page left Australia in the same vulnerable place as Henry Parkes, Duncan Gillies and Samuel Griffith.

It's hard not to wonder about the people Australia missed out on during the half century between the 1890s and the 1930s, when it tried to exclude the world from its fair land. The example of a single Russian refugee in the Great Depression is worth recounting; Australia would have been a different place if others like him had been able to come.

Simcha Baevksi was twenty-one years old when he landed in Melbourne in 1899, in the middle of the depression. He had threepence in his pocket and spent it on a celebratory glass of beer. His brother Elcon had migrated three years earlier, and they worked together for a time in a clothing store in Flinders Lane. They adopted the surname Myer, after the second name of their eldest brother, Jacob. Simcha changed his Christian name to Sidney, and taught himself English.

The Myer brothers began with a small drapery store in Bendigo. 'Prejudice against foreigners had to be contended with, but the young trader regarded his customers' goodwill as more important than high profits, and with undeviating probity and industry he built up that reputation which was the basis for his subsequent business successes,' *The Argus* wrote. Sidney moved back to Melbourne with the purchase of a store in Bourke Street in 1911. Elcon rejoined his brother and together they created a retailing behemoth, gobbling up land across the city. The centrepiece of their operation was the eight-storey Myer Emporium, which took up an entire city block in Melbourne. They also expanded into Adelaide.

Sidney had a knack for riding out the global busts. In 1921, he anticipated the postwar slump in import prices and threw a 'million pound master sale' to clear his old stock. He lost half his fortune but was able to restock with cheaper imports and trade back into profitability.

His strategy to cope with the Great Depression elevated him to national legend. In 1930, Sidney shouted Christmas lunch for ten thousand unemployed people and gave each child a present. He undertook an expensive reconstruction of his Bourke Street store in 1931 to provide jobs and boost confidence. 'All staff, himself included – except for those affected by a wages board – endured a 20 per cent pay-cut for eighteen months, so that no employee need be retrenched,' historian Anthea Hyslop wrote.

He urged the business community to promote jobs, and to donate funds to public works programs, saying, 'It is a responsibility of capital to provide work. If it fails to do this it fails to justify itself.' The Myer method in the Great Depression was the digger's own in Gallipoli: self-sacrifice and good humour.

A friend once advised him, 'You splendid spendthrift – you are wearing yourself out. You will soon have nothing left to give.' Sidney replied, 'He gets most who gives most.'

He died suddenly in 1934, at the age of fifty-six, leaving behind a business with 5300 employees and 10 per cent of his fortune donated to a trust, to assist 'the community in which I made my fortune'. More than 100 000 mourners lined the city streets to observe the funeral procession, and 25 000 people attended his funeral at Box Hill cemetery.

The young Robert Menzies, who was both Sidney's friend and his local member of parliament, wrote in 1936 that Myer was a true Australian pioneer. 'He rose from being an obscure alien peddler to being one of the great merchant princes of Australia.'

The Myer brothers were an anomaly in Australia. They had fled the late nineteenth-century Russian pogroms against the Jews when many of their countrymen had already settled in the United States. If they had delayed their migration until federation, the dictation test might have denied them entry.

When Sidney Myer shouted Christmas lunch for Melbourne's unemployed in 1930, the two main migrant groups from eastern Europe – the Russians and Poles – combined to form just 0.2 per cent of the Australian population. In the United States, they were 1.9 per cent of the population. Likewise Australia's German community was a fraction of America's – 0.3 per cent compared to 1.3 per cent. The Italians were 0.4 per cent of the Australian population, and 1.5 per cent of America's.

Australia bet the future on a single tribe, and kept passing when the world tried to deal it a more favourable hand. The English- and Welsh-born were less than 1 per cent of the US population, but almost 8 per cent of Australia's. It would take another world war to convince Australia to reclaim its true, open migrant self.

PART THREE

THE RETURN

13

WARTIME
AND OUR
MIGRANT SELF

By the 150th anniversary of European settlement in 1938, Australia had enough history to provide two contrasting studies of national development: one open, the other closed. It had dazzled in the nineteenth century, boasting the world's fastest growing economy when people and goods moved freely across the globe. But in the fifty years since the door was shut on Chinese migration Australia's economy flatlined. The poor performance can't be explained by the shocks of two depressions and the First World War, as every other rich nation managed to improve its standard of living over this difficult period. Britain grew twice as fast as Australia, and the settler societies in New Zealand, Canada and the United States grew three times as fast.

White Australia was not the only factor in the nation's decline – economics is never that simple. But it is the reason why Australia could not find new sources of wealth to replace its reliance on wool and gold. As population growth slowed, so did the opportunity to build large domestic markets for the emerging manufacturing sector. The fall was not an inevitable result of the global commodity cycle, but a loss of nerve. Australia turned its back on the world, not the other way around.

The political system was a significant part of the problem, as the reform pioneer of the nineteenth century became a perverse example of mediocrity in the twentieth century. The tension between the Labor Party's shortage of ability and the conservatives' scarcity of compassion was managed but not resolved with shotgun marriages between popular Labor leaders and the conservative establishment. Neither side had a working model for Australia, or any meaningful contribution to international affairs.

The First World War and the Great Depression broke the Labor governments of the day, and the opposition was unready to replace them. Billy Hughes took half the Labor Party across to the conservatives in 1916, while James Scullin's government split even more spectacularly in 1931. One faction, led by Joe Lyons, defected to the conservatives and formed the United Australia Party, which replaced the Nationalist Party, which in turn had replaced the Liberal Party. The other aligned itself with renegade New South Wales Labor premier Jack Lang, and the Right and the Left eventually combined to bring down the government with a vote of no confidence in November 1931. At the election the following month, the people sent Labor back to the political equivalent of year zero, with just fourteen seats – the same number it had won at the first federal election in 1901. The United Australia Party could only muster thirty-four seats in its own name, four short of a majority. Lyons ruled with the informal support of the Country Party.

When Australia did get the world's attention, it was not for the right reasons. Billy Hughes established the precedent for parochialism when he hectored allies and neighbours at the Paris Peace Conference in 1919. He helped thwart Japan's bid to be treated as an equal under the articles of the League of Nations, fearing the implications for the White Australia policy. At the Evian conference in July 1938, which failed to offer help to Germany's persecuted Jews, it was the Australian representative Thomas White who made the most callous remark: 'As we have no racial problem we are not desirous of importing one by encouraging any scheme of large-scale foreign migration.' A short version of the quote is displayed at Yad Vashem, the Holocaust memorial in Jerusalem, Australia's narrow-mindedness juxtaposed with the souls of six million dead.

The habits of political chaos and racial anxiety seemed entrenched, and as the Second World War approached there was no hint that Australia was about to snap out of its half-century-long malaise. The conservatives were in office on the eve of the war, and on cue, the government imploded. Prime Minister Joe Lyons was facing the possibility of a leadership challenge from Robert Menzies when he suddenly passed away on 7 April 1939. Country Party leader Earle Page loathed Menzies and warned the United Australia Party he would not serve in a coalition under him. But the UAP narrowly elected Menzies as its leader. Page was furious. He told parliament on 20 April that Menzies was unfit to rule, accusing him of cowardice for not fighting during the First World War, and of hastening the death of Lyons. The Country Party split, the coalition broke up and Menzies announced Australia's entry to the war on 3 September 1939 as the head of a minority government.

At the federal election on 21 September 1940, an ambivalent electorate returned a hung parliament, thus guaranteeing further instability. Menzies clung to power with the help of two Victorian independents but could not hold his riven government together. He eventually stood down on 28 August 1941 and was replaced as prime minister by the Country Party leader Arthur Fadden. The leadership of the United Australia Party went to the last man standing, Billy Hughes. Fadden was ousted less than six weeks later when the two independents crossed the floor to bring down the government. They transferred their support to John Curtin's Labor Party, avoiding the need for another election. Curtin was the nation's third wartime prime minister in just over a year.

On the surface, Australia appeared to be following the scripts of the First World War and the Great Depression, with the political system exploring every option except the national interest. But something had changed in the Australian people, and on the Labor side of politics. After half a century of isolation, the people were finally open to migrants from somewhere other than the mother country; and Labor was finally ready to govern.

The Hired Military Transport *Dunera* had all the elements of a classic Australian nightmare. As Hitler's troops marched on Paris in 1940, British authorities rounded up 2542 enemy aliens of German, Austrian and Italian stock and sent them to the Antipodes, in a wartime version of transportation. These interns were deemed too dangerous to keep in Britain while the country faced the threat of invasion, although Winston Churchill admitted the boat would include Hitler's opponents. 'I know there are a great many people affected by the orders which we have made who are the passionate enemies of Nazi Germany. I am very sorry for them, but we cannot, at the present time and under the present stress, draw all the distinctions which we should like to do,' he told the House of Commons on 4 June 1940. The 'passionate enemies' he referred to were Jewish refugees, who would be sharing cabin space with Nazi sympathisers.

The *Dunera* left Liverpool in July and docked in Melbourne on 3 September 1940 after eight weeks at sea. The first group of 200 Italians and 344 Germans disembarked and were taken to a detention camp at Tatura in Victoria's north. The remainder went to Sydney where, on 6 September, they received a trembling welcome. Australian soldiers armed with revolvers stood guard, while the police boat *Nemesis* patrolled the harbour.

The *Sydney Morning Herald* didn't know what to make of the new arrivals. 'Most of the internees seemed very young and they smiled as the trains pulled out from the wharf into the sunshine, as if they were delighted at arriving in a safe country,' the newspaper reported. 'A large proportion had grown beards during the voyage – not very vigorous growths as a rule. The result on the boyish faces was often almost comical. Many gave the "thumbs-up" sign to onlookers.'

The British troops that came with the *Dunera* were received like heroes. They were the first to step onto Australian soil since the contingent that celebrated the opening of federal parliament thirty-nine years earlier. The ranking officer, Lieutenant-Colonel William Patrick Scott, was described by the *Herald* as an 'impressive kilted figure'. He left the media with the impression that the detainees had misbehaved, but as he and his men explored Sydney that evening, the Australian troops taking the enemy aliens to Hay decided that these young men were friendly enough. One of the soldiers asked a detainee to hold his rifle while he rolled a cigarette.

There was something else about this boat. It did not provoke angry town hall meetings demanding the human cargo be sent back to where it came from, or a diplomatic row between populist Australian politicians and London. Perhaps public opinion was muted because the community thought Australia was doing its wartime duty in locking up these people. Nonetheless, the *Dunera* contained the single greatest injection of talent from overseas since the Victorian gold rush, and the example of these young men helped to smooth the path for the great postwar migration program.

Their journey to acceptance was, paradoxically, made easier by their mistreatment at the hands of the British. It quickly emerged that the *Dunera* was a 1940s version of the Second Fleet. The vessel had carried at least nine hundred more people than its capacity of sixteen hundred, including officers and crew. The detainees were squeezed onto hammocks, benches and the vomit-soaked floor of the ship. They were physically abused, and their possessions looted. The British had taken what items they needed and discarded overboard everything else, including medicines. The abuse, however, was secondary to the original sin of transportation. Of the 2542 sent to Australia, some two thousand were Jews who had originally fled to Britain to seek protection from the Nazis. Australia's governor-general, the first Earl of Gowrie, wrote to King George VI on 4 November to express his concern. 'We have received a large number of internees . . . dispatched in a great hurry,' he said. 'Some real injustices have been committed.'

Embarrassed, the British sent Scott and two others to court martial. All were found guilty, but only one man, Sergeant-Major Bowles, was sentenced to a year in prison. Churchill agreed to pay compensation to those wrongly interned, and to offer a return to Britain, or the option of joining the Australian Military Forces as labourers. A total of 913 Dunera Boys, as they became affectionately known, chose to become Australians. Artists, academics, engineers, jurists and farmers, they counted among them Franz Philipp, the art historian who was the first to pick the talent of Arthur Boyd; Fred Gruen, the economist who was prominent in the debate to remove tariffs in Australia; and Franz Stampfl, one of world's leading athletics coaches. By their example, the Dunera Boys helped to dissolve public opposition to European migration. The boat that didn't spook Australians proved to be the first tangible sign that the nation would embrace a more open program after the war.

The Second World War was a different experience for the Australian people in every way to that of the First World War. There was unity on the home front, the government was stable, the prime minister inspiring, and the economy finally rose to the challenge of hard times.

John Curtin's personal struggles had reflected those of the nation. He grew up in poverty in Melbourne in the 1890s depression, and was twice a victim of Billy Hughes' police state during the conscription debates. The road to parliament was as tortured as his successful battle to give up the grog. He lost four of the first six elections he contested between 1914 and 1931. Eventually he was elected leader of the opposition in 1935, and then prime minister of a minority government in 1941. Yet he was wracked with self-doubt, unsure he was the right man to lead the country in wartime. He worried also that the community was too blasé. 'The Commonwealth Government found it exceedingly difficult to bring Australian people to a realisation of what, after two years of war, our position had become,' he wrote in his famous new year's message for 1942 that placed the nation on a total war footing. 'Even the entry of Japan, bringing a direct threat in our own waters, was met with a subconscious view that the Americans would deal with the short-sighted, underfed and fanatical Japanese.'

The political system's greatest weakness at that point was that the division of powers between the federal and state governments favoured the states. If Australia was to function as a nation, it needed a national government with genuine authority, and leaders with genuine ability. Curtin answered the call in 1942 with the most far-reaching reforms in federal history. In February, with Singapore in Japanese hands and the first of the bombs raining down on Darwin, he took control of wages, profits and the distribution of labour, and closed non-essential industries. In May, he usurped the powers of the states on behalf of the Commonwealth and introduced a new uniform income tax, which gave his government the funds to extend the safety net that Deakin and Fisher had begun constructing before the First World War. The widow's pension was introduced in 1942, and later the first comprehensive national unemployment, sickness and special benefits scheme. In November, he asked his Labor colleagues for the right to introduce a limited form of conscription to defend Australia and its immediate neighbours New Guinea, Indonesia (then the Dutch East Indies) and the Philippines. The legislation was passed in February

1943, while Labor was still a minority government.

Curtin's difficult choices were vindicated, and Labor redeemed, at the election of 21 August that year, when the party thrashed the Billy Hughes–led United Australia Party. Labor won a record forty-nine of the seventy-four seats in the House of Representatives and control of the Senate, while the UAP was reduced to a rump, with twelve seats. Robert Menzies took on the leadership of the opposition after the election and embarked on his own Curtin-like journey to restore unity to the conservative side of politics through the creation of the modern Liberal Party in 1944.

Labor's supremacy was accompanied by a remarkable improvement in the nation's finances. Where the First World War had been funded by borrowings from London that became a debt trap in peacetime, the second was underwritten primarily by the new federal income tax and war bonds issued to a thrifty and patriotic public. The interest bill on the nation's foreign debt – both public and private – had chewed up more than 40 per cent of export income at the depths of the Great Depression. It started to fall under the Lyons government, and kept falling throughout the Second World War. It was below 10 per cent of export income by the end of the 1940s, providing a stable base from which to rebuild Australia after the war.

This horrible conflict had the unintended consequence of restoring the vitality of the Australian economy after a half-century-long stagnation. The First World War reduced national income in each year, while the Second World War delivered Australia's first genuine surge in economic activity since the 1880s. By 1943, Australia's GDP per person was 31 per cent higher than it had been in the last year of peace, 1938. All the Anglo allies had a similar experience. In Britain, national income rose, despite the Blitz, by 24 per cent; in Canada it jumped by 60 per cent; and in the United States it almost doubled, climbing by 88 per cent.

Australia's rate of unemployment was slashed from 12.5 per cent in July 1939 to 4 per cent two years later. It might have remained there, at around the same rate that applied in the First World War, if Curtin hadn't moved the economy to a total war footing. 'By June, 1943, under conditions of intensive mobilization of man-power for war purposes involuntary unemployment was practically nil,' the Bureau of Statistics reported after the war. Curtin's com-mand economy turned manufacturing into the nation's dominant employer, accounting for more than half of all private-sector jobs. The number of factory workers jumped by 210 000, comprising an additional 130 000 men and 80 000 women, producing tinned food and clothes, arms and ammunition parts, military transports and fighter planes. The only other employer to add more staff from 1939 to 1943 was the government sector, which increased its ranks by 145 000 people – an extra 80 000 women and 65 000 men. The rest of the economy shed 170 000 positions during this period.

Despite this war's much closer proximity, it did not tear the heart out of the nation in quite the same way as its predecessor. Australia sent 65 000 more service personnel overseas in the Sec-ond World War than the first – 397 000 compared to 332 000. But it lost 25 000 fewer people – only 35 000 against 60 000. Almost one in four of those who died in the Second World War fell to 'sickness, disease or injuries' while prisoners of war, mostly at the hands of the Japanese. The total casualty rate was 16 per cent compared to 64 per cent.

There were two exceptions to Australia's magnificent effort in the Second World War. First, the official habits of racial exclusion were hard to shake. The Curtin government's internment policy repeated the mistake of the *Dunera* by lumping together Australia's friends and enemies. The composition of the internment camps reflected the changing migration patterns of the inter-war years. The German-Australians had been the most affected in the First World War; in the second it was the Italian-Australians. They accounted for more than half of the seven thousand detainees, and most came from Queensland. Among them was Francesco Fantin, who was falsely accused by a Brisbane man of being a fascist.

Fantin was sent to Loveday camp in South Australia in February 1942. Under the practice of the time, prisoners were segregated according to nationality. So German Nazi and Jew were placed in one area, and Italian fascist, communist and anarchist were in another. The commandant at Loveday, Lieutenant-Colonel Edwin Theyer Dean, explained that different nationalities required a 'different method of handling and treatment'. The Germans, he wrote, were 'arrogant' and 'appreciated strict discipline and firm control'. The Italians were 'naturally temperamental, needed firm handling, but once shown who was in command had to be led like a schoolboy'. The 'subservient' Japanese, on the other hand, were 'model prisoners'.

The fascists were the dominant bloc at Loveday, and although authorities had fair warning that they were targeting Fantin, they did not move him for his own safety. On the night of 16 November 1942, Fantin was knocked to the ground by Giovanni Bruno Casotti, a fascist recently transported from Western Australia, and died in the military hospital later that evening. Casotti claimed he had been offended when Fantin called him a bastard, and pleaded guilty to manslaughter. The Crown prosecutor Mr Chamberlain said at the sentencing hearing that new evidence had come to light to support a charge of murder, but officials did not want to pursue the matter for fear that it might provoke a public outcry about the internment policy; Casotti was given just two years' hard labour.

But community sympathy was with the victim, and church and other groups eventually persuaded the Curtin government to modify the detention policy. By 1944, four thousand Italian-Australians had won back their freedom, working in the so-called Civil Aliens Corps, which plugged holes in the war economy. Many were deployed to the cane fields of North Queensland, putting them back where they had started.

The second reminder of Australia's prejudice was the attitude of the locals to the United States service personnel who were based in the country. Almost one million Americans passed through the Australia over the course of the war, and their spending power was a valuable source of stimulus for the economy. But they were also a reminder of how far Australia had fallen from its former perch on top of the global income ladder. The better-paid Yanks aroused the most basic jealousy of the diggers in the competition for local women, and the rivalry exploded into a full-scale riot in Brisbane on the night of 26 November 1942. Outnumbered, the Americans called for reinforcements, and in the subsequent scuffle one of the armed military police who arrived at the scene took the life of Australian war hero Edward Webster. Over that night and the next, scores of Americans and Australians were injured, making the Battle of Brisbane one of the worst riots in history. The heavy hand of the Commonwealth censor kept the detail of fighting from the papers at the time, which prevented further clashes.

Despite these disappointing reminders of Australian parochialism, the nation exceeded its own expectations during the Second World War. The home front was more cohesive and the diggers had stopped the Japanese, a people whom the founding fathers of the federation feared would overwhelm Australia with their numbers. In the POW camps, Australian soldiers shared their rations with a fastidious egalitarianism, and reportedly had a higher survival rate than the class-conscious British and the individualistic Americans. Yet it is a single failed campaign in 1915 that virtually monopolises the national commemoration of war. Gallipoli has become so dominant that it has erased the disunity at home of the First World War as well as the triumphs of the second. The most puzzling aspect of the latter is that Curtin himself is written into the background. He doesn't have the same bipartisan status as Churchill as a wartime leader, even though he was at least his equal during the conflict. Today, the achievements of Curtin's government would be less well remembered than those of Don Bradman's Invincibles, who thrashed England in the 1948 test tour.

The Second World War set up Australia for a return to prosperity in the second half of the twentieth century. The lessons that both sides of politics drew from it, and the depression which preceded it, was that Australia could not achieve security or guarantee a high standard of living through isolation. It was finally time to open the door to migrants from across Europe, including from the countries Australia fought with.

One of the forgotten authors of Australia's postwar migration was a conservative politician, Percy Spender. He was the minister for the army under Robert Menzies, and a member of the bipartisan War Advisory Council under John Curtin. In 1943, he broke the ice on the debate by warning that Australia could no longer rely on the mother country for people. He noted the cultural mix of the United States, where 'not more than 30 per cent, of the population is derived from British stock'. If Australia wanted a larger population, it had to follow the American example of diversity. 'Where, then, are we to get our people from? The answer is that they must come – if we seek them in sufficiently large numbers – very largely from eastern European and Mediterranean countries.' But we could not invite people to make a new life here while abusing them as 'aliens'. 'If we really want more people, we must change our attitude towards immigrants from foreign countries. We must encourage such people to become Australians, and to fit into our way of life. They must not be subject to the gibe that they were originally aliens, as is often the case now, even after immigrants have been here for years.'

Curtin prepared the public for the postwar shift following his tour of the United States and Britain in 1944. That trip had underlined allied discomfort with the White Australia policy. The sharpest exchange came at a press conference before more than one hundred American and foreign correspondents in Washington on Anzac Day. Asked if Australia would follow the American lead and ease restrictions on Chinese and Indian immigration, Curtin replied, 'We have not altered any of our laws. All I can say on this subject is that I would not like to have seen 100 000 Japanese in Australia at the time of Pearl Harbor.'

In London on 5 May he declared that Australia expected 'a rapid addition to her numbers' after the war. 'We shall welcome migrants who are prepared to work and who believe that advancement of social standards should come from their own endeavours.'

An Indian journalist then asked him about his 'views on Asiatic migration'. Again he hedged. 'The words "White Australia" have not appeared in any Commonwealth statute. Immigration restrictions are solely designed to guard against cheap slave labour.'

It was essentially the same message Billy Hughes had given the world after the First World War, but without the snarl. Curtin felt that public opinion wasn't ready for Asian migration after the treatment the diggers had received at the hands of the Japanese. But one important change had already been conceded to the White Australia policy. The postwar migration program could not rely on the British alone.

On his return home, Curtin told reporters that Australia had to look beyond the mother country because he had seen 'no evidence that great numbers of British people were anxious to leave home'. They would be too busy rebuilding Britain.

With the opposition offering encouragement on European migration, Curtin prepared an ambitious plan to be released after the war ended. As well as looking beyond Britain for new recruits, he abandoned Labor's hardline policy that no money should be spent to encourage migration while there was unemployment at home. The last time assisted passage had made such overwhelming sense to the political class in Australia was in the late 1830s.

After Curtin suffered a major heart attack on 3 November 1944, the job of preparing the nation for mass migration was passed on to one of the loyal Labor men who had opposed the Italian influx in the 1920s, the acting prime minister, Frank Forde. The Queensland son of Irish migrants, he was an appropriate spokesman for the policy shift. 'We must make a realistic approach to the population problem,' he told parliament on 16 November. 'Australia has an area of 3 000 000 square miles, but carries only 7 300 000 people. In pre-war days, the sharp fall of the birth-rate pointed to a decline of the Australian population, within the next three decades.' Increasing the birth rate alone would not sustain Australia, he explained. 'We must also be realists in regard to the necessity for a scientific migration policy.' Forde said Australia must avoid 'a repetition of the mistakes' made after the last war, alluding to the failed land schemes. 'As our sister dominions and other countries will become keenly interested in securing migrants in the postwar period, Australia will have to bring its plans to the blue-print stage before the end of the war; otherwise, we shall be left behind in the quest for suitable migrants.'

The blueprint was settled in a 'secret' memo dated 11 December 1944: 'A vigorous policy of white alien immigration, complete with an effort to make the individual alien feel he is regarded an asset; assistance to immigrants to meet part of passage costs that may be necessary to induce good flow; a central body of unofficial groups interested in migration to be formed in each State to assist with reception, placement and after-care of migrants, alien and British alike; it should be made clear that Commonwealth immigration policy is based on social, economic and cultural grounds and not on any assumption of racial superiority.'

Curtin had been too sick to announce German's surrender on 9 May 1945. He passed away on 5 July, less than two months before Japan's surrender on 2 September. An estimated hundred thousand people attended his funeral in Perth: one-third of the city's entire population. Among the pallbearers were Liberal Party leader Robert Menzies and Country Party leader Arthur Fadden, testament to a rare Australian leader who was admired across the political spectrum.

Forde was prime minister for a week before Labor elected another son of the 1890s depression, Ben Chifley, as Curtin's successor. As Curtin had transformed from pacifist to wartime leader, it seemed fitting that Chifley, who attacked the Bruce–Page government for putting 'dagoes before heroes' in the 1920s, should become the prime minister to welcome the olive waves.

14

RETURN
TO MELBOURNE:
THE POSTWAR WAVES

The postwar migration program was the greatest social experiment since the 1850s, and it sought to recreate through government planning the diversity achieved through the happy circumstance of gold a century earlier. Within a generation it would turn the Australia that John Curtin described during the war as 'a British land of one race and one tongue' into a European country of many races and mother tongues.

Labor MP Arthur Calwell, who became the nation's first immigration minister, told Ben Chifley in 1944 that he was determined to create a 'heterogeneous society'. 'A society,' he wrote to the then treasurer, 'where Irishness and Roman Catholicism would be as acceptable as Englishness and Protestantism; where an Italian background would be as acceptable as a Greek, a Dutch or any other'. This ambition may well have been informed by his own upbringing as a child of a minority tribe. Calwell's maternal grandparents were exiles of the Irish potato famines who moved to Victoria in the late 1840s, while his Victorian-born father was a child of the gold rush.

Calwell's public argument for European migration was ingenious. It took the nation's perpetual fear of foreign invasion and reframed it. Australia would need foreigners to guard against invasion, he told parliament on 2 August 1945, in the dying days of the war in the Pacific. 'We may have only [the] next 25 years in which to make the best possible use of our second chance to survive. Our first requirement is additional population. We need it for reasons of defence and for the fullest expansion of our economy. We can increase our 7 000 000 by an increased birth-rate and by a policy of planned immigration within the limits of our existing legislation.'

The emphasis on the 'existing legislation' was deliberate. Although the program would be radical from the perspective of recent Australian history, it would not impress the international community. Calwell was merely restoring European migrants to their original position as 'white', before the restrictions of the inter-war period. The White Australia policy would still prohibit the entry of the 'yellow'- and 'black'-skinned, and deny Australia's Indigenous population even the most basic right to be counted in the national census. The global consensus after the horror of Hitler's gas chambers was that institutional racism had no place in the postwar world and by retaining the White Australia policy, successive Labor and coalition governments would risk diplomatic isolation even as they were opening the door to European migration.

What both sides of politics in Australia did appreciate was the economic urgency for large intakes. War, depression and racial selection had prematurely aged the nation. In 1947, there were 120 000 fewer boys and girls aged ten to twenty-four years than there had been just ten years earlier in 1937. Left unchecked, this shortfall would have choked an Australian reconstruction as the nation ran out of workers. The gap can be explained by the absence of new arrivals, which in normal times would have offset the casualties of war and a lower birth rate. By 1947, the overseas-born population had fallen to less than one in ten, which was a record low for the migrant nation. Of this tiny proportion, more than half were from England, which had not happened since the earliest days of convict settlement. In fact, there were 110 000 fewer migrants living in Australia in 1947 than there had been at federation, during which time the population had doubled from 3.774 million to 7.579 million.

The Labor government of Ben Chifley had to counter trade union resistance to the entry of Europe's displaced youth. The Liberal opposition, led by Robert Menzies, had an easier case to make, because its constituency of returned servicemen and middle-class professionals was more open to migration than the workingman. The diggers in particular were returning home with a sense of kinship with the Europeans who had resisted the Nazis. The Greeks were a particular favourite, having sheltered Australian troops.

At the 1946 election, held before the effects of the postwar program were felt, voters might have detected these subtle differences in the campaign launch speeches of the two leaders. Labor's Ben Chifley kept up the appearance of a British bias in the program, even though the first wave of postwar migrants would contain more Italians and Germans than English and Scots. 'Today Australia has become the great bastion of the British-speaking race south of the Equator,' the prime minister said. 'Strategically and economically, our country has assumed a position in the Pacific on behalf of the British Commonwealth of Nations of such importance that development and responsibility go hand in hand.'

Menzies criticised the government for not moving quickly enough to attract migrants. 'It [Labor] has adopted the view that immigration is undesirable so long as we have local problems of an industrial and economic kind to solve. To this we retort that if we wait for economic perfection before building up our population we shall someday find that our lack of population has invited an attack in which our entire economy will be destroyed. Every one of us in this country is either a migrant himself or the descendant of one. We therefore of all people should be prepared to welcome into our community all those who can by their work and citizenship contribute to the strength of this land.'

Menzies had presented as the more optimistic leader, but the people stuck with the party that had seen them through the war. Labor was re-elected in September 1946 with forty-three of the parliament's seventy-five seats – six fewer than the Curtin landslide, but with a largely unchanged primary vote of 49.7 per cent.

By its very nature, the first wave of the postwar program would seek migrants who had been displaced by conflict. Australia recruited from the continent's refugee camps, and were competing with the United States and Canada in the migration marketplace. There was a pressing need to provide assistance to the Jews who had survived the Holocaust, but this immediately hit the pothole of domestic Australian prejudice.

'We are not compelled to accept the unwanted of the world at the dictate of the United Nations or anyone else,' Henry 'Jo' Gullett, the Liberal member for the Melbourne electorate of Henty, told parliament in November 1946, just two months after the election. 'Neither should Australia be the dumping ground for people whom Europe itself, in the course of 2000 years, has not been able to absorb. I am amazed that a Labor Government, of all governments, should sponsor the kind of immigration that is going on at the present time. I am not anti-Semitic. Indeed, very few Australians are.' Yet he went on to describe 'many of the Jews who came to Australia in the year before the war and since the outbreak of the war' as 'notorious exploiters of labour. They set up "sweat shops", and in the records of the industrial courts one may read their names. They have cornered houses, and evaded income tax.'

The most vocal opponent of Jewish migration on the left was Jack Lang, former New South Wales premier and now independent member for the Sydney electorate of Reid. He claimed that wealthy Jews were involved in a 'refugee racket'. They used their money to gain valuable berths on migrant ships at the expense of humble British migrants. 'But, as soon as anybody criticizes this immigration preference, those in authority burst into tears for the poor victims of fascism. They may have been the victims of fascism. Everybody knows that there are millions and millions of victims of fascism. But only a very small proportion of those victims are wealthy and have powerful friends. Why is this Government interested in these victims who are wealthy and who have powerful friends?'

Gullett and Lang were minority voices in the parliament. In the community, the sentiment was mixed. The NSW president of the Returned and Services League, Ken Bolton, was the dial-a-quote of his day, ready with a quick putdown of the Jew who would secure a property ahead of a returned digger. The president of the influential organisation the Australian Natives' Association, Joseph Lynch, said he was 'seriously concerned that Australia was to be made a tip for European refuse'.

The parochial media reverted to type. The Jewish refugees became the latest cartoonish enemy of social cohesion, replacing the Italian migrants of the 1920s, who had replaced the Irish Australians of the conscription debates, who had replaced the Chinese diggers, who had replaced the Irish orphan girls. When a Dutch-flagged ship carrying Jewish refugees was preparing to sail from Shanghai to Sydney, the capital city tabloids informed their readers, without any evidence, that three thousand people were coming on three boats. The correct figure was seven hundred on one boat, and Calwell demanded a retraction from Sydney's *Daily Telegraph* and Melbourne's *Sun News-Pictorial*. But the media wasn't finished yet. When the boat docked on 16 March 1947, the *Courier-Mail* declared: '700 Jews Arrive, Bring Expensive Furs and Jewels'. The refugees carried 'thousands of pounds worth of personal belongings, including jewels, furs, and expensive cameras'. The cameras were rated more newsworthy than the gas chambers they had escaped.

At these tipping points in a migration debate, leaders can turn a media scare into a deep-seated community prejudice. Australia was more than 90 per cent local-born, of essentially Anglo-Celtic stock, and the public was poised between re-engagement with the world and wariness of the damaged people who were coming from Europe. Opinion polls were in their infancy, so the question of whether Australia was prepared for Jewish migration was not put. But the answer would soon be in the affirmative as a Labor government and Liberal opposition argued for the door to be open. Calwell took on every critic, with prompt backing from Menzies, who reaffirmed his party's support for Jewish migration. Between them Calwell and Menzies encouraged community leaders to fly the flag for openness, of whom the most prominent was Melbourne's Catholic archbishop Daniel Mannix.

As the first migrant victims of discrimination in Australia, Catholics were a valuable ally for the Jewish refugees. In an editorial published in February 1947, the *Catholic Weekly* warned 'there has been a dangerous growth of anti-Semitism in Australia over the past year or so'. It was important to stamp it out now before it polarised the country. 'We have not yet a *Der Sturmer* [a Nazi tabloid] in our midst, chanting a hymn of hate against every Jew and all Jewish influence, but we have thousands of otherwise rational Australians who are prepared to curse Hitler for everything except what he did to the Jews. Some are even prepared to give him credit for it.'

Calwell literally debated his opponents into submission. He hectored, he cajoled, and within six years of the bipartisan program, success could be measured by the arrival of fifty thousand migrants from Hitler's killing fields of Poland. However, Calwell did make one unannounced concession to the bigots. Each migrant boat that came on his watch after that poorly received Dutch-flagged vessel would contain a mix of races. As he explained later: 'We had to insist that half the accommodation in these wretched vessels must be sold to non-Jewish people. It would have created a great wave of anti-Semitism and would have been electorally disastrous for the Labor Party had we not made this decision.' It is arguable that his caution was misplaced, as the community proved more welcoming than even the most optimist politician of the day would have hoped. The largest wave of migration since the gold rush carried another resonance of the 1850s, as the city where most new arrivals went was Melbourne.

New arrivals tend to go where there is an established population from their own tribe, and at the end of the Second World War that was anywhere but Melbourne. Western Australia had twice as many migrants as the national average, with almost 20 per cent of the state's population born overseas; Queensland had the most prominent Italian community; and New South Wales was home to more Greeks than Victoria and Queensland combined. Of all the Australian ports, Sydney was the best known overseas.

'Sydney is the second largest "white" city in the British Empire,' Aldwyn Abberley wrote in his popular book *A Manual for Emigrants*. It was a 'miniature Manhattan' and the people who crowded its streets were 'as smart and fast-moving' as their kin in London. 'Every second car is a gigantic six-cylinder limousine. Even dustmen have the appearance of individuals who can afford their hot-shower baths every day and a new suit every year.'

Yet Melbourne proved the most popular destination for five of the six largest non-English-speaking waves after the war – the Italians, the Greeks, the Dutch, the Germans and the Poles. Only the Yugoslavs defied the trend, with a slightly larger number choosing Sydney over Melbourne. The postwar boom couldn't make Victoria the most populous state again – it had fallen too far behind New South Wales to catch up – but it did restore Melbourne to its former position as the migrant capital of Australia. Victoria's population grew faster than New South Wales' in each year from 1950 to 1967. The last time this had happened over the course of an entire decade was in the 1850s.

Melbourne had an economic advantage over Sydney as the nation's manufacturing capital. Manufacturing had become the dominant employer in John Curtin's wartime economy, and it drove the postwar reconstruction, accounting for 25 per cent of the nation's jobs. Propped up by tariffs to keep out foreign goods, and with the centralised wage-fixing system to maintain high incomes, the assembly lines and factories making Australian cars and white goods became an industrial melting pot for blue-collar local and migrant workers.

Melbourne had another, less well-understood economic reason for its migrant renaissance: cheap housing. Incredibly, the property bust of the 1890s was still playing out all these decades later. In the inner-city suburb of Carlton, where the Italian wave was most concentrated, real house prices, after adjusting for inflation, would not return to their late 1880s levels until the early 1980s.

Melbourne also received a publicity boost from staging the 1956 Olympic Games. The forgotten capital of a long-lost gold rush had re-entered the global consciousness as a city of cheery sporting enthusiasts even though Melbourne was not physically equipped to host the event. There was a shortage of hotel accommodation and visitors were billeted to Melbourne families. But it was the first televised games, and it sent a message of welcome to would-be migrants to Australia. Dubbed the Friendly Games, Melbourne was also first to have all athletes marching together in the closing ceremony, an idea that had come from a young Chinese-Australian man, John Wing, an apprentice carpenter.

Neither Arthur Calwell nor Robert Menzies planned for their hometown to dominate. Rather, they had intended to steer the new arrival away from the cities. The nation-building propaganda of the time focused on the Snowy Mountains hydro-electric and irrigation scheme. It was a powerful symbol, uniting the young men of the continent in the postwar equivalent of the goldfields: foreign mates digging together. But once again the reality of inland development

never matched the rhetoric, and the scheme only employed a fraction of the migrant workforce. Agriculture had less than 10 per
cent of the nation's jobs. The retail sector employed twice as many
people, adding yet another reason for migrants to cluster in the cities as this was the sector that typically provided work for the young
women coming from Europe.

Manufacturing had a similar economic effect to gold, concen-
trating the European wave in Melbourne and to a lesser extent
Sydney. This left cities like Adelaide and Perth with above-average
shares of British migrants. The postwar wave missed the less industrialised Queensland, and by 1971 the state had become the least
diverse on the mainland. British Australia was still in the ascendancy outside the nation's two biggest cities, and the emotional
appeal of White Australia remained undiminished for the politicians who grew up with it.

The loudest echo of the gold rush was heard in 1949, just two
years after Labor formally introduced its assisted-passage program. Arthur Calwell picked a fight with Robert Menzies over the
fate of wartime refugees from Asia with the political intention of
reaffirming Labor's status as the party of White Australia. Like a
colonial politician, Calwell drew the colour line between the welcome European diggers and the unwelcome Chinese prospectors
and assumed he had the public on side. But the immigration minister didn't count on Menzies defending the refugees, and the fallout
from their argument would leave the door ajar for an unexpected
intake from Asia within the confines of the White Australia policy.

During the war, Australia had given sanctuary to some 4400
refugees from China, Malaysia and the Dutch East Indies (now
Indonesia). By 1947, an estimated 550 wanted to remain in Australia. Calwell declared he had 'not one ounce of sympathy' for these
people and demanded they leave – even those who had married

Australians – because they had defied his lawful order to go back home. The opposition took the side of the refugees and peppered the minister with questions on individual cases. That parliamentary scrutiny yielded the White Australia policy's most infamous quote. Calwell conceded that a Chinese man had been wrongly targeted for deportation, but went on, with an attempt at humour, 'The gentleman's name is Wong. There are many Wongs in the Chinese community, but I have to say – and I am sure that the honorable member for Balaclava will not mind me doing so – that "two Wongs do not make a White".' By White, Calwell was referring to Thomas White, the conservative member for Balaclava, who had, by coincidence, been the minister representing the Lyons government at the Evian conference. White was sitting in the chamber, but had not asked the question.

Calwell fell pitifully short of his desire for a 'heterogeneous society' in this debate. He did not want the assisted-passage scheme for Europeans to be misread as an invitation to Asia, and to make this distinction clear, Calwell decided to publicly humiliate any wartime refugees who overstayed their welcome. Mother-of-eight Annie O'Keefe provided him with an ideal scapegoat.

Annie was a war widow. She had been born in the Dutch East Indies island of Celebes in 1908, and her husband, Samuel Jacob, was a Dutch intelligence officer. They were evacuated with their seven children on the HMAS *Warrnambool* in September 1942, and an eighth child was born in Australia. Samuel returned to battle and was killed in 1944. In 1947, Victorian John William O'Keefe offered to marry Annie, trusting that this would allow her and the children to remain in Australia. But in early 1949, an election year, Calwell ordered Annie and her eight children – including the youngest, born in Australia – to leave the country by 28 February. 'Mrs. O'Keefe and her children are not important,' he told parliament. 'It is the precedent that is important. If we allow these people to stay we shall have to leave the floodgates open to any Asiatics who want to come here.' He did not want Europeans and Asians mating on Australian soil. 'We can have a white Australia, we can have a black Australia, but a mongrel Australia is impossible.'

When the High Court ruled in Annie O'Keefe's favour in March that year, Calwell retaliated by asking parliament to give him explicit powers to deport her, and anyone else who didn't want to leave. He called it the War-time Refugees Removal Bill. In addressing the Australian Natives' Association, a group he had condemned two years earlier for its anti-Semitism, Calwell said the High Court had threatened the government's right to decide who comes to this country. 'I am determined that the flag of White Australia will not be lowered. So long as the Labor Party remains in power we shall insist on maintaining our sovereign rights to determine what people shall make up our population.'

The opposition supported the White Australia policy, but refused to be bluffed by Calwell's appeal to race pride. Menzies criticised Calwell for his disregard of morality and law. 'In the name of common sense what harm would have come to Australia or to a policy supported by every Australian political party if Mrs. O'Keefe and her children had been allowed to remain here for some years longer, or – let's face it – even permanently?' Menzies thought the title of Calwell's bill was 'internationally offensive'. He was concerned that it placed the White Australia policy at risk of challenge in the United Nations. On a personal level, he thought the pursuit of the O'Keefe family was vindictive. 'There will be a widespread impression in this country that the Minister, by not making an exception in the case of the O'Keefes is not only taking away from them at one stroke the fruits of their successful appeal to the law of this country and to the High Court as its interpreter, but is also engaging in a singularly unpleasant process of victimization.'

The legislation was passed in July 1949, and in August the NSW police began arresting Chinese refugees who had not heeded Calwell's order to go back to where they came from. But condemnation

of Calwell was building. Victoria's Liberal premier, Thomas Holl-
way, said Calwell's 'blundering policy had already built up a solid
hatred against Australia in the countries to the near north'. It
would take 'years of wise administration before Australia could
again establish good relationships' with those he had insulted. The
High Court ordered a freeze on all deportations so it could hear an
appeal from thirty-eight Chinese men. Meanwhile, the secretary
of Calwell's own department, Tas Heyes, exercised his discretion.
He did not pass on the legislation to the governor-general for royal
assent, placing the law in limbo as the government prepared for
another election. It was at this point that history both repeated,
and changed. White Australia would endure for another generation, but the race card that Calwell played rebounded against him.

No prime minister has faced the electorate with a prouder record
of economic achievement. Ben Chifley's government had surpassed
its targets for migration and growth. From a modest start of 11 000
in 1947, net migration jumped to 53 000 in 1948 and then soared
to 147 000 in 1949. In each of the first three years of the assisted-
passage program, unemployment fell, from 2.9 per cent, to 2 per
cent and then 1.5 per cent, removing the risk of an immediate trade
union backlash. Public opinion quickly moved in favour of the program. As early as 1949, a majority of voters (54 per cent) thought
non-British migration from the continent of Europe would be good
for the country. One third (32 per cent) thought it would be bad,
while the rest were undecided. Confident in his national planning
regime, Chifley now set an ambitious population target: ten million by 1957, and, with a Henry Hayter–like flourish, double that
number within a lifetime.

Robert Menzies used his campaign to call out Arthur Calwell's
inflexibility on the Asian refugee question. 'We will continue to
maintain Australia's settled immigration policy, known as "The

White Australia policy"; well justified as it is on grounds of national homogeneity and economic standards. At the same time we believe in humane and commonsense ministration. All cases of aliens resident in Australia should be considered, not as if the law allowed no human discretion but in the light of the circumstances of each case.'

Both sides were talking up the future, but the incumbent was weighed down by unpopular policies of petrol rationing and bank nationalisation. The labour movement had also fractured. A national coal strike in the winter of 1949 was broken when Chifley sent in the troops to work the open-cut mines. Meanwhile, the opposition lobbed cash at the electorate. Menzies promised to remove petrol rationing and offered mothers a child endowment for their first-born. But he also stoked voter fears of communism. The Cold War between the United States and the Soviet Union was underway, and Menzies was keen to paint Labor as socialist, and tainted by association with the Reds.

Australians were ready for change, and they followed the example of the British, who had not long thrown out Winston Churchill's wartime government. At the previous election, Labor had won a majority of seats in every state with the exception of Menzies' home state of Victoria. In this election, the coalition prevailed in every state, and for the first time claimed more than 50 per cent of the primary vote. The parliament had expanded from 75 to 121 seats for this election to account for the growing population, and almost all those new seats were taken by Liberal or Country Party candidates. The final seat count was 55 Liberal and 19 Country Party for a coalition total of 74, while Labor had 47. Menzies, the man who could not hold his government together in war, was now trusted to manage the postwar reconstruction.

Despite this decisive shift to the right, there was more continuity between the Chifley and Menzies governments than is often assumed. Menzies largely accepted Labor's model for national development, and he signalled this bipartisanship by reappointing

Labor's chief economic adviser Nugget Coombs. In time, coalition policy would creep towards its own form of socialism as industry protection, originally crafted by Alfred Deakin and extended by both Labor and conservative governments, was pushed to the point of unviability. But the immediate consequence of the change of government was at the margin of Australia's ethnic face. In May 1950, the High Court finally overturned Calwell's War-time Refugees Removal Act. The new immigration minister in Menzies' government, Harold Holt, allowed all remaining wartime refugees to stay in Australia, and allowed Japanese war brides to enter.

Although the White Australia policy would remain under Menzies, the colour line was no longer rigidly enforced. The removal of the anti-refugee bill and the coalition's subsequent program encouraging Asians students to study in Australia saw the Chinese-born population increase for the first time since the 1880s. Their number almost doubled from six thousand in 1947 to more than ten thousand by 1954 and barely a whisper of protest was heard. The first quiet step to a Eurasian future had already been taken before the full force of the olive waves had been felt.

15

THE SUBURBAN
DREAM: STABILITY
AND STAGNATION

The Europeans were accepted by the economy almost immediately, with work on arrival. Australia enjoyed full, or near-full
employment throughout the 1950s and '60s, and this helped the
newcomers join the locals on the middle of the income ladder.
But cultural acceptance was slow in coming. Although a majority
of people thought European migration would be good for Australia, there was resistance to particular groups. The most revealing
survey, taken in March 1951, tested community attitudes towards
what would become the five largest non-English intakes: the Italians, Greeks, Yugoslavs, Germans and the Dutch. A clear line was
drawn between north and south. The most popular source country was the Netherlands, which secured the favour of 81 per cent
of those who responded. Less popular were wartime allies from
Greece (only 43 per cent of Australians wanted them) and Yugosla-
via (34 per cent). It is in the attitude to migrants from the former
enemies Germany and Italy where the preconceptions of White
Australia were most obvious. The Germans saw their fair skin
reflected in an approval rating of 55 per cent, double the score for
the Italians (27 per cent).

Bipartisan support for mass migration had begun to fray in 1951. In April that year Robert Menzies called an early election after the Labor-controlled Senate refused to pass the coalition's banking legislation. Late in the campaign, the opposition leader Ben Chifley accused the coalition of going too far with the assisted-passage program. 'The Labor Party stresses that the plans of the Menzies Government on immigration differ from those of the last Labor Government in that proper regard is not now being paid to the numbers and the selection of those migrants likely to make the best contribution to the solution of our housing and economic problems.'

Menzies did not take the bait, saying he would continue the program in which his opponent had, until recently taken 'great pride' 'This policy,' the prime minister told voters, 'involves constant effort'. Menzies prevailed at the election, but migration would continue to attract sniper fire from Labor whenever unemployment crept up.

The early 1950s was a period of extreme volatility for the Australian economy. The Korean War had created a shortage in wool, and the boom in prices led to a surge in domestic inflation that threatened to cut short the postwar reconstruction. Inflation topped 20 per cent in 1951 and the economy fell into recession the next year, but the coalition treasurer Arthur Fadden passed that policy test with a tough budget that knocked inflation on the head. When the recovery came in 1953, inflation did not return, and the economy cruised for the remainder of the decade. But the next deep recession in 1961 once again threatened the bipartisanship on migration.

In that year's election campaign, Arthur Calwell was opposition leader, and he took Labor back to the 1920s with the mantra that migrants were not welcome while the economy was weak. Labor, he said, 'will resume large scale immigration when it restores full employment'. The opinion polls at the time suggested Calwell's race card would yield political gold. By 1961, 44 per cent of voters wanted to reduce the migrant intake, while only 15 per cent wanted to increase it.

Labor won the popular vote at the 1961 election, but fell one seat short of defeating the coalition government. Interestingly, the state that defied the national swing to Labor and saved Menzies was his own Victoria. It was here that migration was most popular, and Labor most divided because of its most recent split; the combination of these two unrelated factors secured not just the long conservative rule but probably ensured the postwar program as well.

Australia's ethnic face would have been radically different if Calwell had become prime minister at that election. The 1950s had been the Italian decade, with the community almost doubling in number from 120 000 in 1954 to 230 000 in 1961. The 1960s would be the decade when the largest number of Greeks and Yugoslavs arrived. Each community doubled in size between 1961 and 1971; the Greeks from 80 000 to 160 000 and the Yugoslavs from 50 000 to 130 000. Whether Calwell would have accepted a large portion of these intakes cannot be known. But it seems likely that my mother would not have been invited to migrate to Australia in 1962 if Labor were in power that year.

My family's story is typical of the most consistent pattern of migration, in which the men arrive first, and then, after a decade or so, women are recruited to help close the gender gap. The European wave started out as masculine as the Victoria of the gold rush, and by 1954, the Italian- and Greek-born populations were two-thirds male. My father had arrived in 1950, when public opinion preferred German over Greek migrants. His one-month journey from the Greek Island of Ithaca for Australia was almost worthy of Ulysses. He took the local ferry from Piraeus, the main port of Athens, to Port Said in Egypt via Lebanon and Cyprus. At Port Said he checked into his first ever hotel, before boarding the Greek-flagged migrant ship the *Cyrenia* five days later. There were eight hundred migrants on board and all had purchased second- or third-class tickets. The Greek captain didn't want to see the first-class deck go to waste so he grabbed his passenger list and called out the Greek names on it. He told the startled passengers that he was giving them a free upgrade. Dad still had a rough trip. He caught chicken pox and was quarantined from his fellow first-class travellers.

When the *Cyrenia* docked in Melbourne on 26 May, the media was in its element. *The Argus* reported that two hundred Greeks on the wharf had tried to invade the ship. 'About 10 Customs officers formed a human barrier, and forced the people back behind the wooden barriers protecting the wharf. In a desperate effort to get off the ship to meet the waiting people, many of the 800 Greek migrants aboard the *Cyrenia* lowered their luggage over the ship's side on ropes.'

Dad shook his head when I read him the passage. According to him, there were only fifty Greeks on board, and as first-class passengers, they were allowed to disembark ahead of the others. The journalist appears to have confused the small Greek contingent with the much larger group of Italians on board. But who could really blame him? To an Australian eye in 1950, the southern Europeans all looked the same.

When my father got off the boat, his expectations were modest. He was chasing a better life, like all of his peers, and was astounded by Australia's wealth compared to Greece. His father was a fisherman, and one of the poorest men in a poor village. The family lived in what the colonial statistician in Victoria would have described as a one-room house. It was no bigger than a modern bathroom.

Dad found work immediately in Melbourne as a kitchen hand at a city cafe. He didn't last long, but there was always another job to go to. He washed dishes, served spaghetti, sold fruit and sat at the conveyor belt at the Rosella factory. He sent money back to his family every fortnight, and repaid his relatives for his 170-pound trip after two ferocious years of thrift. In 1955, he joined the Victorian Railways, where he remained for the next thirty-five years until poor health forced him to an early retirement.

By contrast, my mother had no relatives in Australia to pay her fare. She had been raised in war in the northern Greek village of Nestorio, with the first seven of years of her life straddling the German occupation and the Greek Civil War. Her father was a builder, and as a young girl she learned to mix cement with a shovel and a bucket of water. When her parents took their one holiday to Australia in the summer of 1980–81, I watched in bemused awe as father and daughter laid a concrete path along the side of our house. I often asked my grandparents why they sent their teenage daughter halfway around the world. The question always opened a wound. My grandmother didn't want her to go, but they were poor, she would sigh, and when the Menzies government offered free air travel to the girls in the village in 1962, Mum was asked to take the leap of faith on behalf of the family.

Her sponsor in Melbourne was a Greek lady who ran a fish'n' chip shop in Victoria Street, Richmond, in the heart of Arthur Calwell's electorate. Mum shared two rooms above the shop with eight other homesick Greek girls. They all cried, every night. Each morning the fish'n'chip proprietor took her young charges to local factories for job interviews. By the time Mum met my father, she was working at the Ithaca House on Elizabeth Street. Dad swept her off her feet, proposed and then showed her the house he wanted to buy for them.

Support for migration was at its lowest ebb when she arrived, but within two years, the unemployment rate was back below 2 per cent and the published polls reflected that in renewed approval for the Menzies program. By 1964, public opinion had swung decisively in favour of more migration, with 29 per cent wanting to increase the intake and only 21 per cent wanting to reduce it. By 1966, the assisted passage of young women from Greece had virtually closed the gender gap in that community, although it persisted in the Italian community.

There is a myth, shaped by the 1960s movie *They're a Weird Mob*, that the European men charmed the local-born women while the local-born men were more distrustful of the new arrivals. This romantic notion of integration through mixed marriage, and resistance due to economic competition, is not borne out by the opinion polls of the time. In fact, the reverse is the case. The voters who were most likely to express concern about migration were women, while it was the men who were first to support the program. This political gender gap remained until the early 1990s and can be explained by the relatively low rates of female participation in work in the 1960s, '70s and into the '80s. Mothers who stayed at home to raise young children had, by definition, less contact with migrants than their partners. Because they were less familiar with migrants, they were more likely to be concerned.

This is not to suggest that the local-born workingman was free of bigotry. Many children of non-English-speaking migrants would likely have a memory of fathers who were picked on at work. Many would themselves have been subjected to taunts at school, or in cases such as my own, regular beltings. Yet the postwar program succeeded, in the end, because it restored the link between migration and economic growth.

The overseas-born population trebled from just under 750 000 in 1947 to 2.55 million in 1971, and the Europeans outnumbered the British across the country. The migrants' share of the total population doubled from 10 to 20 per cent. In that period, the Australian economy grew faster than its peers for the first time since the 1860s and 1870s. GDP per person rose by 84 per cent, compared to Canada's 77 per cent, the United States' 72 per cent, Great Britain's 66 per cent and New Zealand's 48 per cent.

Unemployment, the scourge of the first half century of White Australia, averaged less than 2 per cent over the course of the 1950s and '60s; about half the rate in the United States at the time. With a stronger economy, the local-born men came to associate their higher standard of living with the new arrivals who they worked alongside. This, in turn, reduced the scope for politicians who wanted to stifle the program with appeals to protect Australian jobs.

Menzies was a more generous host than his Labor opponents, and contemporary Liberal politicians might be shocked that their mantras on border protection sound more like Calwell than the founder of their party. Although Menzies was implacably British in his outlook, he saw the non-English-speaking migrant as a human being, not just a cog in the machine of national development. He also believed that a new arrival should be allowed to bring his kin. Chifley and Calwell may have introduced the mass-migration scheme, but it was Menzies who persisted with the program when they, in opposition, took the populist option of questioning the pace of change.

Decades later, John Howard would be approached by women of my mother's generation to offer their thanks to that nice man Mr Menzies. 'I've never forgotten the experience as prime minister. I'd go around to various functions and older ladies who'd been born in say Latvia, or Italy, or Greece, they'd come up to me and they'd say, "I came here when Mr Menzies was running the country. Mr Menzies gave me a new home in a good country. And my children have grown up in this country." [The postwar migration program] was a time of enormous optimism. We felt we were participating in quite an adventure.'

Yet even as Australia was opening itself to Europe, it remained an insular society, one step behind global policy trends.

Paul Keating and Peter Costello were born thirteen years apart, but they describe very similar childhoods growing up in the Australia of the 1950s and '60s. Life was centred on suburb and church.

Keating was born in Sydney's west in 1944. 'Bankstown, where I lived, had a great clannishness about it. There was a lot of society around the Catholic Church. Treats would involve visits to the city, to the beaches. If you were lucky you'd go to the theatre. I remember seeing with my father a film called *The Robe*, which is a quasi-religious epic. Our local parish priest took all the altar boys – and I was one – to see *Roman Holiday* with Gregory Peck and Audrey Hepburn. These were big events.'

Costello was born in Melbourne's east in 1957: different city, different side of the tracks, different faith, but the same socially conservative upbringing. 'Australia was a pretty stable place. The norm was the two-parent family with Mum at home looking after the kids. Some people would say it was probably a bit boring, by recent standards. There were no Sunday newspapers – that was a good thing, in my view. Society got destroyed when Sunday newspapers came in. There was no current affairs on television on a Sunday. Everybody worked their nine to five, or seven to four, Monday to Friday, and went to the football on Saturday and church on Sunday.'

One decade snoozed into the next so that by the end of the 1960s it could safely be said that Australia missed the decade as it was lived in the United States and Britain, without the social movements and the glamour, or the political chaos. With good reason, Australian writers at the time eviscerated the ugliness of the cities, the languor of suburbia, and the lack of imagination in the federal parliament. Some of the nation's finest young talents fled for London and New York, including the celebrated quartet of Germaine Greer, Barry Humphries, Robert Hughes and Clive James. The Australian people made their isolation evident every time someone famous visited from overseas. Actor, musician, politician; it didn't matter who they were – the fact they had taken the trouble to come to this lonely corner of the globe was a cause for celebration. By all accounts, Australia shrieked the loudest for the Beatles, and in Adelaide, 350 000 people – half the population – lined the route from the airport to the city to greet John, Paul, George and Ringo's substitute on their 1964 tour. But that adolescent energy did not translate to civil strife, as it did elsewhere. The Vietnam War, the cause of much political and social disruption in the United States, was supported by a majority of the Australian population until 1969. When people did march against the war, there were no riots.

Labor was in no position to challenge the conservative hegemony because it was split, and because its own leader, Arthur Calwell, was even more reactionary than Robert Menzies, with his literal defence of a White Australia. The two-party system was placed in cold storage as the coalition ruled the national parliament for twenty-three years between December 1949 and December 1972, and Menzies was prime minister for just over sixteen of those years.

That second decade of power, which allowed Menzies to maintain the momentum for European migration, held the nation back in other ways. The prime minister simply wasn't interested in the social change that John F. Kennedy and Lyndon Johnson were pursuing in the United States, or Harold Wilson in Great Britain. They were progressive politicians for a progressive decade. Menzies saw the 1960s as a decade of consolidation for Australia, not change. And so Australia was up to a decade late to reforms that would likely have been embraced by colonial politicians, or by Alfred Deakin, Andrew Fisher or John Curtin. President Johnson introduced the Civil Rights Act, banning discrimination based on race, colour, religion or national origin; started affirmative action for women; and embarked on his Great Society spending program to alleviate poverty. Menzies left it to his successor Harold Holt to expunge some of the original sins of federation by including Indigenous people in the census, and by dismantling the White Australia policy.

When Holt became prime minister on 26 January 1966, he was greeted as the beginning of a new era. Holt moved first on the White Australia policy. In March, less than two months into his term, he amended the rules to allow 'well qualified' non-Europeans to migrate. It was a guarded formula, designed to play down the revolutionary nature of the change. Those who were already in Australia on a temporary basis, as, for example, students, would be allowed to stay, and become citizens after five years – granting them the same rights as Europeans. Under the old rules, non-Europeans had to wait fifteen years for citizenship, which deterred family reunion. The total non-European intake had been restricted to five hundred per year under Menzies. Holt doubled it to a thousand. In November that year, polls found the electorate divided five ways on the subject of Asian migration, between those who were happy with the intake as announced (25 per cent), those who wanted more Asians allowed in (18 per cent), those who wanted to stick with the old quota of five hundred (19 per cent), those who wanted to 'admit none' (18 per cent) and those who had 'no idea' (20 per cent). The pollsters concluded: 'At least 6 out of 10 Australians favour some migration from Asia, and they are inclined to approve this year's increase to 1000 a year.' This, incidentally, was a much better result than the Italians and Greeks achieved in the opinion polls of the early 1950s. Evidentially Australians were more welcoming of Asians than their politicians had presumed them to be.

Even after this change, Australia was viewed as backward. On Holt's official visit to the United States in June 1967, he was confronted with the same niggling question that had embarrassed John Curtin during the Second World War: when will you abandon the White Australia policy? He should have expected the backlash, given the civil rights agenda of his good friend LBJ. That month, the US Supreme Court would rule that banning interracial marriage was unconstitutional. But Holt's response was defensive, and his discomfort betrayed how much further Australia had to travel before it caught up with the rest of the world.

Appearing on NBC television's *Meet the Press* program, Holt was asked how a country that 'by geography is Asian [but] by race is white' could continue to exclude its neighbours from migrating. Holt replied he had 'liberalised the arrangements quite a good deal'.

There were twelve thousand Asian students studying in Australia at that time, and more than thirty thousand migrants had been accepted in the two decades since the war.

The American journalist persisted. He had met many Southeast Asians 'who had a lot of antagonisms' against Australia's 'racial immigration laws'. 'Are you saying that you are going to moderate those even more and more as time goes on?'

'I have said we have moderated them,' Holt replied. 'I emphasise that not one representative of an Asian government has ever raised with me in my many travels around the area the question of our immigration policy.'

It is to Holt's credit that he began the process of dismantling the White Australia policy at a time when the nation was embroiled in the Vietnam War. He had wanted to do it earlier, but Menzies would not countenance such a change on his watch. Holt's death in December 1967 left the business of removing the final traces of the colour line to his successors. John Gorton did not act, and nor did Billy McMahon, although they were quietly shifting the composition of the postwar program. One in ten migrants who arrived in 1971 were either fully or partly Asian. It would take a change of government to finally terminate the White Australia policy. But while the political system dithered and the nation seemed frozen in another age, the European wave was slowly changing the culture at home and in the workplace.

The nineteenth-century influx of migration had triggered a long housing boom. The postwar intakes replicated that experience, but without the bust. The home-ownership rate surged from around 50 per cent at the end of the war to 70 per cent by the early 1960s, where it remained, more or less, until the end of the century. The new members of the property class were returned servicemen, the local-born and European migrants. The locals purchased large houses in the outer suburbs with mortgages that could be serviced on a single income; the migrants moved first into the old workers' cottages in the inner city and then traded up to the leafier suburbs.

Australia's property obsession can be traced back to Lachlan Macquarie's day, but the realisation of a home-ownership society would not have been possible without the European wave. By 1981, every major migrant household from the continent was comfortably above the 70 per cent figure for Australian-born home ownership. The Italians had the highest rate at 86 per cent, followed by the Maltese (81 per cent), the Poles (81 per cent), the Greeks (80 per cent), the Yugoslavs (77 per cent), the Dutch (76 per cent) and the Germans (74 per cent). But the English and Welsh (69 per cent), the Irish (68 per cent) and the Scots (67 per cent) all fell just below the local-born benchmark.

The difference between the English- and non-English-speaking migrant can be explained by their sense of place. Australia was familiar ground for the British and Irish. For the migrants of my parents' generation, Australia was friendly but alien territory. They would learn to trust the system, but their life experience had taught them to fear for the future. Property gave them a stake in the country. My father never understood why someone would rent, or even take the slow road to paying off a mortgage. Only freehold title gave him security. No landlord or banker could throw him out. No regime could dispossess him. One could dress up the higher home-ownership rates for migrants as an entrepreneurial spirit, but it was something more primal: the rational paranoia of someone who grew up in the broken continent of Europe.

Unlike the housing boom of the nineteenth century, this rush to the suburbs was characterised by stability. First, population growth remained strong throughout, and second, the automobile allowed the boundaries of the city to extend well beyond existing tram and rail lines, so cheaper land was accessed before supply overran demand and prices collapsed. Deep recessions in the early 1950s and the early 1960s proved to be temporary interruptions only, and it wasn't until the early 1970s that house prices first jumped beyond the reach of the workingman.

The typical migrant household of the 1950s and '60s predicted the most fundamental shift in Australia society: the feminisation of the workforce. It appears the most unlikely change to come from intakes that began with an excess of males. Yet the very nature of migrant life made this shift inevitable.

At the end of the Second World War, local-born women made way for returning soldiers in the workforce. They gave up their jobs in manufacturing and in the public service when they started families, and many never took up paid employment again. The majority of mothers did not return to work until their youngest child was in primary school, at age six. For those with two or more children, that meant more than a decade out of work. In the case of the public service, women were required to give up their jobs as soon as they married. Australia was one of the last countries to remove this restriction.

Migrant families were more likely run on two incomes, with both parents working. The example of Julia Gillard, who is just four years younger than Peter Costello, demonstrates the contrast between the migrant and the local-born experience.

Gillard was born in Wales in 1961, and migrated with her family to Australia in 1966, after Robert Menzies had retired as prime minister. 'We were ten-pound Poms,' she tells me. 'Both my mother and my father had served as police officers so that was viewed as a qualification and good work experience. They had to come with a housing deposit, which they had saved up.' They were destined for Melbourne, but the Gillards befriended another Welsh couple on the boat who was returning to Australia. 'They lived in Adelaide and so they thought to themselves, Well we only know two people in the whole of Australia, we might as well go to the city where they are.'

Her father found the employment market tough. 'It was in the middle of a very bad drought. He went through a few different jobs – cheese factory, security guard and a few others. He ended up training as a psychiatric nurse.' Her mother also worked, a fairly shocking idea to most Australians of the time.

As Gillard was completing primary school, Paul Keating entered parliament at the 1969 election, and his maiden speech criticised John Gorton's government for forcing mothers to find work. 'In the last couple of years, the Government has boasted about the increasing number of women in the work force. Rather than something to be proud of I feel that this is something of which we should be ashamed.' Keating's mother had never worked. 'In the world I grew up in most women stayed at home and looked after their children,' he explains. What concerned him at the time was the cost of living, which was rising, and how this placed pressure on families to find a second income. 'I held a view then and I hold a view today: if you take a baby or a child up to, say, two years, are they best in their perpetual mother's care or in a childcare centre? They're obviously best in their perpetual mother's care. But that doesn't speak of the changing nature of our society, particularly the opportunities for women, which I hope I [as prime minister] had some substantial measure in creating.'

Gillard's mother ran a babysitting business from the family home, then, when the young Julia went to primary school, she took a part-time job as a cook in an aged-care home. 'She would pick me up from school and have me sit there until she finished work, my sister and I. So it was just natural to us, but looking back on it now with an adult's eyes, I remember many kids at school that I would go and visit whose mums didn't work at all.'

As Gillard grew older, she began to help her mother in the kitchen of the nursing home. Her first task was to put out the afternoon tea. In her teenage years she took a part-time job serving the evening meals and, for three hours on Saturdays, peeling potatoes.

'Getting a job where Mum worked, I suppose it's a bit of nepotism,' she jokes. 'I was pretty proud of that little pay packet when I was a teenager.'

Many of her girlfriends still expected to live as their mothers had: marry young, raise children and perhaps never work again. But Gillard was a member of the generation where that stopped being the social norm. Women went to university in large numbers from the 1970s, and by the early 1980s more girls than boys were arriving on campus. Coincidentally, Australia finally achieved gender balance in 1979, with more women than men across the population. Australia was the last settler nation to reach this position, three years after Canada, ten years after New Zealand and twenty years after the United States.

The postwar migrants had presaged the trend for both parents to work when their children were young. When Keating was treasurer in Bob Hawke's government in the 1980s, the majority of mothers still waited until their youngest child was ready for primary school before returning to work, usually part-time. But this time away from work was reduced by two parallel trends – the rise of education for women, and higher property prices, which meant the typical mortgage could no longer be serviced on one income alone. In 1996, when Costello became treasurer in John Howard's government, the majority of mothers were back at work when their youngest was aged three. By 2011, when Gillard was prime minister, the threshold between home and work had been reduced to a single year – most mothers were back at work after their baby had celebrated their first birthday.

The reservations that women had about migration during the European wave had disappeared by the early 1990s, when their views aligned with those of men, reflecting their greater familiarity with the cosmopolitan workplace of new Australia. The children of the golden intakes of the 1850s had ultimately closed Australia to the rest of the world, on behalf of the male labourer. The children of the European intakes and their local-born peers had inverted that history, laying an unexpected foundation for an open Australia in which the best qualified worker was female.

Hard work defines the migrants of the postwar era. But the most productive migrants are not the first generation, who rebuild the nation and acquire the property, but the second, their local-born children who rise through education. The second generation of the postwar migrants began topping the class in the 1980s and '90s, as Australia moved from a single-income to dual-income society, and from a blue- to a pink-collar economy. By 2002, the advance of the second generation could be measured in the success of those who grew up in non-English-speaking households. 'Those whose parents arrived in Australia in the postwar years have achieved better educational and occupational outcomes than those with Australian-born parents,' according to a report prepared for John Howard's government. 'The study also found the second generation of people from southern and eastern Europe and Asia had a higher proportion of people with university qualifications and in professional occupations than the second generation whose parents migrated from the United Kingdom or other Western European countries.' Even those migrants who struggled on arrival were more likely to lift their children out of poverty than Australian-born parents on the same rung of the ladder. 'In circumstances where the parental generation is economically disadvantaged, the second generation seems more able to overcome this disadvantage – through greater participation in education and achievement of tertiary qualifications – than their peers who are at least third generation.'

The move to European migration had paid off, across two generations, with Australia's greatest migrants since the gold rush still to come. But before they could be received there was the unfinished business of White Australia. Asian migration had to flow as naturally to Australia as from Europe or Britain, Indigenous Australians had to be treated as equals in their own country, and the economy had to be reopened to the world. This final break with the past required a level of political unity Australia had not witnessed before, not even in wartime.

16

REOPENING
THE DOORS

Every innovation in Australian public policy after the Second World War restored the nation, almost by serendipity, to the position that the colonies had enjoyed in the 1850s, before the colour line and tariffs stopped people and goods flowing freely across the continent. These reforms to open the society and then the economy were not inevitable. They required a degree of goodwill across the parties of capital and labour that past experience suggested was fanciful, and which the present, conflicted polity may never repeat. The previous examples of bipartisanship, between Deakin and Fisher, and between Curtin, Chifley and Menzies, lasted barely a decade before national politics resumed its regular programming of division. Yet the critical decisions to encourage mass migration from Asia and to embrace the market economy required at least double that time to secure, and they were taken from a position of material weakness. The global economy, an agent of stability for Australia in the 1950s and '60s, collapsed in the '70s and behaved erratically in the '80s.

Open Australia was born on 2 December 1972 with the election of Gough Whitlam's Labor government. Whitlam, the grandson of a convicted forgerer, was a lawyer by training and only the second Labor leader after Doc Evatt who could be classed as a white-collar professional. His social-policy agenda represented catch-up for Australia, bringing the nation closer to the progressive models of the United States and Great Britain in the 1960s. Whitlam's program included universal health care, free university education, equal pay for women and no-fault divorce. It was a testament to both Whitlam's ambition and the inertia of the previous regime that so much was achieved in the three controversial years of his government. One of his first priorities was to establish diplomatic relations with communist China. In 1973, he removed White Australia from the statute books, and Australian embassies around the world were instructed that no prospective migrant could be denied entry on the basis of their race. In 1975 he enacted the Racial Discrimination Act, and introduced the Land Rights Act. He handed over the title of Wattie Creek, at Daguragu in the Northern Territory, to the Gurindji people.

Whitlam imagined a Eurasian future for Australia, but he passed up an opportunity to give practical effect to his vision. When Saigon fell at the end of the Vietnam War in April 1975, the Labor prime minister resisted calls from the opposition leader, Malcolm Fraser, and diplomatic pressure from the United States, to accept more refugees from South Vietnam. Whitlam reportedly told his immigration minister Clyde Cameron at the time, 'I'm not having hundreds of fucking Vietnamese Balts coming into this country with their political and religious hatreds against us.' The comment was made privately, and Cameron gave his version of their conversation after Whitlam left politics. By 'Balts' Whitlam appeared to mean anti-communists, who were therefore more likely to vote Liberal. Whitlam was more open to refugees fleeing right-wing regimes. He welcomed eight thousand people from Cyprus and six thousand from Chile, but only two thousand from Vietnam.

It would take the next prime minister, the Liberal Malcolm

Fraser, to fully open the door to the Vietnamese. Fraser was the grandson of a gold-rush migrant, and his policies made the most substantial change to Australia's ethnic face since the 1850s. His motivation was both simple and profound. He had a particular empathy for the Vietnamese that he extended across the entire Asian region, inverting the old Australian motto that anyone with yellow skin should be kept out.

'Once it was all over in Vietnam,' he told me, 'one of the first things to come to my mind: What was going to happen to the people who had worked with and supported Australian troops, and the Australian Embassy? I felt all along, maybe particularly because I'd been army minister and defence minister in earlier times, that we had a very particular obligation – ethical, moral – to people from Vietnam.'

Fraser recalled the official reception for the first boat. The deputy prime minister and leader of the Country Party, Doug Anthony, happened to be in Darwin at the time, and telephoned Fraser with the news. 'He just told me he'd seen the first refugee boat. It was not a big boat. And Doug's advice to them was, "Well, just do everything you're asked to." And I said to Doug, "Make sure they've got medical attention, make sure they've got food, make sure they're billeted somewhere comfortable and we'll take it all from there."'

Three boats arrived in 1976, and twenty-four the following year. Among the first to land was the 22-year-old Hieu Van Le, a future governor of South Australia. Le fled South Vietnam with his wife in 1977, part of a group of fifty who took a fishing boat to Malaysia. After a few months in a refugee camp, they headed for Darwin by sea. As they approached the Australian mainland, they were greeted by two local men in a tinnie. 'They waved at us and they come very close, very close and very fast to our boat and one of them raises the stubbie up as if proposing a toast. "G'day, mate," he shouted. "Welcome to Australia."'

The Labor opposition did not provide uncritical support for the Fraser policy. The party's immigration spokesman, Senator Tony Mulvihill, said many of the Vietnamese leaving the country were not legitimate refugees. 'Without reopening old sores, it is my honest opinion that the people with the wealth did not have the heart to fight,' he told the Senate in March 1977. 'Now that there is to be a redistribution of wealth many people are attempting to leave as pseudorefugees.'

At the 1977 election, a future Labor prime minister also took aim at the Vietnamese. 'Of course, we should have compassion, but people who are coming in this way are not the only people in the world who have rights to our compassion,' Bob Hawke, the president of the Australian Council of Trade Unions, told reporters. 'Any sovereign nation has the right to determine how it will exercise its compassion and how it will increase its population.'

The political animosity between Whitlam and Fraser had the potential to poison the reception for the Vietnamese refugees. Whitlam, still bruised from his dismissal by the governor-general, could have sought a shortcut back to office by playing to old fears of the yellow peril. But he did not follow his colleagues down the low road of demonisation, earning Fraser's respect. 'Even though Gough Whitlam and his government didn't want to bring in large numbers from Vietnam, when my government later made a decision to do so, Gough did not oppose it. And that meant that the bipartisan approach to a humanitarian Australian policy remained bipartisan.'

Fraser had always felt that he and Whitlam were continuing the work of Chifley and Menzies in bringing migrants ahead of public opinion, but in the national interest. 'If we asked voters, "Do you want Melbourne to be the biggest Greek city outside of Greece?" they would have said no. If I had bothered to take some polls about Vietnamese and Cambodians, people would have said no. Whoever was in government thought that it was something that Australia had to do, and whoever was in opposition, in the national interest happened to agree.'

The critical decision Fraser took later in his second term was to arrange airlifts of refugees from camps in South-East Asia. The image of refugees stepping off Australian airlines gave a legitimacy to the exercise for a public that Fraser well understood was wary of these new arrivals. The policy slowed the boat arrivals, but did not stop them altogether. The new opposition leader, Bill Hayden, supported the program, and his Labor colleagues finally stopped sniping from the sidelines. Almost forty thousand Vietnamese refugees were accepted in the first five years of Fraser's program to 1981 – the largest intake from Asia since the Chinese on the goldfields. Only New Zealand delivered more migrants in this difficult period of transition from old to new Australia, when people were no longer coming from Europe and the economy no longer worked.

The global economic disease of the 1970s was stagflation – rising inflation and unemployment. It terminated the long postwar boom, and Australia was unprepared for the shock. The economy that had exceeded expectations in the good times of the 1950s and '60s became, once again, one of the worst in the bust of the '70s. And once again, international opinion of Australia was scathing. Ian Macfarlane, Reserve Bank governor from 1996 to 2006, received these criticisms firsthand as a young economist at the Organisation for Economic Development and Co-operation in Paris. 'Australia was looked upon as sort of one of the juvenile delinquents of the world, because of its poor economic performance in the '70s.'

'A lot went wrong,' Macfarlane tells me. 'It was our worst decade. We had an antiquated system of economic control, one that had sort of worked reasonably well during the '50s and '60s, the period of postwar reconstruction. But it came under increasing pressure in the '70s. It was the decade where we went from being

a low-unemployment economy to a high-unemployment economy, and from being a low-inflation economy to a high-inflation
economy.'

Two deep recessions in 1974–75 and 1982–83, one occurring on
the watch of the Whitlam government, the other under the Fraser
government, convinced both sides of politics that the economic
crutches of the White Australia policy – industry and wage protection – had to be removed.

Paul Keating says the worst thing about the closed economic
model 'was that the price of all of our goods was set by officials'.
'So when I became treasurer [in 1983], on the cabinet table sat the
rate of exchange and interest rates. Wages [were set] under the centralised wage-fixing system with the national wage cases and, of
course, tariffs and quotas. I had to decide whether to be a passive
participant in the scam or to blow the scam up.'

Bob Hawke returned Labor to office in 1983, after just seven
years in opposition – the shortest period in the wilderness for the
party of the workingman in the postwar era. But this was like no
Labor government before or since, as it sought to promote the
interests of workers by favouring business. Over the next thirteen
years, Hawke and Keating successfully floated the dollar, opened
the financial sector, pulled down the tariff wall, and allowed workers and employers to negotiate wages at the enterprise level, without
officials looking over their shoulder.

These pro-market policies were sold to the public by reframing
the fear of foreign invasion as the fear of foreign derision. Keating
famously warned that Australia would become a 'banana republic'
if the economy was not opened to international competition. However, the government did not give up all controls. It still placed a
value on fairness through a means-tested social safety net, a public health system, universal superannuation and the guarantee of
minimum wages.

The payoff from the reforms was not apparent until the end of the

century, when Australia proved able to avoid the new crises of glo-
balisation. The economy kept growing during the Asian financial
crisis of 1997–98 and then the global recession of 2000–01. What
is easily forgotten in light of this success is that Australia continued to lag behind the rest of the world while Hawke and Keating
were changing the nation. Like a form of economic chemotherapy,
the medicine they administered involved a period of pain before
the patient was restored to health. Australia's unemployment rate
was higher than the Unites States' in every month of the thirteen
years of the Hawke–Keating government from April 1983 to March
1996. Australia was also one of the worst affected during the global
recession of 1990–91. In fact, the twenty-year period from the first
oil shock in 1973 to the peak in unemployment in 1993 echoed that
of the depressions of the 1890s and 1930s, when Australia was the
world's great underachiever.

Australia had turned inward during the two earlier depressions
with self-defeating policies of protection. The Hawke–Keating program broke that legacy by securing an open economy and society
at a time of crisis, a first for Australia. Labor did so with coalition
support for the pivotal decisions on the dollar, financial deregulation and the tariffs.

But the bipartisanship on the economy did not extend to migration policy because the Liberal Party adopted the old Labor position
on the politics of race. It was a deliberate tactic, designed to capital-
ise on the fallout from economic reform. Blue-collar workers made
redundant by the Hawke–Keating program wanted protection
restored. Although the coalition had no interest in that agenda,
they could offer another version of the White Australia policy in
return – the slowing of Asian migration.

Every record was broken in the 1980s. It was the first big decade of Asian migration, and the first decade in which the Chinese
were actively recruited as migrants. For the first time, the top five
intakes to Australia were all from the neighbourhood: more than a

hundred thousand from New Zealand, ninety-five thousand from China and Hong Kong, more than eighty thousand from Vietnam, almost sixty thousand from the Philippines and forty thousand from Malaysia.

The first Liberal leader to question Australia's new ethnic face was Andrew Peacock, the member for Kooyong, Robert Menzies' old seat. In May 1984, Peacock suggested the rate of Asian migration should be lowered to preserve the 'European nature' of the migration program. Not by reducing the intake, he explained, but by rebooting the European component. The comment angered many within the opposition, and Peacock quickly retreated.

Among the Liberals to slap him down was John Howard, who had been treasurer in the Fraser government. In a widely praised speech in August that year, Howard said politicians had a higher duty to 'keep race out of debate in Australia'. He reminded both sides that Bob Hawke had played this card against the Vietnamese as ACTU president just seven years earlier. 'Of course,' he told parliament, '[Hawke] was then conscious that immigration and unemployment were potential issues in that election campaign, and he was fairly short on liberalism and fairly strong on opportunism in the remarks that he made in 1977. He did not mind if those remarks were interpreted by Australian workers as hitting out against Asian immigration and the potential threat that that might represent to the jobs of Australians.'

But Howard forgot his own advice. Almost four years to the day from that speech, Howard, now the opposition leader, made a more explicit call than Peacock. He wanted to slow down Asian migration. 'I wouldn't like to see it greater, I'm not in favour of going back to a White Australia policy,' Howard said in a radio interview on 1 August 1988. 'I do believe that if it is in the eyes of some in the community that it's too great, it would be in our immediate-term interest and supporting of social cohesion if it were slowed down a little, so the capacity of the community to absorb it was greater.'

Howard's timing was uncanny. It was the bicentenary of European settlement, and a hundred years since Henry Parkes had slammed the colonial door on the Chinese. The opposition leader was met with a tsunami of protest from colleagues, business and community groups, and senior members of the media. But if Howard backed down, he knew he would lose the votes of those he had aroused with his call. If Labor blinked, either by modifying its migration policy, or by trying to change the debate to another topic, Howard would be declared the winner of this divisive contest.

The opinion polls at the time showed coalition voters were more concerned about migration than Labor voters, reflecting a number of complex trends. In the 1960s, it was Labor voters who were more concerned about migration, but this changed from the middle of that decade as the party attracted two new constituents who were pro-migration – local-born professionals, and migrants from southern Europe. Coalition voters, by contrast, moved from being pro-migration in the mid-1960s to being more concerned about migration by the late 1970s. The decisions by Harold Holt and Malcolm Fraser to terminate the White Australia policy were ultimately not popular with coalition voters. It was into this electoral reality that Peacock and Howard played their cards in the 1980s. Howard's comments in particular provoked the nastiest race debate since Labor's campaign against the Bruce–Page government some sixty years earlier.

Bob Hawke confronted the opposition leader on the floor of the House of Representatives. The prime minister wasn't accusing Howard of racism, but 'the more serious charge of cynical opportunism'. 'His [Howard's] polling shows that there is this prejudice in the community and he has unleashed within his coalition and within the wider community the most malevolent, the most hurtful, the most damaging and the most uncohesive forces.' Hawke moved a parliamentary motion to reaffirm Australia's non-discriminatory migration policy. It acknowledged 'the historic action of the Holt

Government, with bipartisan support from the Australian Labor Party, in initiating the dismantling of the White Australia policy'.

Howard was defiant: 'I would never want to see Asian immigration stopped, because I think that would be politically and socially and emotionally stupid. We have moved on from the days of the White Australia policy, but I do think it is legitimate for any government to worry about the capacity of the community to absorb change, and there is some concern about the pace of change involved in the present level of Asian migration. I think any government is entitled to take that into account and it ought not to be accused of being racist.'

He had, in continuing to question the rate of Asian migration, made the Billy Hughes–like suggestion that some members of the existing Australian community were not welcome. It was only many years later that he apologised for the offence he may have caused.

At the time, the row cost him his job. Three Liberal MPs crossed the floor to vote with the government in the lower house, while two others walked out of the chamber. Peacock was also a notable absentee, citing a prior commitment in Melbourne. A fourth Liberal MP voted with the government when the resolution was put to the Senate.

The following May, Howard was ousted by Peacock in a countercoup. 'I think one of the reasons why I lost the Liberal Party leadership in '89 was because of some disquiet about the comments I had made on Asian immigration,' Howard tells me. He concedes now that he misjudged the capacity of the community to absorb Asian migration. Even in 1988, the opinion polls showed support for Asian migration actually improved once Hawke confronted Howard.

Hawke believes that the argument he had with Howard made it easier to convince the community to accept forty thousand Chinese asylum-seeking students after the massacre at Beijing's Tiananmen Square in June 1989. 'The Australian people understood precisely where we [Labor] stood on the question of race and colour, and the fact that we had that sort of background did assist when we came to the events of 1989. When I was just about to go on television that day I received a cable from our embassy in Beijing, and it had some rather gruesome details of the people [who] had been killed. And so I was emotionally moved. I said that those students here who wanted to stay would be welcome. When I went off the stage the senior public servant said to me, "Prime Minister you can't do that." I said, "It's done." And those people have made a massive contribution to our country.'

Race as a political tool should have been thoroughly discredited at the end of the 1980s, with Hawke's decisive action and Howard's departure. But the deep recession of 1990–91 – the third in just sixteen years for the nation – meant that race could be used once more by politicians who wished to harness voter discontent with economic reform, while keeping those reforms in place.

The next target of this cynical calculation by politicians and media was Australia's Indigenous community. Although Labor won this encounter, the fallout from this debate changed the behaviour of both sides. The coalition became more assertive on questions of national identity, while Labor would become more timid.

The issue was forced on the political system by the High Court's June 1992 judgement in the Mabo case that the land had been occupied before British settlement. Paul Keating was now prime minister, having toppled Bob Hawke in a party room ballot the previous December. Mindful that the Hawke government had failed to act on the issue of land rights in the 1980s, Keating wanted to use Mabo to make amends. 'I saw this as a huge opportunity to address the original colonial grievance, the dispossession of the Aboriginal people,' he tells me. 'But more than that – to come clean with them about the nature of the dispossession. I said, "We took the children from their families, we did the murders, we introduced the alcohol and the diseases." Because a country can't come to terms with its history without the truth being there. And I used to say to my staff: "We'll never do any good with the blacks until we own up to it all.'"

He made his intentions clear in his famous Redfern speech in December 1992, and after winning the election in March 1993 devoted his time to securing native title legislation to provide Indigenous people access to Crown land where their prior rights had not been extinguished. Pastoral and mining interests were vehemently opposed, and the coalition refused to offer Labor any assistance in the Senate, even voting against amendments that their own rural constituency had demanded. One of the most inflammatory and inaccurate assertions at the time came from Victorian Liberal premier Jeff Kennett, who warned that claims for native title could be made on suburban backyards. 'Every property in Australia could be at risk,' he said.

The issue also threatened to split the Labor side. 'Most of the members and ministers from the outlying states, particularly Western Australia and Queensland, were never in favour of native title, nor the [debate on the] republic which followed,' Keating says. He ignored his internal critics, and the Native Title Act was eventually passed in December 1993. The Liberal leader of the time, Dr John Hewson, did not accept the verdict of the parliament. He called it a 'day of shame' but lost his job the following May – the second Liberal leader to fall after challenging the bipartisanship on issues of race. His replacement, Alexander Downer, was gaffe-prone, and in January 1995 the opposition returned in desperation to John Howard.

The Labor program of an open market and open society seemed assured because Howard very quickly agreed with Keating on native title, and he apologised for his earlier comments on Asian migration. If the Chinese had reservations about Howard in 1988, they had disappeared by the 1996 election. Late in the campaign, Keating clipped a page-one article from the *Australian Financial Review* for his personal archive and underlined two passages. One quoted Labor's deputy lord mayor of Sydney, Henry Tsang, who said, 'The Chinese community is swinging to the Liberals.' The other referred to an opinion poll showing Labor's vote among the Chinese had been 70 per cent at the 1993 election but 'had fallen by 20 percentage points by last week'.

The Chinese support for Howard was a surprise at the time, although it need not have been. The Chinese who came to Australia were anti-communist, which meant they would lean towards the Liberal Party. They were socially conservative and entrepreneurial – values the Liberals held dear. The Italians had, by a similar logic, gravitated towards Labor, even though Labor had traditionally demonised them. The Italians in Australia were generally anti-fascist and pro-trade union.

There was an edge to the 1996 election. The economy had been growing strongly since the last recession, but the unemployment rate remained stuck at around 8 per cent. Most of the 250 000 men who had lost their jobs in the crash would never work again. Many blamed Labor, and a significant portion associated Keating's progressive agenda, for Indigenous rights and engagement with Asia, with their unemployment. They thought their country had been taken from them.

Howard did not court these voters with appeals to the old certainties of racial selection and industry protection. In 1996, he was on a unity ticket with Keating on native title and Asian migration. But after winning the election in a landslide, Howard found that these voters carried a disproportionate power in the electorate. They had swung from Labor to the coalition, but if Howard could not appease them they would move further to the right, to a new protest movement led by Pauline Hanson. Hanson had claimed the safe Labor seat of Oxley as an independent by attacking Indigenous welfare and migration. She used her maiden speech to parliament to fly the flag for White Australia, warning that the nation was 'in danger of being swamped by Asians'. It should have been a footnote to a debate already resolved, but Howard didn't use the authority of his office to rebuke her quickly enough. He was caught between carefully worded statements disagreeing with her on Asian migration and hailing her right to free speech.

'Hanson really represented the people who wanted no change,' says Peter Costello, the treasurer in the Howard government. 'No change on the ethnic composition of Australia, no change on the gun laws.' Costello believes Howard should have made a strong statement at the outset, before Hanson established her One Nation Party. 'Howard didn't want to take it on. He thought that you could manage it by being nice, and appealing to the better instincts of the One Nation people. And, in my view, [he] waited far too long and had to be pushed, basically, into taking it on full frontal.'

Howard believes his gun law reforms of 1996, following the Port Arthur massacre, gave oxygen to One Nation. Today those reforms are recognised globally for their political bravery, and policy innovation. But in 1996, they had the same effect on the conservative side of politics that native title had had on Labor three years earlier. 'I have no doubt that her appeal to the flannel shirts was very strong when it came to guns,' Howard says of the blue-collar voters who switched from Labor to the coalition to One Nation. 'She felt she saw an opportunity, you know: "This bloke is taking away your freedom to have a gun." Now I just think the American culture on guns is crazy beyond belief, and it's probably the greatest single thing that I did to make Australia a safer country and I'm very proud of it.'

But it was surely about more than guns. Hanson's home state of Queensland had missed both the European and Asian waves of migration. By 1996, it was the only mainland state with 80 per cent of its population Australian-born. Although Hanson proved to be a political flash-in-the-pan, losing her seat at the next election in 1998, Queensland remained the state most likely to tip the policy scales back towards insularity. At the 2001 election, One

Nation again threatened the coalition's majority, forcing Howard to strike a dramatic new bargain on migration. It had been half a century since Arthur Calwell had targeted wartime refugees from Asia while keeping the door open to mass migration from Europe. Howard would now close the door on asylum seekers fleeing tyranny in Afghanistan and Iraq while increasing the intake of migrants from Asia to record levels. But there would be no Robert Menzies or Malcolm Fraser on the Labor side to fly the flag for the refugee.

17

THE LONGEST BOOM:
AUSTRALIA IN THE
TWENTY-FIRST CENTURY

The opening of the economy pulled migration back towards the old free-trade capital of Sydney in the 1980s and '90s. By 2001, the Chinese-born population in Australia had reached 200 000, and more than half lived in Sydney. John Howard was himself host to the second-largest Chinese community in the nation as the member for the federal seat of Bennelong, in the city's inner north-west. But Sydney proved to be an ambivalent host. While it welcomed the Chinese, it also led a new backlash against asylum seekers from the Middle East. The juxtaposition of one door opening and another closing is as old as the gold rush, when the colonies were happy to receive every nationality of digger except the Chinese. As Australia returns to the very top of the global income ladder, it is once again trying to stop the world's tired, poor huddled masses from coming to its shores.

The anxiety appears to be out of proportion to the numbers involved. In the first decade and a half of the new millennium, almost 63 000 asylum seekers have either arrived in Australia by boat, or been intercepted by the Australian Navy and transported to detention centres on the tiny Pacific island of Nauru or Papua

New Guinea's Manus Island. In that same period, a record 2.732 million migrants were added to the Australian population with barely a murmur of discontent.

The refugees who sailed into a political storm in 2001 were the twenty-first-century equivalents of the Vietnamese. They were fleeing regimes in Afghanistan and Iraq that Australia would soon be at war with. But the political system did not extend to them the same welcome as it had to the Vietnamese, placing Australia in the morally ambiguous position of being at war with both the oppressed and their oppressors. What changed between these two eras was not just political attitudes, but the very nature of migration to Australia. Support for Asian migrants and the hardening of opinion against asylum seekers were part of the same process.

By the time the Afghanis and Iraqis were seeking Australia's protection, the migration program had been running on the Keating–Howard model for almost a decade. Political and ideological rivals, there was nonetheless an important continuity between their policies.

Following the recession of 1990–91, Paul Keating shifted the migration program from family reunion towards a greater emphasis on skills. John Howard accelerated this process after 1996. This meant the migrants who arrived in the 1990s were more likely to find work, and thus were not seen as a drain on the public purse. Most of these qualified recruits were from Asia, and in particular from China. Yet their success had the unintended consequence of undermining public sympathy for refugees. In the electorate's mind, it didn't matter if the asylum seekers had a genuine claim. They were seen as unauthorised arrivals who lacked the skills for the open economy. The losers of economic reform saw these people as competitors for government welfare.

Keating did not have an electoral dilemma to confront on asylum seekers in part because he enjoyed warm relations with Indonesia, which was the final port of departure for boatpeople originally from Afghanistan and Iraq. That relationship cooled on Howard's watch after East Timor won its independence in 1999. It is clear from the numbers that Jakarta took less interest in preventing boats from making the journey to Australia at this point. In 1998, just 17 boats carrying 200 asylum seekers arrived in Australia. In 1999, there were 86 boats with 3721 asylum seekers. The previous record had been 18 boats with 953 asylum seekers in 1994.

The issue did not seem to trouble voters all that much in 1999, or in 2000 when a further 51 boats carrying 2939 asylum seekers arrived on Australia's shores. Media and political attention was fixated on the implementation of the coalition's goods and services tax. It was the pressure cooker of the 2001 election campaign that turned this matter into a national crisis. Public attitudes have remained remarkably consistent in the decade and a half since Howard first declared war on boatpeople in August 2001. The most vocal opposition to asylum seekers has tended to come from electorates with higher-than-average Australian-born populations and higher-than-average rates of unemployment. The most politically influential of these voters cluster in coastal and regional electorates either side of Brisbane in Queensland, and in the outer western suburbs of Sydney. The main parties have lived in terror of these voters ever since Pauline Hanson demonstrated how to mobilise them with appeals to bigotry. Asylum seekers are more welcome in the inner cities of all the capital cities, and across Victoria, but these voters have yet to pull the main parties in the opposite direction, where politicians identify themselves as advocates for refugees in the manner of Robert Menzies and Malcolm Fraser. Menzies and Fraser created constituencies for refugees by treating them as the equal of migrants. Howard created an alternate constituency for their demonisation, and his Labor opponents did not contest the characterisation of asylum seekers as 'illegal immigrants'.

Origin plays a role in this debate. Menzies and Fraser represented the moderate Victorian wing of the Liberal Party, which had been pro-migration since its formation in 1944. Howard was the first successful Liberal prime minister from Sydney, where migration has historically been more polarising. It is notable that the backlash against Jewish refugees after the Second World War was centred in Sydney, the home of tribal politicians like Jack Lang, not Melbourne, the home of beloved refugee businessmen like Sidney Myer.

Howard undoubtedly had public opinion on his side, and a little bit of luck. He framed his standoff with the *Tampa*, the Norwegian vessel that had rescued 433 mainly Afghan asylum seekers at Australia's request, as a question of national sovereignty. The asylum seekers wanted to go to Christmas Island, from where they would make their claim for settlement in Australia. Howard demanded that they return to Indonesia, the previous stop in their journey. He ordered the SAS to take over the vessel, and after a few days of diplomatic haggling, struck a deal with Nauru to detain the asylum seekers, pending their resettlement to other countries. He vowed none would set foot in Australia. The confrontation began on 27 August 2001, and might have faded as an issue in the election later that year if not for events a fortnight later. On 11 September, Islamic terrorists flew hijacked planes into the Twin Towers in New York and the Pentagon in Washington. In the public's mind, the boat-people and the terrorists became indistinguishable, even though the asylum seekers were themselves victims of the Taliban.

At Howard's election campaign launch on 28 October, he delivered his most memorable phrase in politics: 'We will decide who comes to this country and the circumstances in which they come.' This sentiment is as old as British settlement, and it has been expressed by political figures though the ages, from Henry Parkes protesting the arrival of the *Hashemy* convict ship to Bob Hawke questioning the Vietnamese intake.

On election day 10 November 2001, the prime minister was pressing flesh in his electorate of Bennelong when two Sri

Lankan women approached him with words of encouragement. He recounted the conversation to me after the election. 'They said, "We strongly agree with you because we are trying to get our relatives and parents in through the regular way and we can't, and we don't like people pushing their way in." That may be a simplistic way of putting it, but that's quite a strongly held view.'

There was, in fact, no queue for the asylum seekers to jump. Later, it would emerge that seven out of ten boatpeople who had their claims processed on Nauru or Manus Island under Howard's so-called Pacific Solution were found to be genuine refugees. Australia accepted 705 out of the 1153 who were resettled.

At the time of the crisis, Malcolm Fraser lobbied the Labor opposition to reject the Howard policy. 'I tried to say to one of the most senior Labor people at the time, "Look there are tens upon tens of thousands of Liberals who hate this, there are a lot of Labor people who hate it, why don't you oppose it?"' Fraser told me. 'And he just looked at me pityingly and said, "Malcolm, you don't understand. The Liberal Party have ripped so many rednecks out of the Labor Party, I'm not going to let them rip any more."'

The *Tampa* recalled the *Afghan* crisis in 1888. Coincidentally 2001 was the centenary of federation, the housing market was booming, and the government worried that the nation's economic winning streak looked in danger of ending. Although Australia avoided being dragged into the US recession that year, the threat of a homegrown crash remained. By 2003, the Reserve Bank's Ian Macfarlane was concerned that the property market was overheated.

'I thought we were very close to having a bubble,' he says. 'We had house prices going up by 20 per cent per annum; we had lending for housing going up by 20 per cent plus per annum. We had nearly half of it going into speculative investment housing. We had all these spruikers going around telling you how to get rich quick and we had something like seven programs on prime-time television telling you how to get rich quick through property development.

So you put all those things together, and it sounds like you're getting very close to a bubble.'

A disaster was averted through a combination of good management and unexpected fortune. The Reserve Bank deflated the
bubble by increasing interest rates, and the rise of China created a
new driver of growth for Australia. The history that was about to
repeat was not the decline of the 1890s, but the gold rush of the
1850s.

Australia enjoyed two unique economic advantages in the opening decade of the twenty-first century. The first was in the earth.
Once China and then India emerged as economic powerhouses,
Australia's coal and iron ore resources became as valuable as gold.
The terms of trade – the prices Australia received for its exports
relative to the prices it paid for its imports – surged to levels not
seen since the 1850s. But the transformation of the society did not
come from mining, which accounted for less than 2.5 per cent of
all jobs in the economy. What drew more people to Australia was
the second economic advantage: education. Overseas students from
China and India were the vanguard of a new type of migrant who
came to Australia to study, and on completing their degrees applied
for permanent residency. In the five years preceding the mining
and education booms, between 1999 and 2003, net migration to
Australia was just under six hundred thousand. In the first five
years of the boom to 2008, it was one million.

Once migration rose, it almost guaranteed a second decade of
uninterrupted growth for the Australian economy. Enough time has
passed since Australia's remarkable escape from the global financial
crisis in 2008–09 to give migration the full credit it deserves. The
crisis was sourced to something that would have been familiar to
Australians of the late nineteenth century. In the first decade of the
twenty-first century the United States indulged in a housing boom

with the same dangerous characteristics of the Melbourne and Sydney land bubbles of the 1880s. People who could never afford to repay loans had borrowed on the assumption that house prices would continue rising.

'The problem with the US was the underlying incentives were to cause people to take massive risks,' Macfarlane says. 'The mortgage originator had a huge incentive to lend money to someone who couldn't pay it back. He'd pass it onto the investment bank, which had a huge incentive to put them all together and make them look better, then take it to the rating agency. The rating agency had a huge incentive to put a triple A on it and then it went back to the investment bank. The salesman at the investment bank had a huge incentive to sell it to an obscure Landesbank in Germany. All the way through, the system was full of incentives to take risks and push them onto someone else.'

Australia's banks were better regulated than their US counterparts and were not fooled by the so-called subprime mortgage. When the US housing market collapsed in 2007 it triggered a global debt crisis that ultimately brought down every rich nation in the world except one. Australia not only broke with its own past record of suffering the worst of global downturns, it broke with the world itself, by continuing to grow when rich nations such as the United States, Japan, Germany, Britain and Canada tumbled into their worst recessions since the Great Depression. The relative strength of the Chinese economy was clearly a factor in Australia's stellar performance, but it was not the only one.

The Reserve Bank had built an interest-rate buffer during the boom to check the rise of inflation, and was able to deploy it with rapid and large cuts when the crisis came. The Howard government had left behind a surplus budget, which its Labor successor, led by Kevin Rudd, was able to raid for cash handouts to keep consumers spending through the crisis.

The Treasury secretary at the time, Dr Ken Henry, says the claim that Australia survived simply because of China is not supported by the data. 'There's no doubt in the minds of people in the Treasury at the time, and a lot of work has been done on this, that without those fiscal stimulus packages the Australian economy would have gone into a very deep recession.' China did play an important role, but not immediately. 'The Chinese economy actually suffered a bigger slowdown than any of the industrialised countries in 2008–09. A bigger slowdown than the United States, a bigger slowdown than Europe. Of course, subsequently, the support provided by China and Korea – but by China in particular – was very important in providing support to the Australian economy through the second half of 2009, through 2010 and so on.'

But Henry says the critics of the Labor government's stimulus try to have it both ways by pointing to China's stimulus. 'And some of those who say, "But it was China who saved the Australian economy from recession" will even admit that it was the Chinese fiscal stimulus that did the work. Curiously, Chinese fiscal stimulus saves the Australian economy from recession, not Australian fiscal stimulus. I don't believe a word of it.'

All of the government's actions mattered, Macfarlane says, but he believes China was the main reason Australia pulled through. 'The first and immediate thing is the banking system didn't fail. So we didn't have bank runs and panics. The more fundamental reason is that our economy was plugged into the strong Asian part, producing products that went up in price, and we had much less connection with the extremely weak North Atlantic part. Our policies were right. I think our monetary [interest rate] policy and our fiscal [government stimulus] policy, or certainly the initial phase of fiscal policy, were right.'

Economists will argue the detail for many more years. What is apparent now, but was not as obvious at the time, is how migration kept the economy growing after the sugar hit of the stimulus faded in the second half of 2009, and after the peak of the mining boom itself, which was reached in 2011. Across this entire period, when the rest of the world was still counting the cost of the Great Recession, net migration to Australia actually beat its previous five-year record. Between 2009 and 2013, it increased by a further 1.1 million.

The mining boom could have been cancelled out by poor policy responses. But the open economic model handled this episode far better than the previous commodity boom of the late 1960s and early 1970s, when the fixed exchange rate and centralised wage system fuelled inflation, which led to a deep recession.

Consumers found this boom came with cheaper prices, because while China's demand increased the price of Australia's primary exports, its manufacturing sector reduced the cost of imported goods. Reserve Bank governor Glenn Stevens described Australia's unusual position by comparing a shipload of iron ore with imported flat-screen television sets. In 2005, one shipload could buy 2200 TVs. Five years later, it could buy 22 000 – 'partly due to TV prices falling but more due to the price of iron ore rising by a factor of six'. 'This is, of course, a trivialised example – we do not want to use the proceeds of exports entirely to purchase TV sets. But the general point is that high terms of trade, all other things being equal, will raise living standards, while low terms of trade will reduce them.'

Australia's economic success should be a cause for national celebration, and reflection. Opportunities like this are rare in any country's history. In Australia's case, this is the second occasion since the 1850s that its star has shone so brightly.

The simplest measure of Australia's success is its winning streak. At the time of writing, the economy has been growing for twenty-four years without the interruption of a deep recession. Although a downturn is inevitable at some point, it is testament to the open market and open-migration model that it could handle every one of the global and domestic shocks of the age, from the Asian financial crisis and the rise of Hansonism in the late 1990s to the disruption of the lost American decade of the 2000s.

The second decade of Australia's boom is certainly tied to the rise of China. This is demonstrated by the parallel climb of the two economies up the global production ladder. China's emergence actually restores it to the place it held from at least the birth of Christ until the early 1800s. Until that point, global production was distributed according to population, meaning China and India were the world's two largest economies. They still accounted for the majority of global output in 1820, when Lachlan Macquarie was duelling with John Thomas Bigge about the place of convicts in Sydney society. The Industrial Revolution and colonisation expanded production in Europe and North America, and sent China and India down the ladder. From the mid-nineteenth century, productivity, not population, was pivotal in determining both the absolute size of an economy and the standard of living. Australia was on the right side of this transaction while Britain remained a powerful empire.

The short story of the twenty-first century has been the catch-up of China and India, and the closer realignment of global production with population. In 2003, China was the world's sixth-largest economy and Australia was ranked fifteenth. Economists at the time did not see the connection between these nations because they did not foresee the resources boom that would herald their symbiotic ascent. China passed France in 2005, the United Kingdom in 2006, Germany in 2007 and Japan in 2010. Only the United States is ahead of it now. Australia followed China, rung for rung, passing the Netherlands in 2005, South Korea in 2008, Mexico in 2009 and Spain in 2011. The latest available rankings for 2014 have Australia in twelfth place, just behind Canada and Russia.

Yet Australia's political system has been in a state of high anxiety ever since the economy survived the Great Recession. The crisis in national confidence was apparent as soon as the asylum-seeker boats returned in 2009, after a relative absence of eight years. One boat in particular, carrying seventy-eight Sri Lankan asylum seekers bound for Christmas Island, set off a chain reaction that has changed the way Australia is viewed in Asia. This vessel had run into trouble while it was still in Indonesian waters in October 2009. Jakarta asked Canberra for help, and Labor prime minister Kevin Rudd obliged by sending the *Oceanic Viking*, a Customs patrol boat, to rescue the Sri Lankans at sea. The asylum seekers were taken back to Indonesia, but they refused to disembark until Australia guaranteed them safety.

Rudd had excelled during the financial crisis. The big decisions to stimulate the economy and guarantee all bank deposits were taken quickly, and explained to an anxious but trusting public. 'He was the right person in the right chair at the right time,' Julia Gillard says. 'Everything about his work capacity, his leadership style, came to the fore in a good way during those very difficult days.'

But the standoff with the asylum seekers gave voters their first real glimpse of another, more hesitant Rudd. Nothing would entice the Sri Lankans off the boat. Days passed, then weeks without a resolution. After a month, a deal was finally struck in favour of the asylum seekers. The US embassy in Canberra wrote a cable to Washington to record the damage to the prime minister's personal standing with the electorate. 'The duration of the saga undermined the government's border protection credentials with the public, while the PM's heavy-handed and increasingly awkward spinmeistering has alienated a media corps that has previously given him the benefit of the doubt on most issues,' according to the document dated 18 November 2009. That leaked analysis also noted that Australia's relations with Indonesia were tested by the episode. 'One theory is that Rudd's "megaphone diplomacy" on the 78 Tamils caused political pressure for [Indonesian president] Yudhoyono; that the Indonesian public don't want to be a dumping ground for what they perceive is Australia's problem.'

In a reversal of roles, Australia has become like the mother country of old, pushing people it does not want onto its allies. The lack of self-awareness is concerning because Indonesia is the third nation after China and India that is expected to thrive economically in the twenty-first century as global production realigns more with population. Indonesia was the sixteenth-largest economy in the world in 2013, just four places behind Australia. Ten years earlier, Indonesia was ranked twenty-second, seven behind Australia.

The escalation of politics made the second round of the asylum-seeker debate even more toxic than the first. Measures that John Howard would not have contemplated are now policy. Under the original Pacific Solution, Australia paid the poor countries of Nauru and Papua New Guinea to detain asylum seekers. But those found to be genuine refugees were ultimately resettled in Australia, or in other rich nations such as New Zealand. Now the poor countries of Papua New Guinea and Cambodia are paid to give the refugees a new home. No refugee who arrives by boat, regardless of the persecution they suffered in their home land, or any mistreatment they may receive in detention, is allowed to settle in Australia any more. It is a form of transportation in which Australia seeks to scrub her ethnicity clean of boatpeople.

What is missing is a common policy in the same bipartisan spirit that previous governments had shown towards regular migration. Australia does not lack the experience in integrating asylum seekers, and policy makers are certainly aware of the advantages that these people can bring to the economy and society. The local-born children of the Vietnamese have already matched the overachievement of the second-generation Greeks and Italians. The danger now is that this debate risks alienating not just Indonesia but other countries in the region from which Australia may seek migrants in the future.

The research of the main parties shows that public opinion separates asylum seekers from those who arrive through the regular program. John Howard goes so far as to argue that he was able to increase the migration intake because of his 'border protection' policies. Yet it is not entirely clear that politicians have maintained the distinction between the boatperson and the migrant. The asylum seekers who have tried to come to Australia in the new millennium have tended to be Muslims, and perhaps not coincidentally Muslim Australians have been the people on the receiving end of most of the recent media vilification and political point scoring. It has become almost normal practice now for conservative leaders and commentators to question the loyalty of Muslim Australians. In 2006, Howard said there was a 'fragment' of the Muslim community 'which is utterly antagonistic to our kind of society, and that is a difficulty'. 'You can't find any equivalent in Italian, or Greek, or Lebanese, or Chinese or Baltic immigration to Australia. There is no equivalent of raving on about jihad.'

The political appeal of this language may not be as strong as the main parties might assume. By the 2007 election, voters had tired of the terror card and Howard's government fell to the Kevin Rudd–led Labor Party. Howard even lost his own seat of Bennelong.

But the divisive politics of fear had a second coming following Tony Abbott's election in 2013. Abbott has been the most provocative prime minister since Billy Hughes, leaving entire sections of the Australian society with the impression that he doubts their patriotism, from the national broadcaster, the ABC, to the Muslim community. Voters may shrug at a leader who tries to bully the media, but it is another matter to target minority groups. 'I've often heard Western leaders describe Islam as a "religion of peace,"' Abbott said in 2015. 'I wish more Muslim leaders would say that more often, and mean it.' The echo of the conscription debate almost one hundred years earlier is unmistakable.

An optimistic reading of history is that Muslim Australians are merely the latest temporary victims of xenophobia, soon to be replaced by the next arrival. Yet the lesson of White Australia's sectarianism is that religious divisions can outlast by many decades the leaders who play the loyalty card.

But if any nation can secure a union between Muslim and

Christian it is Australia. It has a proud record of forging alliances that would have seemed ridiculous in the old world, beginning with the English and the Irish. The most significant postwar intakes from Europe and Asia had been bitter rivals before landing in Australia. The Greeks and Italians were on opposite sides of the Second World War. The Vietnamese and Chinese had been rivals for centuries, and were at war as recently as 1979.

Australians have proven remarkably adept at absorbing new arrivals without losing the national value of fairness. No migrant group has ever formed a permanent economic underclass in Australia. The only people with poverty, health problems, and rates of imprisonment well above the national average can be found in Australia's Indigenous communities. Of the non-Indigenous groups, the most disadvantaged happen to be 'white' – Australian-born single mothers. The most successful communities today are the migrants from China and India. The challenge for Australia is no longer the integration of European and Asian migrants. That mission has been accomplished. Having restored prosperity and diversity after the disaster of the White Australia policy, the test now is whether Australia can build on that success and create the world's first rich Eurasian nation.

18

AUSTRALIA'S
SECOND CHANCE

Australia's future had been foretold in the most astonishing place. In 1881, the British colony of Queensland was home to more migrants from Asia than from Europe, and to more men in total from China, Germany and the Pacific Islands than from England and Wales. That diversity was so frightening in the nineteenth century that it helped trigger the White Australia policy.

Today, that diversity defines Australia almost everywhere except Queensland. People born in Asia are the largest ethnic group in the country, accounting for 10 per cent of the total population. In New South Wales and Victoria they are closer to 12 per cent, and the only mainland state below 6 per cent is Queensland.

In the past, regardless of whether a state had a high or low proportion of people born overseas, the distribution in each was the same. The British were the top migrant community, followed after the war by the Italians. From the 1970s onward the New Zealanders took second place. This meant high and low migration states remained broadly familiar to one another.

Today the nation is moving in three different directions – one part leans towards China and India, another towards the mother country and the third towards the Pacific. Australia's Eurasian self is concentrated in Sydney and Melbourne, its Anglo-Celtic self in Perth and Adelaide, and a new Pacific identity is taking shape in Brisbane. The Chinese have already replaced the British as the largest overseas-born group in Sydney. The British still have the largest migrant community in Melbourne, but are likely to drop to third behind the Indians and the Chinese by the end of the next decade. Among migrants aged under thirty-five in Sydney and Melbourne, the British are already ranked third behind the Chinese and Indians. In Perth and Adelaide, the British remain unchallenged with almost the same population share that they had under White Australia. But in Brisbane, Australia's most parochial mainland capital, the New Zealand–born are poised to overtake the British.

The shift occurred in the blink of a decade, but it has been coming since the 1950s, when the postwar wave bypassed Queensland entirely and the European and British waves broke in different directions – the British headed to Adelaide and Perth while the Greeks and Italians went to Melbourne and Sydney. It is time to discard the old incantation that Australia is the sum of its Anglo-Celtic parts. Our heritage may be British and Irish, but our location has always been Asian. Now the demography is Eurasian.

The postwar restoration raised the migrant from 10 per cent of the Australian population in 1947 to 22 per cent by the mid-1970s. The most recent surge in migration has taken that figure from 23 per cent in 1999 to 28 per cent by 2014, and it has still further to rise. When the United States had the same population base as Australia does today, in 1850, its overseas-born were less than 10 per cent of the total. Today, only one of the fifty American states – California – has an overseas-born population comparable to Australia's – 27 per cent. Only two others, New York and New Jersey, have rates above 20 per cent. New South Wales, Victoria and Western Australia have a higher share than California, and all five mainland states – even the outlier of Queensland – have a greater proportion of migrants than New York and New Jersey.

The most revealing difference between Australia and the United States is not just the proportions of their respective migrant communities, but their compositions. Australia has been increasing migrant diversity at the very time that the United States is losing it. The best way to see this is to look at the origin of each nation's overseas-born population. Australia's 28 per cent comprises 10 percentage points from Asia, 9 from the old empire quartet of Britain, Ireland, New Zealand and South Africa, 5 from Europe, and just under 2 from the Middle East. In the United States, almost 7 of the 13 per cent total overseas-born population is from Latin America, 4 is from Asia and less than 2 from Europe. There is a logic to both flows. The ethnic faces of Australia and the United States are now inexorably linked to their respective locations. Each is essentially bilingual. Australia's main languages are English and Asian ones; America's are English and Spanish. Given the shift in global economic power from the North Atlantic to Asia, Australia now enjoys its greatest advantage over the United States in the global competition for migration since the gold rush.

In Australia's three cosmopolitan capitals, migrants already account for more than a third of the population – Sydney at 39 per cent, Perth at 37 per cent and Melbourne at 35 per cent. These proportions were last seen in the 1870s. Add the second generation – the local-born with at least one parent who was born overseas – and two-thirds of the population has a dual identity. In the inner suburbs of each city, the overseas-born account for more than half the total population. In Sydney's central business district they are 78 per cent of the population, while in the adjacent Haymarket they are 88 per cent, and across the railway line at Ultimo, 72 per cent. In Melbourne's CBD it is 68 per cent, and to the immediate north in Carlton it is 61 per cent. In Perth's Northbridge it is

68 per cent. The boom in international students explains almost half the migrants in each of these suburbs, and based on recent trends, most can be expected to settle permanently.

The migrants being drawn to Australia today are the best qualified since the golden intake of the 1850s. The Chinese and Indians carry the elevated expectations of rising nations, last seen in the British migrants of the Victorian era. Rapid development in these countries has drawn people from rural to urban areas, and encouraged the middle class to leave crowded, corrupted and polluted cities for a better life overseas. The new empire migrants don't have the overwhelming numbers of the golden intake, which overran a small colony and trebled the settler population in a decade. Even so, the Chinese and Indians pose the equivalent challenge to the nation that colonial authorities faced in the 1850s. If they are given prosperity without cultural acceptance – that is, if an old, white, macho media ridicules them; if they are shut out of the boardrooms and the parliament – they will simply move elsewhere, or go back home with reports that Australia is not the promised land. Australia's prosperity is contigent on their continued arrival.

The Chinese and Indian migrants of the twenty-first century are younger and better educated than their own predecessors who arrived in the Hawke–Keating era. The median age for both communities in 1999 was 42 years – six and a half years older than the Australia-wide figure. Today, the national median age is 37 years, but for the much larger Chinese-born population it is 35.5 years, and for the Indians 33 years. The British, on the other hand, are much older than the nation, with a median age of 54 years.

There is another empire wave worth recording: the Americans. Their numbers have almost doubled in the last decade, from 53 000 in 2001 to 104 000 in 2014. Australia now has more residents born in the United States than those from Ireland, Lebanon or the Netherlands. On present trends, the American migrant community will surpass the German, Greek and even the Scottish by

2020. American-Australian doesn't quite roll off the tongue yet, but it may well if Australia maintains its present path of prosperity. The opening decade of the twenty-first century marked the first occasion since the 1870s that the Australian economy soared while the US economy stagnated.

Australia has moved onto a new migration trajectory that is more dynamic than that of the postwar program from Europe. In the second half of the twentieth century, the population grew by 2.2 million per decade, and migration accounted for a third of that total, or just over 800 000. The latest available figures between 2003 and 2013 show that migration was responsible for almost two-thirds of a much larger increase in population – 2.1 million out of 3.3 million. The last decade when migration was responsible for more than half of Australia's population growth was the 1850s.

Without migration, the Australian population would stagnate at twenty-four million by 2050. With migration, the population is projected to grow to thirty-eight million. The migration program, like the economy, is no longer in the day-to-day control of politicians. If the economy remains strong, migrants will come. But if they do not feel welcome, they won't, and the economy and society will count the cost of their absence in lost demand and output, and a diminution of national creativity and energy.

The political system has been slow to grasp the change of the past decade and a half. For a while it saw the resources boom as a licence to bribe voters. Then, when the windfalls passed and the budget returned to deficit, fear became the default currency. It is telling that the national parliament is notably less diverse than the nation itself. Just 13 per cent of federal politicians in 2010 were born overseas, almost half of whom were, like Julia Gillard and Tony Abbott, born in Britain. It is this narrow political class that poses the greatest threat to Australia's second chance since the gold rush.

———

There have only been two periods in Australia's modern history that genuinely combined policy innovation, political stability and a shared sense of purpose across the parties of labour and capital. The first was the Curtin–Chifley–Menzies era between 1941 and 1966; the second was the Hawke–Keating–Howard era between 1983 and 2007. Each period was preceded by global humiliation for Australia – as the crash test dummy for austerity in the Great Depression of the 1930s and with the reputation of being the 'juvenile delinquent' economy of the 1970s and early 1980s.

Both eras commenced with the Halley's Comet of federal politics – a long-term Labor government – and ended with the complacency of a conservative government that secured one too many re-elections. Interestingly, the time spans were identical at almost a quarter of a century apiece, and when the eras closed they were followed by an extended period of volatility that was more in keeping with the first decade and a half of federation, when the nation had ten changes of prime minister and the parties of labour and capital each had spectacular ideological splits.

The political instability following the departure of Robert Menzies did have some redeeming features. Between them, Holt, Whitlam and Fraser opened up the society. The prime ministers who came after Howard have only chaos to their names. Rudd, Gillard and Abbott are united by failures of policy nerve, which, uncharacteristically for open Australia, have left the nation on the wrong side of international debates.

This difficulty is exemplified in the issue that all sides of politics agree poses the greatest long-term threat to Australia's prosperity – climate change. The system has veered between extremes of world-leading reform and wilful isolation, between building on our second chance and raising a twenty-first-century version of White Australia's tariff wall.

No policy debate in federal history has claimed more leaders or seen more policy U-turns than climate change. In 1998 the Howard government signed the so-called Kyoto Protocol, with twenty other nations, pledging to restrict greenhouse gas emissions. In 2002, the coalition changed its mind and said it would not ratify the deal. But the Australian public wanted action on climate change, and in 2007 John Howard had a late-career conversion to environmentalism. Although he still refused to ratify Kyoto he would now introduce a market-based scheme to reduce carbon emissions. This concession did not save his coalition government at the 2007 election. But the new Labor government of Kevin Rudd fared no better, even though it described climate change as the greatest moral and economic challenge of the generation.

Rudd abandoned his policy in 2010, after the coalition parties again changed their own position from support back to opposition. He suffered a stunning drop in his polling numbers; his colleagues panicked and ousted him in a leadership coup. Labor went to the 2010 election with a platform as convoluted as Howard's earlier policy. The new leader, Julia Gillard, promised there would be no carbon tax, while reserving the right to place a price on carbon through a market-based mechanism. That formula made no policy sense, because any market-based scheme would have to commence with a fixed price. Gillard changed her mind after the election and introduced a carbon tax to run for three years before moving to a market-based scheme. The policy did work to reduce emissions, but there was no political reward for Gillard and she lost her leadership to Rudd on the eve of the 2013 election. He disowned the carbon tax, while supporting a market-based scheme. Tony Abbott went to the election promising to scrap the entire scheme, and was rewarded with a thumping majority.

Abbott calculated that Australia could wait for the rest of the world to act on climate change, and that the nation would not be punished for its recalcitrance. But that strategy seems increasingly risky. In China's provinces, and in South Korea, the abolished Australian scheme is being used as a template for their emissions trading schemes. And the world's leaders have been moving towards a stronger public commitment to action. Australia was the odd nation out when Abbott hosted the summit of the world's twenty largest economies in Brisbane in September 2014. He insisted that climate change not be on the agenda, but the Americans and the Chinese coordinated a calculated diplomatic snub by announcing an agreement to reduce greenhouse gas emissions on the eve of the meeting. US president Barack Obama made his displeasure plain in Brisbane with a speech urging young Australians to stand up for action on climate change. 'One of the things we have in common is we produce a lot of carbon. Part of it's this legacy of wide-open spaces and the frontier mentality, and this incredible abundance of resources. And so, historically, we have not been the most energy-efficient of nations, which means we've got to step up.' Not since Harold Holt and John Curtin faced uncomfortable questions on the White Australia policy has a prime minister been challenged as directly on the world stage as Tony Abbott.

As a resource-dependent economy, Australia will always be prone to big swings in national income, in both directions. Climate change has all the hallmarks of a terms-of-trade bust for Australia, with a chief source of export wealth – coal – losing international favour. It happened with wool, and it would be naive for any political party to discount this risk. The weight of history is against isolationism; whenever Australia tried it in the twentieth century, the penalty was an extended stagnation. Yet the Abbott government has taken a perverse pride in its climate change scepticism, and has gone as far as to punish the renewable energy industry with funding cuts. If this attitude persists, it will mark something more than a reversion to protectionism. Australia built its tariff wall in an era when other nations were doing the same. But it did distinguish itself by being one of the first to remove protection in the 1980s. On climate change, Australia has turned inward against its own recent history of engagement, at a time when the rest of the world is becoming more engaged on the issue.

The Abbott approach is characteristic of his generation of politicians, who entered parliament after the last recession in 1990–91. They have governed in a long boom, at a time of disruptions in media technology and a decline in trust for all institutions. Typically, their road to parliament has been a straight line from student politics at university, to staff work for a politician or a trade union or business association, to preselection for a safe seat. They think short-term, and while their method is effective in crisis management, as witnessed by the Rudd government's deft handling of the global financial crisis, it is ill-equipped for identifying and dealing with long-term challenges.

The best of Australia's political culture was pragmatic in the true sense of the word. It resisted the extremes of Reaganism and Thatcherism in the 1980s, and avoided the celebrity traps of Clinton and Blair in the '90s. Hawke and Keating were trusted to open the economy while maintaining a social safety net. Howard reaffirmed Australian cohesion with his gun controls.

Previous reform eras had a sense of shared mission between the parties of labour and capital. There was not always agreement on the policy detail. But the nature of the problem was understood by both sides. Today neither party wants to concede even the smallest human error for fear of losing that minute's news cycle. If one side nominates an issue, the other feels compelled to deny its importance. And so the coalition argued that the global financial crisis and climate change were both beat-ups, while Labor refused to concede that the federal budget was in need of structural repair. The main parties are so immersed in the game of politics that they have imported the very thing the Americans hate about their own system – political gridlock by partisanship.

Both sides underestimate the economic danger of their behaviour. They have sped up the political cycle at the very time when governments need to return to a form of economic planning last seen in the postwar years. Climate change is the most diabolical example, requiring sacrifices that may not yield conclusive benefits for many deacdes. Another is urban infrastructure. Both federal and state governments have been slow to grasp the need for traditional nation-building policies to cope with record levels of migration. They are still trapped in the 1980s thinking that the public sector should be wound back in favour of the market. This has now proven to be a false economy, as the capital cities have struggled to cope with the influx. The danger is that Australia's ambition once again runs ahead of its fragile environment, as it did with the failed land settlement schemes of the 1920s.

In the last available statistics, Australia had four capitals rated in the top ten cities in the world for 'liveability'. Melbourne was first, Adelaide was equal fifth, Sydney seventh and Perth ninth. The economic evidence suggests that cities start to become unliveable – that is, gridlocked, polluted and with widening gaps between rich and poor – once they pass a population of four or five million. That is where Melbourne and Sydney are headed, and without a concerted effort to plan for this growth, the capitals will succumb to the same dysfunction as the crowded cities the British left in the nineteenth century, and those the Chinese and India are fleeing today. Australia cannot continue to prosper if Melbourne and Sydney are allowed to sprawl through policy neglect into replicas of Mumbai and Shanghai.

The NSW Labor government of Bob Carr took a novel approach to this challenge by declaring Sydney full, and encouraging migrants to go somewhere else. All this achieved was slower population growth and the weakest mainland economy in the first decade of the twenty-first century. Overseas migration didn't stop, but its effect on the economy was diluted by the exodus of a significant number of local-born families leaving for Queensland, Western Australia and Victoria. While Carr tried to contain growth, the more welcoming and relatively better-functioning Melbourne once again became the capital of open Australia. But even Melbourne is facing problems of congestion now because Steve Bracks' state Labor government did not sufficiently expand its public transport system in anticipation of a larger population.

It was one of the issues that kept Dr Ken Henry awake at night when he was Treasury secretary between 2001 and 2011. 'In the second half of the twentieth century, in those five decades, the Australian population increased by between 2.1 million and 2.4 million people [per decade],' he says. 'In the first decade of this century the Australian population increased by 3 million people. According to the mid-case projections, in each of the next four decades, the Australian population is going to grow by between 3.8 and 4.1 million. That's in each of those decades. Now, I was secretary to the Treasury during pretty much the first decade of this century, and one of the things that was very evident to me was that coping with an increase in the Australian population of 3 million people was more than the Australian policy system could handle.'

History does not offer much comfort as even the innovative postwar migration scheme was stymied by the refusal of the Menzies government to follow up with basic services such as sewerage for the new housing estates being developed in the outer suburbs.

Henry believes that all levels of government have yet to appreciate the need for planning. 'Australia has never had to deliver the sorts of infrastructure requirements that we're looking to over the next four decades. In fact, nothing, nothing remotely like it. I'm obviously a baby boomer. My experience of the government's provision of infrastructure is actually not that positive. The high school that I went to was opened in 1966, when governments knew there was a baby boomer cohort coming through; they even knew the size of it.' But governments did not build the extra schools to cater for these students. 'By the time I left Year 12 we had something like thirty demountable classrooms that had been brought in on the back of trucks, scattered around the school yard.'

Those same foreseeable demands have been unmet in recent years as hospitals have been caught without enough maternity beds, schools without enough classrooms, and the public transport network without enough trains. The short-term governing cycles of politics, and the shorter attention span of the media, have conspired to prevent a rational debate on the future of Australia's cities. When Kevin Rudd said in 2010 that he was an advocate for a Big Australia, his own ministers thought he was crazy for raising the issue and the electoral backlash was immediate. But the migrants are coming anyway, and if politics continues to duck this debate, the risk is that cities will begin to implode. Chinese and Indian migrants might not see it as a crisis because they will carry the skills and the wallets to live in the wealthy suburbs. But Australia could eventually find itself with entrenched pockets of disadvantage in the outer suburbs, where the less educated local-born and migrants will cluster, and congestion in the cosmopolitan centre. To head off this worst-case scenario, governments must think of their cities as fragile ecosystems.

Henry says if government gets it right, Australia would become a much more vibrant place. '[It could be] a country that has all the good things that large cities in other parts of the world demonstrate in terms of dynamism and cultural diversity. It could and, if done properly, it will. But as we've discovered in the past decade, if we don't do it well it could be truly bad.'

The short-term risks are in fact as deadly as the long-term. The absence of any tangible policies to prepare for the growth of the past decade has inflated property prices to the point where the new Treasury secretary, John Fraser, warns there may be a bubble in parts of Sydney and Melbourne. Supply has not kept up with demand, and investors have been crowding out first-home buyers because the tax system encourages speculation. A crash of 1890s proportions is unlikely while the banks remain better regulated and migration continues to prop up demand and prices. But house prices do fall in

Australia. They dropped sharply at the end of the 1980s, ahead of the recession of 1990–91, and remained flat across most of the 1990s.

The key indicators of social cohesion in Australia have been drifting in the wrong direction despite the winning streak since 1991. Income inequality has risen, the home ownership rate has declined markedly and Australia has now lost the most obvious advantage it enjoyed over the United States. Australia's unemployment rate first fell below America's in the open economic era in 2003 but the gap had closed by late 2013. By mid-2015, Australia's unemployment rate was 6 per cent – half a percentage point higher than America's. A 6 per cent unemployment rate after twenty-four years of uninterrupted growth is a poor return for those who have been left on the margins of society.

The fear of foreign competition used to hinge on the migrant dragging down Australia's standard of living. Now that standard of living depends on the migrant. This is the ultimate irony of Australia's return to an open market and open society; its vindication and the sting in the tail. The challenge now is to ensure that old Australia does not lose touch with new Australia.

Conclusion

The cycles of Australian prosperity are unlike those of any other country. The booms and the busts can run for decades, while the national personality reflects and reinforces these cycles. The decades of isolation from 1788 to the foundation of Melbourne in 1835 created a national inferiority complex that will always be with us. The windfalls of wool and gold that followed this period brought metropolitan settlement and migration, and the beginnings of an essential Australian optimism. Yet by the end of the 1880s we had literally got too rich for our own good, behaving like the spoilt brat of wealthy parents. The architects of the White Australia policy felt we had to keep out people and goods to preserve our standard of living. That miscalculation left Australia unprepared for multiple global shocks between the 1890s and 1940s. As we lost touch with the world, our old inferiority complex returned.

The mix of optimism and victimhood is the migrant's own personality: the overachiever who is unsure of their place in the new world. Australians crave attention and status, but we can't take a compliment when we've earned it. This is the Australian duality – we are a seemingly confident but ultimately anxious people. We are engaged with the world, but carrying a cultural chip on the shoulder. We never had the American assurance to seize independence from Britain, or even the Canadian cheek to remove the Union Jack from the flag. We clung to Britain from the final years of the nineteenth century until the Second World

War; transferred our affections to the United States until the end
of the twentieth century; and have been toying with the idea of
China as national saviour in the twenty-first century. At each
point, Australians assumed, correctly, that the mother country,
the big brother and the business partner didn't think about them
a great deal – but their indifference only made us more willing
to please.

We still worry that our leaders will embarrass us on the world
stage. When I see an Australian prime minister snuggle up to a
US or Chinese leader, I hear Mum asking my sixth-grade pals,
'Tell me, now, has Georgie been good at school?' I'd like to see
the day when we are comfortable enough in our own skin to
let others ask the first question: 'How did you make the world's
greatest migrant nation?'

Understanding the false pride that undermined us in the past,
and true source of our success – people, not resources – has never
been more critical. Australia can only survive in a neighbourhood
of giants if it thinks big. It is not necessarily a matter of size,
because the continent may not be able to carry a very large
population. It is a question of ambition. To reach a position of
national maturity, we must maintain our openness, and take the
lead in a global conversation. Role model is the wrong term –
it reeks of that cloying superiority of the golden intake, which
quickly turned to hubris. Australia is too small to dictate to the
world. But the idea of Australia has been big enough to inspire
millions to make a new home here over almost two hundred
years. Only the United States has attracted and retained more
people since mass migration commenced in the 1830s.

Australia matters more than most nations because it remains
a settlement with potential. Our unique strengths are our social
cohesion, our ability to turn the disparate, querulous cultures of
the world into a unified people, and a long tradition of pragmatic
policy innovation. But these advantages come with a burden.

The rest of the world expects Australia to succeed, given our small population and resource endowment. Our previous eras of poor performance were punished so severely because the world believed we had let it down. This is the pragmatic argument for openness, because history tells us the alternative is an isolated, belittled Australia. A globally minded Australia will continue to thrive, because the world will project its best self onto us.

Most nations don't get a first chance to prosper. Australia is on its second. It would be a shame if we passed up this opportunity because we were afraid of success.

ACKNOWLEDGEMENTS

Thank you to family and friends who have tolerated my absences in the preparation of this book. In alphabetical order, Allison Sloan, Anna Ferguson, Anna Megalogenis, Anna Ziaras, Annabel Crabb, Bronwen Colman, Erin Vincent, Esther Anatolitis, Fiona Hando, Foong Ling Kong, Gabrielle Chan, Gavan Randles, Geoff Ginn, Gigi Megalogenis, Jeff Jenkins, Joe Setright, Joe Fulco, Joel Deane, Kate Legge, Kellie Mayo, Louise Perry, Lynne Gallagher, Margaret Easterbrook, Marie Claire Gateaux, Michael Williams, Natasha Cica, Nick Harford, Nick Leys, Nina Field, Patricia Karvelas, Paul Daley, Peta Stevenson, Rebecca Huntley, Sean O'Beirne, Susan Hornbeck, Tom Dusevic and Waleed Aly.

Thank you to Glyn Davis, Anthony Page, Shaun Ratcliff and Julianne Schultz for invaluable advice on areas of research to pursue, and to all those above who helped workshop the ideas. Special thanks to David and Meryl at Lorne Books and Toby Colman for the use of your brilliant library.

This project coincided with the ABC documentary *Making Australia Great*, and is the richer for it. Three cheers to series producer Alex West, director Bruce Permezel, and the team, Miriam Kenter, Robyn Young, Zac Grant, Dan Thomas, and Nicole Curby. And at ABC HQ, Mark Scott, Kate Torney and Phil Craig.

Finally, and most importantly, thank you to the crew at Penguin: Ben Ball, Gabrielle Coyne, Heidi McCourt, John Canty, Johannes Jakob, Nikki Lusk, Glenda Browne and especially the book's editor, Arwen Summers.

NOTES

MAIN SOURCES:

Unless noted otherwise, the dispatches from governors are taken
  from the *Historical Record of Australia*. See: archive.org/
  details/historicalrecordoooust; volume II: archive.org/details/
  historicalrecordoov2aust; etc.

Basic overview of the Australian population, including gender, colonial
  and state breakdowns, net migration, country of birth and
  Indigenous population drawn from Australian Bureau of
  Statistics (ABS) catalogue 3105.0.65.001 – Australian Historical
  Population Statistics, 2014: www.abs.gov.au/AUSSTATS/abs@.
  nsf/DetailsPage/3105.0.65.0012014?OpenDocument_

Detail of colonial censuses: hccda.ada.edu.au/

Convict statistics, 1787 to 1837, taken from Martin, Robert
  Montgomery, *Statistics of the Colonies of the British Empire*,
  Allen and Co, 1839, Appendix V Australasia, 176,

Emigration from the United Kingdom 1815–1872 taken from *Emigration
  Commission, Thirty-third general report of the emigration
  commissioners*, Appendix No. 1, 48–9

Latest overseas-born statistics: stat.abs.gov.au//Index.
  aspx?QueryId=743

Latest migration report: 3412.0 – Migration, Australia, 2013–14.
  See: www.abs.gov.au/AUSSTATS/abs@.nsf/allprimarymainfea
  tures/66CDB63F615CF0A2CA257C4400190026?opendocument

Summary of nineteenth-century population censuses from the United
  Kingdom: www.visionofbritain.org.uk/census/table_page.
  jsp?tab_id=EW1911GEN_A_C1&show=DB

Detailed United Kingdom censuses from 1801 to 1971: www.
  visionofbritain.org.uk/census/

United States historical censuses: www.census.gov/population/www/
      censusdata/hiscendata.html

Detailed United States censuses of foreign-born populations since 1850:
      www.census.gov/population/www/documentation/twps0029/
      tab04.html

National comparisons of economic growth between AD 1 and 2010,
      which shows Australia's rise to the top of the global income
      ladder in the nineteenth century and subsequent fall, taken from
      the New Maddison Project Database: www.ggdc.net/maddison/
      maddison-project/data.htm; see also Maddison, Angus, *The
      World Economy: A Millennial Perspective*, OECD, 2001

Unless otherwise noted, biographical information for colonial figures
      is taken from the *Australian Dictionary of Biography:*
      adb.anu.edu.au/

Prime ministers: primeministers.naa.gov.au/primeministers/

Election results: elections.uwa.edu.au/electionsearch.lasso?ID=2; and
      Parliamentary Library research paper, *Federal Election Results
      1901–2014*, 17 July 2004

All newspaper articles quoted can be searched at trove.nla.gov.au/

Main interviews conducted for this book: Malcolm Fraser, 29 January
      and 11 March 2014; Peter Costello, 28 March 2014; Ken Henry,
      9 April 2014; Ian Macfarlane, 10 April 2014; John Howard, 29
      April 2014; Bob Hawke, 15 May 2014; Mark Textor, 17 June 2014;
      Julia Gillard, 4 July 2014; Paul Keating, 8 and 9 July 2014.

INTRODUCTION

ix   **Twenty-four years have passed** The only developed economy
      to have grown for longer than Australia was the Netherlands,
      which grew for twenty-six and a half years from 1981 to 2008.
      Its winning streak ended with the global financial crisis. See:
      www.treasury.gov.au/PublicationsAndMedia/Speeches/2014/
      Fiscal_sustainability

      'poor white trash of Asia' The best summary of Lee Kuan
      Yew's famous quote was written by Graeme Dobell, for the
      Australian Strategic Policy Institute. www.aspistrategist.org.au/
      lee-kuan-yew-and-oz-white-trash-or-white-tribe-of-asia-1/

CHAPTER ONE

3   **They had spent the previous seventeen thousand years**
Summarised from Blainey, Geoffrey, 'I see parts of history with
fresh eyes', the *Weekend Australian*, 21–22 February 2015.

6   **When Phillip and Bennelong reunited** I relied on two
comprehensive accounts of the spearing of Arthur Phillip:
Clendinnen, Inga, *Dancing with Strangers*, Text Publishing, 2003,
110–132; Champion, Shelagh and George Champion, 'The Spearing
of Governor Phillip at Collins Cove (now Manly Cove), 7
September, 1790', 1989. See: www.manly.nsw.gov.au/IgnitionSuite/
uploads/docs/The%20Spearing%20of%20Governor%20Phillip%20
at%20Collins%20Cove.pdf
While this argument 'seemed at first to threaten the colony'
Collins, David, 'An Account of the English Colony in New South
Wales', 1798

7   **By 1775, some fifty thousand felons** The figure comes from Butler,
James, 'British Convicts Shipped to American Colonies', the
American Historical Review, Vol. 2, No. 1 (Oct., 1896), 12–33. See:
www.jstor.org/stable/1833611?seq=1#page_scan_tab_contents

8   **One third of the First Fleet intake** Ratio calculated from the
University of Wollongong's online database: firstfleet.uow.edu.au/
download.html

9–10   **'The men convicts got to them very soon after'** The full diary of
Arthur Bowes Smyth: www.sl.nsw.gov.au/discover_collections/
history_nation/terra_australis/journals/bowes_smyth/index.html
See also 'The women come ashore': firstfleet.uow.edu.au/s_women.
html; and 'Phillip addresses the convicts': firstfleet.uow.edu.au/s_
harang.html

12   **six marines were hanged** Private John Easty's diary: www.sl.nsw.
gov.au/discover_collections/history_nation/terra_australis/
journals/easty/index.html

12-13   **At the final muster of 1789** Calculations from ABS data set
3105.0.65.001 *Australian Historical Population Statistics, 2014*
Table 1.1

CHAPTER TWO

17   **the military got fatter** Although the rule prohibiting government
staff and marines from owning land had been scrapped just before

Arthur Phillip left for London, Francis Grose still went further than intended. As B H Fletcher wrote in the *Australian Dictionary of Biography*, 'Without specific instructions and apparently on his own initiative he issued land grants of about twenty-five acres (10 ha) apiece to serving members of the corps who requested them.' Officers were still prohibited from using convicts for their own private gain.

18   **Almost five hundred migrants** Clendinnen, *Dancing With Strangers*, 285. Phillip had moved most of the settlement to Parramatta from 1788 because it had superior soil to Sydney Cove. The soil at the Hawkesbury and Nepean Rivers was even better, but according to his *Australian Dictionary of Biography* entry, by B H Fletcher, 'Phillip opposed the settlement of the Hawkesbury because the area was too isolated and too little known, and "proper people to conduct it" were lacking'.

20   **Macquarie . . . found the colony upbeat, but in disrepair** Account written after he had left the colony, in a letter to Lord Bathurst dated 27 July 1822.

21   **animals jostled with people for the right of way** Summary of Haskell, Arnold, *The Australians*, Adam & Charles Black, 1943, 45.

23   **At 'Aboriginal Feast Day'** Full account of meeting published in the *Sydney Gazette*, 31 December 1814, www.mq.edu.au/macquarie-archive/lema/documents.html

24   **The relationship broke down at Appin** Macquarie's reasons for the punitive strike against the locals are contained in his diary entry of 10 April 1816: www.mq.edu.au/macquarie-archive/lema/1816/1816april.html#apr16

25   **He declared mission accomplished on 4 May** www.mq.edu.au/macquarie-archive/lema/1816/1816may.html#may1
The *Australian Dictionary of Biography* entry for Lachlan Macquarie by N D McLachlan gives an unsatisfactory one-sentence account of the massacre. 'The results of this naive policy [of engagement] were not very encouraging and in 1816, when the natives showed signs of ungrateful hostility, he organized a military drive to chasten them. But no other governor since Phillip had shown them so much sympathy.'

25   **George Arthur vowed to punish all wrongdoers equally** Summary of Arthur's *Australian Dictionary of Biography* entry, by A G L

Shaw; and Boyce, James, *Van Diemen's Land,* Black Inc, 2014 reprint, 261–94.

26 **Although outnumbered three-to-one** See Stirling's *Australian Dictionary of Biography* entry by F K Crowley.

A local population of up to one million There is no reliable estimate of the Indigenous population at 1788. According to the ABS summary in *Year Book Australia, 2003* '. . . the absolute minimum pre-1788 population [was estimated] at 315 000. Other estimates have put the figure at over 1 million, while recent archaeological finds suggest that a population of 750 000 could have been sustained.' See: www.abs.gov.au/AUSSTATS/abs@.nsf/Previousproducts/2F6A3D06D66A12A5CA256CAE00053F9C?opendocument

perhaps twenty thousand, according to a summary Hirst, John, *Looking for Australia,* Black Inc., 2010, 24.

28 **By 1820 . . . the majority of the New South Wales population was already free** Table taken from the Bigge report, and published in Greenwood, Gordon (ed), *Australia: A Social and Political History,* Angus and Robertson, 1955, 13. Note the breakdown between the mainland and Van Diemen's Land. Of the 2021 free migrants in the colony, New South Wales had 1307, or just 5.5 per cent of its population, and Van Diemen's Land had 714, or 13.1 per cent of a much smaller population. But Van Diemen's Land had a higher proportion of serving convicts at the time, and therefore would receive a disproportionate share of the next wave of convicts.

28–29 **The first volume of the Bigge report** *Report of the Commissioner of Inquiry into the State of the Colony,* House of Commons, 1822.

29 **Fifty thousand convicts** Summary of data drawn from *Statistics of the Colonies of the British Empire,* 176; *Emigration Commission,* 48–9 (see main sources) and William Molesworth's speech to the House of Commons, 5 May 1840, archive.org/stream/cihm_39569#page/n3/mode/2up

CHAPTER THREE

30 **The convicts were excessively English** '. . . the vast majority of the convicts to Australia were English and Welsh (70%), Irish (24%) or Scottish (5%)'. By contrast, the English and Welsh were 59 per

cent of the UK population in 1841, the Irish 31 per cent and the
Scottish 10 per cent. See: www.australia.gov.au/about-australia/
australian-story/convicts-and-the-british-colonies

31   **The architect of the Irish massacre** Summary of Keneally, Thomas,
Australians: Origins to Eureka, Allen & Unwin, 2010, 225–35. See
also: www.bbc.co.uk/history/british/empire_seapower/irish_
reb_01.shtml_

33   **Castle Hill** Summary of the uprising is drawn from Keneally, ibid.
See also Anne-Maree Whitaker: dictionaryofsydney.org/entry/
castle_hill_convict_rebellion_1804

36   **women were ten times more likely to be raped** Statistics drawn
from Molesworth's speech, House of Commons, 29–30. He wrote
that the general crime rate in the colonies was 'about one in a
hundred of the whole population' compared to about one in a
thousand in England and one in thirteen hundred in Scotland.
Britain's population was majority female The gender gaps were
calculated using the nineteenth-century census data for the United
Kingdom, United States, Canada and Australia. The male deficits
in Britain and Ireland were virtually equal to the surpluses in the
settler societies. For example, in 1881, the UK had 972 249 fewer
men than women. They seem to have gone to the three settler
societies. The US had 779 898 more men than women in 1880;
Canada 52 895 in 1881 and Australia 156 948 in 1881, for a total
of 989 741. Because of its smaller population, Australia was the
most masculine of the trio (54.1 per cent male) while the US (50.8
per cent) and Canada (50.6 per cent) were approaching gender
balance.

38   **mass emigration** Figures from Britain and Ireland adapted from
Baines, Dudley, *Emigration from Europe, 1815–1930*, Cambridge
University Press, 1995, 3; and *Emigration Commission* (see main
sources).

40   **As the wool boom accelerated** The final report of Bourke's
immigration committee, presented to London in 1837,
emphasised the need for agricultural workers. 'The want of
shepherds, stockmen, agricultural laborers [sic] in general, and
of mechanics in a smaller proportion has become so alarming
and necessitous . . . that unless Immigration be immediately
encouraged to the full extent of the present demand for labour out

of the funds set apart for that purpose, the consequences will be most fatal to the best interests of the colony.' 'Immigration', *Sydney Monitor*, 6 September 1837, 2–3.

43   **'God's police'** Summary of Caroline Chisholm's letter to Earl Grey, *Sydney Chronicle*, 6 January 1848, 3.

44   **The mother of the Australian nation** The first censuses to be taken at the same time across all six colonies were conducted in 1881. They showed the British-born in Australia were 59.9 per cent male, while the Irish had achieved gender balance – 50.1 per cent male and 49.9 per cent female. Women were the majority in the Irish communities of Victoria (52.5 per cent) and South Australia (50.3 per cent). They had also been the majority in New South in 1856, and in Victoria and South Australia between 1861 and 1921. Calculations made using ABS data set 3105.0.65.001 *Australian Historical Population Statistics*, 2014, Table 8.

45   **'The real evil'** Charles Trevelyan's comment on 6 January 1847, as cited in Keneally, Thomas, *Three Famines*, Vintage Books, 2011, 65. Trevelyan followed up these controversial thoughts in his 1848 book, *The Irish Crisis*, archive.org/details/irishcrisi00trev
One million Irish perished Official Irish record: www.parliament.uk/about/living-heritage/evolutionofparliament/legislativescrutiny/parliamentandireland/overview/the-great-famine/
And another two million abandoned the country Willcox, Walter F. (ed), *International Migrations, Volume II: Interpretations*, National Bureau of Economic Research, 1931, 265, table 93. Note Australia received just 75 000 or 3.6 per cent of the total in that period. See: www.nber.org/chapters/c5112.pdf

47-8   **The *Sydney Morning Herald* had also had enough** Editorial, the *Sydney Morning Herald*, 13 March 1850, 2.

CHAPTER FOUR

52   **cultivation by fire had created a 'park-like' estate** See Gammage, Bill, *The Biggest Estate on Earth: How Aborigines Made Australia*, Allen & Unwin, 2012.

53   **the newspaper cheerfully announced the acquisition of five hundred thousand acres** The *Hobart Courier* of 26 June 1835 contained two articles on the Batman venture, on pages 2 and 4. The article on page 2 describes the 'compact which Mr. Batman

has so wisely made with the original owners of the soil' and regrets
that a similar arrangement hadn't been taken when Van Diemen's
Land was settled.

53–4   **When Fawkner joined the camp** As quoted in Greenwood, *Social and Political History*, 77.

54   'It obviously helped' Boyce, James, *1835: The Founding of Melbourne and the Conquest of Australia,* Black Inc., 2012, 86–7.
   'The background of most was middle class' Greenwood, *Social and Political History*, 71.

55   **'The colonists had little idea'** Ibid, 74.

58–9   **The Orange Riots** James Palmer's official report on the riots appeared in *The Argus*, 4 August 1846, 4; the New South Wales parliamentary debate on 21 October 1846, including details of the Party Procession Bill, appeared in the *Maitland Mercury and Hunter River General Advertiser*, 24 October 1846, 2.

60   **Port Phillip surged** The population of 76 000 at the end of 1850 is an estimate. At the census of 2 March 1851, the last before Victoria separated from New South Wales, the population was recorded at 77 345. Figures for Van Diemen's Land, South Australia and Western Australia are for 31 December 1850. From ABS data set 3105.0.65.001 *Australian Historical Population Statistics, 2014,* Table 1.1.

61   **Taking the long view** GDP per capita for all counties from 1835 to 1850 calculated from raw tables on the New Maddison Project Database: www.ggdc.net/maddison/maddison-project/data.htm. Australia's advantage was even greater over the 1840s, with national income increasing by 93 per cent from 1839 to 1849 compared to 4 per cent for the United States and 14 per cent for the United Kingdom.

62–3   **in early 1849, something snapped** 'The Great Protest Meeting', the *Sydney Morning Herald*, 12 June 1849, 2; *The Argus* account of the *Randolph* protest meeting, 'Last Night's Meeting', 21 August 1849, 2.

63   **The *Hashemy* wasn't sent back** Among the convicts on this ship was English apprentice baker William Groom, who was thirteen when he was convicted of stealing in 1846. His reformation took him from publican to newspaper publisher and eventually to the first mayor of Toowoomba, Queensland. He was elected to the

first federal parliament in 1901 as the member for Darling Downs. Our first convict MP unfortunately became the first federal politician to die in office, passing away in August 1901.

64 **Earl Grey had given the House of Lords a stirring account** 10 August 1848, speech extracted in the *Sydney Morning Herald*, 9 December 1848, 3–4.

CHAPTER FIVE

67 **California's 210 000** Estimate for 1854, based on census results of 92 597 in 1850 and 379 994 in 1860.

at least four migrants from Sydney were lynched McAllister, Peter, 'Sydney Ducks', *The Monthly*, February 2015. See: www.themonthly. com.au/issue/2015/february/1422709200/peter-mcallister/ sydney-ducks

72-3 **The mother county . . . encouraged her sons** Quotes attributed to Charles Dickens, and the article in *Punch* as cited in Serle, Geoffrey, *The Golden Age*, Melbourne University Press, 1963, 37.

76 **The Times wrote** 'The Progress of Victoria', *The Argus*, 9 December 1856, 5

80-1 **Rafaello Carboni** As cited by Serle, *Golden Age*, 162–3.

CHAPTER SIX

83 **But Hotham was in a supercilious mood** Account of the lieutenant governor's meeting with the diggers on 27 November 1854 taken from 'Sir Charles Hotham and the Ballarat Deputation', the *Sydney Morning Herald*, 5 December 1854, 5.

85 **He asked for volunteers** Peter Lalor, 'To the colonists of Victoria', *The Argus*, 10 April 1855, 7.

'the greatest scoundrels in the colony' As cited by Serle, *Golden Age*, 168.

at least 'thirty killed on the spot' The account by J W Thomas, captain commanding troops at Ballarat, published in 'The disturbances at Ballarat', *The Age*, 21 December 1854, 4–5. Lalor's account listed fourteen 'killed' and twelve 'wounded, and since died'.

88 **'drawn from the middle class'** Serle, *Golden Age*, 372.

91 **Elections under the new system** Summary of colonial democratic reforms can be found on the website of the Australian Electoral

Commission: www.aec.gov.au/elections/australian_electoral_
history/reform.htm and the Museum of Australian Democracy:
www.foundingdocs.gov.au/timeline-b-1837-t-1899.html

95　　**'A man of Yankee temperament'** 'The "short hours" question', *The
Argus*, 2 April 1856, 4.

96　　**'some stupid mischievous blockhead'** Full quote in Kimber, Julie
and Peter Love (eds) *The Time of their Lives*, Australian Society for
the Study of Labour History, 2007, 10. See also: ergo.slv.vic.gov.au/
explore-history/fight-rights/workers-rights/james-stephens
The eight-hour day became the norm Summary of legislation
across the colonies from Clark, C H H (ed), *Select Documents
in Australian History 1851–1900*, Angus and Roberstson, 1955,
734–5.

CHAPTER SEVEN

104　　**the Chinese would lose almost fifty million** Maddison, *The World
Economy*, 39–40 (see main sources).

108　　**'Even if the Chinese were considered desirable colonists'** 'Report
from the Commission Appointed to Inquire into the Conditions of
the Gold-fields of Victoria', *The Argus*, 3 April 1855, 6.

108-9　　**'What we mainly wish to guard against'** 'Law for the Chinese', *The
Argus*, 28 May 1855, 5.

111　　**'the whole white population'** 'Riot at the Buckland', the *Sydney
Morning Herald*, 13 July 1857, 5.

113–4　　**One of the few politicians to defend the Chinese unconditionally**
Extracts from the parliamentary debate of 25 September 1857
published in the next day's 'Parliamentary Intelligence', *The Argus*, 4.

115　　**Miner George Preshaw** 'Lambing Flat', the *Sydney Morning
Herald*, 13 July 1861, 5.

CHAPTER EIGHT

119　　**The Sydney newspapers joined the chorus** *The Empire* condemned
the Towns scheme in its page 5 editorial on 3 September 1863.

119-20　　**Towns wrote to the Queensland premier** *The Empire* ran the
letter in full on page 8 of the edition mentioned above, under the
headline 'The Honorable Robert Towns M.L.C [Member of the
Legislative Council], Sydney to the Honorable R. G. W. Herbert,
Esq, Colonial Secretary. Queensland'.

120 **'great ignorance' and 'strange ideas'** Raymond Evans' observation, as cited in Banisch, Mark, *Queensland*, NewSouth Publishing, 2015, 158.

127 **'We are now threatened'** John Douglas's letter to his fellow premiers, and Earl Carnarvon's objections to the original Queensland legislation: 'Chinese Immigration', the *Brisbane Courier*, 30 May 1877, 3.

128 **'A great number were shot during the night'** 'Sydney Summary', the *Goulburn Herald and Chronicle*, 23 November 1872, 5.

129 **'the life of a black man'** 'Supreme Court', the *Brisbane Courier*, 28 November 1884, 5.

130 **At a mass public rally** 'The case of McNeill and Williams', *The Queenslander*, 27 December 1884, 1031 [sic]. See also: Wiener, Martin J., *An Empire on Trial: Race, Murder, and Justice Under British Rule 1870–1935*, Cambridge University Press, 2009, 39–70; Finger, Jarvis, *A Cavalcade of Queensland's Crimes and Criminals*, Boolarong Press, 2012, 87–8

131 **'My objection to Polynesian labour'** 'Sir S. W. Griffith's Manifesto, the government resolved on a ten years' extension of Pacific Island labour for tropical agriculture', the *Brisbane Courier*, 13 February 1892, 5.

CHAPTER NINE

134 **almost six in ten dwellings** The number of houses in Victoria increased by 45 484, from 134 332 in 1861 to 179 816 in 1881. The number with one or two rooms also decreased by 36 206, which suggests for every new home built another existing dwelling had one or more rooms added to it.

135 **the precision of his confidence** *Victorian Year-Book, 1887–8*, 54

136 **'Australia for the White Man'** www.federationstory.com/the-bulletin-magazine-first-published-in-sydney/

137-141 Summary of the land boom from Fisher, Chay and Christopher Kent, 'Two Depressions, one banking collapse', Research Discussion Paper 1999-06, June 1999, System Stability Department, Reserve Bank of Australia (RBA); Simon, John, 'Three Australian asset-price bubbles', RBA, Conference Volume 2003 (see: www.rba.gov.au/publications/confs/2003/simon.html); Cannon, Michael, *The Land Boomers*, Melbourne University Press,

Melbourne, 1966; McLean, Ian W., *Why Australia Prospered*,
Princeton University Press, 2013, 113–43.

142   **The *Sydney Morning Herald* sided with the upfront Queenslanders**
Editorial 4 August 1887, 6-7. This commentary predicted the
Afghan crisis of 1888. 'The restrictions which have been placed upon
Chinese immigration have been adopted deliberately, and with
the determination that Australia shall be essentially a European
community. We have made up our minds not to be overrun by
the Chinese or any other inferior race, and no proposal to relax
the precautions which serve to keep back the threatened Chinese
invasion would be listened to for a moment.'

145   **His name was Lo Pak** Justice Windeyer's judgment, the *Sydney
Morning Herald*, 19 May 1888, 10.

145-6 **The legislation Parkes rushed through** Full transcript of the
debate: 'Legislative Assembly', the *Sydney Morning Herald*, 17 May
1888, 5-6. Further reading for chapters eight and nine: Griffiths,
Philip Gavin, 'The making of White Australia: Ruling Class
Agendas, 1876–1888', Australian National University, 2006. See:
espace.library.uq.edu.au/view/UQ:265385/Griffiths_thesis.pdf

CHAPTER TEN

150   **In 1893, the global economy fell** Whitten, David, 'Depression
of 1893', EH.Net Encyclopedia, 2001, eh.net/encyclopedia/
the-depression-of-1893/

158-61 **A sample of both conservative and Labor views** *Hansard*: Edmund
Barton, 26 September 1901; Alfred Deakin, 12 September 1901;
Chris Watson, 6 September 1901; Billy Hughes, 12 September 1901;
Henry Higgins, 20 September 1901; Isaac Isaacs, 12 September
1901; Bruce Smith, 25 September 1901.

161   **'In some respects it must be slavery'** *Hansard*, 2 October 1901.

163   **'they are not always trustworthy'** 'Queensland sugar industry,
the deportation of the Kanaka, statement by the prime minister',
the *Western Australian*, 16 January 1907, 7. Deakin played down the
number who had been deported illegally, saying: 'I have inquired
carefully into this matter, and find that in only two instances can
there be any doubt about the fullest information not having been
given.'

CHAPTER ELEVEN

165   **The economy went backward in every year** I have used GDP per capita throughout the nineteenth century, and in the two world wars for sake of consistency and because it is the best available measure for comparing Australia's performance against other nations. On the other hand, annual GDP did not fall in every year of the First World War. See 'Australia's century since Federation at a glance', Australian Treasury, Chart 1: archive.treasury.gov.au/documents/110/PDF/round3.pdf

166   **'What sort of peculiar capitalist country is this'** Lenin, V. I., *Lenin Collected Works,* Progress Publishers, 1977, Volume 19, 216-7. www.marxists.org/archive/lenin/works/1913/jun/13.htm

167   **'to our last man and our last shilling'** www.aph.gov.au/About_Parliament/Parliamentary_Departments/Parliamentary_Library/pubs/rp/rp1415/AustToWar1914

167-8   **'If I were German'** *Hansard,* 28 October 1914

169   **'drunk with the lust of power'** 'An appeal to all who love liberty', *The Worker,* 21 September 1916, 14.

171   **'There is a war to the knife'** Hughes, Aneurin, *Billy Hughes,* Wiley, 2005, 64–5. Hughes sent his secret cable to Lloyd George on 30 December 1916.

172   **Charles Heydon** 'Archbishop Mannix, criticised by Justice Heydon', *Riverine Herald,* 20 November 1917, 3. Mannix's reply, reported in the *Freeman's Journal,* 22 November 1917, 23, was caustic. 'People are under the impression that this person is an Irishman. He is not an Irishman. His father was an Englishman, and I believe he was born in Australia. People are also under the impression that he is a Judge of the High Court. He is not. He is a judge of the second or third class of some kind or other.'

173   **'this meeting of loyal citizens'** 'Great protest rally, prosecution of traitors urged', *Bendigonian,* 22 November 1917, 22.

174-5   **'the Prime Minister was daunted by nothing'** Summary of accounts in 'Riot at Warwick', the *Brisbane Courier,* 30 November 1917, 7, and 'Reinforcements Referendum', *The Register,* 30 November 1917, 7. See also: www.naa.gov.au/collection/fact-sheets/fs161.aspx

CHAPTER TWELVE

180   'loss of population growth' 'Characteristics of the Development of the Population of Australia and the Effect of the War thereupon', ABS: 1301.0 – *Year Book Australia, 1920*, 1128. The Spanish flu claimed a further twelve thousand lives.

181   'The soldiers made a rush' 'Soldier settlement, Royal Commission's report, why the scheme failed', *The Mercury*, 30 September 1926, 7, 9.

183   'Australia is part of the British Empire' *Hansard*, 28 May 1926.

184   the new Canadian wave Data from Martel, Laurent and Jonathan Chagnon, 'Population growth in Canada: From 1851 to 2061', Statistics Canada, 2013, figure 1: www12.statcan.gc.ca/census-recensement/2011/as-sa/98-310-x/98-310-x2011003_1-eng.cfm

185   the US Congress moved to shut the door Summary of 1924 Immigration Act (an act to limit the immigration of aliens into the United States, and for other purposes): library.uwb.edu/guides/usimmigration/1924_immigration_act.html (note the annual quota for Australians was 121, three fewer than Armenians).

186   'refrain from granting passport facilities to Spanish or Greek intending migrants' Letter from Bruce to Gunn, 9 September 1924, National Archives of Australia (NAA) A1, 1936/13639 13.

191   'dagoes before heroes' Ben Chifley's quote as cited by Day, David, 'Beazley's tempted to appeal to the fickle mob', *The Age*, 19 September 2006, www.theage.com.au/news/opinion/beazleys-tempted-to-appeal-to-the-fickle-mob/2006/09/18/1158431641212.html?page=fullpage#contentSwap1.
See also the NAA entry: primeministers.naa.gov.au/primeministers/chifley/before-office.aspx

192   'The Dagoes' friend' 'Federal election campaign', *The Mercury*, 10 October 1929, 9. One of the subheadings for the article betrayed the newspaper's misreading of the coming election result: 'Nationalist gains predicted'.

194   'Australia must reassure the world' 'Sir Otto Niemeyer, statement to conference', the *Sydney Morning Herald*, 22 August 1930, 11–12

195   'Prejudice against foreigners' 'Death of Mr. Sidney Myer, career of achievement, citizen and philanthropist', *The Argus*, 6 September 1934, 9

197   The young Robert Menzies Pratt, Ambrose, *Sidney Myer*, Quartet Books, 1978, viii

CHAPTER THIRTEEN

203   **'As we have no racial problem'** *Australian Dictionary of Biography* entry for Thomas White, by John Rickard.

204   **Churchill admitted the boat would contain Hitler's opponents** His speech to the House of Commons on 4 June 1940 is more famous for its bulldog declaration: 'We shall fight on the beaches'. **'Most of the internees seemed very young'** 'War prisoners arrive from England', the *Sydney Morning Herald,* 7 September 1940, 13. Almost every assumption made in the article proved to be false. See also: guides.naa.gov.au/safe-haven/chapter5/dunera-affair.aspx

209   **'involuntary unemployment was practically nil'** ABS 1301.0 – *Year Book Australia, 1946-47,* 492. Employment by industry, raw tables, 491
Despite this war's much closer proximity 'Australians at War', ABS 1301.0 – *Year Book Australia, 1988.* See: www.abs.gov.au/ausstats/ abs@.nsf/featurearticlesbytitle/00753BC276CCB154CA2570FF0 00075A8?OpenDocument. Overseas deployment and casualties rates for the First and Second World Wars taken from Long, G., *The Final Campaigns,* Australian War Memorial, 1963, 'Appendix 7 – Some Statistics'. Long's death toll for the First World War is 60 284 and for the second 24 751. The War Memorial's 'Roll of Honour' has higher counts for both wars, which include those servicemen who died later from wounds: the figure for the first is 61 524 and the second 39 649. Although the latter is substantially higher than the Long estimate, it does not alter the general point that the second had a much lower casualty rate. See: www.awm.gov.au/ encyclopedia/war_casualties/

210   **The commandant at Loveday** As cited in Nursey-Bray, Paul, 'Anti-Fascism and Internment: The Case of Francesco Fantin', *Journal of the Historical Society of South Australia,* Number 17, 1989, 88–111.

212   **'we must change our attitudes'** *Hansard,* 28 September 1943.

212-3   **Curtin prepared the public** 'Mr Curtin Adroitly Answers Questions', *The Argus,* 26 April 1944, 16; 'All Migrants Welcome, says Curtin', *Daily News,* 5 May 1944, 2; 'Mr. Curtin Home Again', *The Examiner,* 27 June 1944, 5.

214   **'the population problem'** *Hansard,* 16 November 1944. **'A vigorous policy of white alien immigration'** As cited in Zubrzycki, Jerzy, 'Arthur Calwell and the Origin of Post-War

Immigration Canberra', Bureau of Immigration, Multicultural and
Population Research, 1995.

CHAPTER FOURTEEN

216 **'a British land of one race and one land'** As cited in Curran, James,
Curtin's Empire, Cambridge University Press, 2011, 84. Calwell's
'heterogeneous society' quoted in Zubrzycki, 'Calwell and the
Origin'.

218 **'the great bastion of the British-speaking race'** Chifley's 1946
campaign address was delivered to Australian radio stations on
2 September 1946. Menzies' speech was made on 20 August 1946.
All election speeches can be found at the Museum of Australian
Democracy: electionspeeches.moadoph.gov.au/speeches/

219 **'I am not anti-Semitic'** *Hansard*, 27 November 1946.

219-20 **'refugee racket'** Jack Lang's comments were made the following
day, 28 November 1946. Arthur Calwell replied by accusing Lang
of 'anti-alienism'.

221 **'concession to the bigots'** As cited in the *Australian Dictionary of
Biography* entry for Arthur Calwell, by Graham Freudenberg.

222 **'the second largest "white" city'** Abberley, Aldwyn, *A Manual for
Emigrants,* the Tantivy Press, 1947, 90–2.

223 **'two Wongs don't make a white'** *Hansard*, 2 December 1947.
Calwell detailed how the colour line would apply to wartime
refugees. 'In all, 15 000 evacuees of all nationalities came to
Australia during, the war. Of that number, 4400 were Asiatics.
Most of the evacuees, including the Asiatics, have gone. There
are about 500 Chinese, mostly, seamen, and about 50 Malays left.
All of these people will have to leave Australia.'

226 **'I am determined to fly the flag of White Australia'** 'Moves against
deportation', the *Sydney Morning Herald*, 24 March 1949, 1. In
his address, detailed further on page 4, Calwell used the Henry
Parkes argument that Asians should be kept out to protect social
cohesion. 'The influx of so many Asiatics of different religion,
standards of living, culture, and national characteristics, inevitably
leads to friction and eventually to rioting as has happened in South
Africa, the United States of America, and other countries where
people of different races and living standards live side by side in
the same community.'

'a singularly unpleasant process of victimization' *Hansard,* 16 June
1949.

227   'blundering policy' 'Judge warns against "weekend deportations"',
Northern Star, 30 August 1949, 5.
Public opinion moved quickly in favour The Australian Gallup
Poll of 2 December 1949 asked: 'As you know, many thousands
of NON-BRITISH immigrants, mostly displaced persons, have
come to Australia from the continent of Europe since the war. IN
THE LONG RUN, do you think their coming here will be good,
or bad, for Australia?' The answers were: Good 53.5 per cent; Bad
31.5 per cent; Undecided 15 per cent. Total responses 1873.

227-8 **'We will continue'** Menzies' campaign speech, 10 November 1949.
Note how hard he went after Calwell: 'Nothing has done both
the Policy and our relations with Asiatic countries more harm
than some of the stupid and provocative decisions of the present
Government.'

CHAPTER FIFTEEN

230   **Less popular were wartime allies** The Australian Gallup Poll of 30
March 1951 asked: 'Here is a list of European countries from which
Aust. [sic] could get immigrants. As I name each country, would you
please say whether or not Aust. should get immigrants from there?'
The answers were, in order of countries asked: France 59.4 per cent;
Italy 27.3 per cent; Sweden 76.8 per cent; Holland 80.6 per cent;
Germany 55.4 per cent; Jugoslavia [sic] 33.5 per cent; Greece 42.7
per cent; None wanted 6.0 per cent. Total responses 1730.

231   **'The Labor Party stresses'** Note Ben Chifley's formula (which
would be echoed three decades later by John Howard): 'The
urgency of the housing problem throughout Australia today calls
for an immediate review or the Menzies-Fadden Government's
immigration policy with a view to determining an annual number
of arrivals that is within the capacity of the country to absorb',
28 March 1951. Menzies' policy speech was made on 3 April 1951,
and Calwell's was made on 16 November 1961.

233   **When the *Cyrenia* docked** The ship my dad came to Australia
on had a reputation for poor hospitality. On its first voyage from
Italy to Australia in 1949, it carried 663 passengers, from thirty
nationalities. Only seventeen English migrants had secured

tickets, and when the vessel docked at Fremantle on 2 April they made a beeline for the reporter from the *Sunday Times* to unload. 'This is the worst ship anyone could hope to travel on,' Mr J A Baxter, of Lancashire, said. 'It might be alright for foreigners but it's not alright for us.' He complained about the pita bread, dips and spaghetti. 'Hungry? You're telling me,' Mrs C. Davies from Stratford-on-Avon said. 'We could all do with a nice chop and egg when we get ashore.'

234 **public opinion had swung decisively** The Australian Gallup Poll of August 1964 reminded those questioned that 120 000 migrants had come to Australia to live permanently last year. 'Do you think the number of people coming here each year to live permanently should be increased, reduced or remain about the same?' Total responses: 1800. In a related poll in July, voters were asked what seemed to be a leading question: 'Do you think Asian migration should be prohibited altogether, or allowed in small numbers, or allowed without restriction?' Only 22 per cent wanted no migrants from Asia, while 73 per cent wanted 'small numbers' and 5 per cent wanted the door completely open.

235 **There is a myth** Attitudes to migration based on research by Shaun Ratcliff, PhD candidate, political science, School of Social Sciences, Monash University.

239 **the electorate divided five ways** The Australian Gallup Poll of November 1966 asked: 'About how many Asians should be given permanent residential status in Australia each year?' Total responses: 2020.

239–40 **NBC televisions 'Meet the Press' program** Interview aired 11 June 1967. Holt pointed out that Australia's commercial interests had switched from Britain to Asia. '[In] the 1950s 15 per cent of our export trade was east of Suez, it is 43 per cent today. Japan has become the biggest customer in the world for Australian goods. These things have a bearing on all this. But I emphasise that not one representative of an Asian government has ever raised with me in my many travels around the area the question of our immigration policy.'

241 **Australia's property obsession** Home ownership rates from customised tables supplied by the ABS.

245 **'Those whose parents arrived'** 'Second Generation Australians',

report for the Department of Immigration and Multicultural and
Indigenous Affairs, 2002.

CHAPTER SIXTEEN

249 **two local men in a tinnie** Mann, Alex, 'Former Vietnam refugee
Hieu Van Le set to be installed as governor of South Australia',
ABC, 30 August 2014, www.abc.net.au/news/2014-08-30/
former-vietnam-refugee-hieu-van-le-installed-governor-sa/5707742

250 **'Without reopening old sores'** *Hansard*, 22 March 1977.
Senator Mulvihill said he was happy for Australia to receive
some people from Vietnam, but said the Americans had 'a bigger
obligation than we do'. 'Of course, there was a natural link
between Vietnam and France, because many of the aristocrats in
Vietnam had a French education. They were more identified with
France. Because of this France has an obligation to do something
as well.'
'Of course, we should have compassion' 'Hawke: return bogus
refugees', *The Australian*, 29 November 1977, 1. The report
said: 'Mr Hawke did not consider his stance inhumane and he
questioned the compassion of those who advocated that the
refugees should all sail under the unsafest conditions in the
world.' Gough Whitlam was more measured, and his comments
appeared below Hawke's: 'Any genuine refugee should be
accepted but the Government has a responsibility to ensure they
are genuine refugees. It should also see that they don't get ahead
in the queue over people who have been sponsored and who are
already coming here.'

253-4 **Every record was broken in the 1980s** Overseas-born figures
calculated from censuses in 1981 and 1991. These numbers will
be lower than the annual intakes published by the government
at the time because they are net of departures and deaths. The
same method is used to calculate all postwar intakes, and for
all migration to the United States. The only time I use the raw
intakes is for the nineteenth-century emigration from the United
Kingdom.

254 **'keep race out of debate in Australia'** *Hansard*, 23 August 1984.

255-6 **'His polling shows'** *Hansard*, 25 August 1988.

258 **Keating clipped a page one article** A post-election editorial from

the *Australian Financial Review* was headlined: 'Racism the worst part of election. Paul Keating underlined the word 'worst' and wrote a brief comment: 'Pity the AFR didn't say so at the time.' Keating says now that he had run ahead of public opinion on the subject. 'They [the public] were probably not ready and tired of me too.'

CHAPTER SEVENTEEN

262　**The Chinese-born population in Australia** The 2001 census figure comprises 142 781 people from China and 67 121 from Hong Kong. **almost 63 000 asylum seekers** Phillips, Janet, 'Boat arrivals in Australia: a quick guide to the statistics', Parliamentary Library, 23 January 2014. Between 1999 and 2013, Australia received 62 572 asylum seekers. Half that total – 36 755 – came in 2012 and 2013.

270　**this boom came with cheaper prices** Glenn Stevens' speech to the Committee for Economic Development of Australia, 29 November 2010, www.rba.gov.au/speeches/2010/sp-gov-291110.html

271　**Australia in twelfth place** The global production ladder based on data from the World Bank using 'GDP (current US$)'. See: data.worldbank.org/indicator/NY.GDP.MKTP.CD
It is interesting to compare the top six in 2003, when the China boom commenced, with the latest result for 2014. Back then, the US was first, Japan second, Germany third, the United Kingdom fourth, France fifth and China sixth. Essentially China's rise to second place has meant that Japan, Germany, the UK and France each drop one place to make way. The bigger changes have been in the next six places. Brazil has jumped from fourteenth to seventh, and India from twelfth to ninth. The most significant falls have been Spain, from seventh to fourteenth, and Mexico, from tenth to fifteenth.

272　**'megaphone diplomacy'** 'US thought Rudd handling of Oceanic Viking asylum seeker crisis "awkward"', WikiLeaks' AAP, published on *The Australian* website, 30 August 2011.

274　**'raving on about jihad'** John Howard interview with author, 9 December 2005, for Cater, Nick (ed.), *The Howard Factor*, MUP, 2006.

CHAPTER EIGHTEEN

276   **People born in Asia** ABS estimates for 2014 show the Asian-born number 2.348 million, or 10 per cent of the population. Almost one in four are Chinese, with 447 370 born in China and another 94 420 in Hong Kong. The Indian-born figure is 397 180.

277-8   **only one of the fifty American states** The top five US states for overseas born in 2013: California 26.9 per cent; New York 22.3 per cent; New Jersey 21.6 per cent; Florida 19.4 per cent; and Nevada 19 per cent. Source: Migration Policy Institute, 'Immigrant Population by State, 1990-Present', www.migrationpolicy.org
The 2011 census for Australia had the state migrant shares as follows: Western Australia 33.4 per cent; Victoria 28.7 per cent; New South Wales 28.3 per cent; South Australia 23.7 per cent; Queensland 22.5 per cent and Tasmania 12.6 per cent. Note the national figure in 2011 was 26.9 per cent. In 2014 it was 28.1 per cent, so state shares will have also risen.

278   **The most revealing difference** Latest US figures are for 2012, two years behind the Australian breakdowns by region. See: United States Census Bureau, Current Population Survey – March 2012 Detailed Tables, Table 3.1., www.census.gov/population/foreign/data/cps2012.html
The US details: Overseas-born 13.1 per cent, of which 6.9 percentage points are from Latin America. Mexico alone (3.8 points) has supplied more migrants to the US than Asia (also 3.8 points). Europe accounts for 1.5 percentage points.

285   **four capitals rated in the top ten cities in the world** 'A Summary of the Liveability Ranking and Overview August 2014', *The Economist* Intelligence Unit, 2014. Key lines in this report for Australia's future: '. . . there does appear to be a correlation between the types of cities that sit right at the very top of the ranking. Those that score best tend to be mid-sized cities in wealthier countries with a relatively low population density. This can foster a range of recreational activities without leading to high crime levels or overburdened infrastructure.' See: pages.eiu.com/rs/eiu2/images/Liveability_rankings_2014.pdf

For follow-up questions on individual references, please contact me on Twitter@GMegalogenis

INDEX